ABSTRACTION FOR PROGRAMMERS

ABSTRACTION FOR PROGRAMMERS

J. A. Zimmer, Ph.D.

Spoon Software
Northboro, Massachusetts

McGRAW-HILL BOOK COMPANY

New York   St. Louis   San Francisco   Auckland   Bogotá
Hamburg   Johannesburg   London   Madrid   Mexico   Montreal   New Delhi
Panama   Paris   São Paulo   Singapore   Sydney   Tokyo   Toronto

ABSTRACTION FOR PROGRAMMERS

Copyright © 1985 by McGraw-Hill, Inc. All rights reserved. Printed in the United States of America. Except as permitted under the United States Copyright Act of 1976, no part of this publication may be reproduced or distributed in any form or by any means, or stored in a data base or retrieval system, without the prior written permission of the publisher.

1 2 3 4 5 6 7 8 9 0   DOCDOC   8 9 8 7 6 5

ISBN 0-07-072832-1

This book was set in Times Roman by Monotype Composition Company, Inc.
The editors were Eric M. Munson, Kaye Pace, and Sheila H. Gillams;
the production supervisor was Charles Hess.
The cover was designed by Cynthia Iron.
R. R. Donnelley & Sons Company was printer and binder.

Library of Congress Cataloging in Publication Data

Zimmer, J. A.
    Abstraction for programmers.

    Includes indexes.
    1. Electronic digital computers—Programming.
2. Algorithms. 3. Abstraction. I. Title.
QA76.6.Z56 1985   001.64′2   84-21874
ISBN 0-07-072832-1

To Edwin Halfar,
who taught me to love abstractions

and C. St. J. A. Nash-Williams,
who taught me to create them.

CONTENTS

PREFACE

PURPOSE

It used to be thought that learning to program a computer was something like learning a foreign language. Having learned a computer language, such as FORTRAN or Pascal, a person could translate her intentions into that language in a way that caused the machine to do her bidding. A person skilled in making such translations was called a programmer. Everybody knew that programmers controlled computers. The skill of translating into a computer language was confused with the skill of planning the way in which a computer would carry out a given task. The word "programming" was used to cover these concepts. (Sometimes it even covered the activity of planning what a computer *should* do.) Today many people recognize the distinction by reserving the word "coding" for the part of programming which is mere translation. Others use the word "analyst" for a programmer who plans the way computers carry out given tasks. Unfortunately, there are still people who do not recognize the distinction between coding and designing or who think that coding is all there is to programming. This is unfortunate, because designing a plan for a computer program is much harder than coding a design that already exists.

Niklaus Wirth, who gave us the Pascal language, has written, "our most important mental tool for coping with complexity is abstraction" [WIR]. Abstraction is the way we carry out a divide-and-conquer approach to the solution of complex problems. It is the way we tell others what we have done—without boring them. It is the way we coordinate the mental work of several people who are working together on one project. It is an important part of the training of both designers and coders, both analysts and programmers.

Without good training in the use of abstraction, designers of computer programs create software that is unnecessarily difficult to maintain. *Maintenance* is the work that comes after a program is declared finished and debugged. It involves fixing mistakes that have not yet been caught and changing the program to provide new services or to run on different computers. More money is spent on maintenance than on the development of new software [PARI]. Further, an unknown but possibly large amount of new software is written from scratch that should have utilized building blocks of existing code, had that code been more maintainable. For these reasons, the creation of maintainable software is very important to the software industry.

Without good training in the use of abstraction, designers of computer programs cannot communicate those designs to coders. The combination of functions implied in the term "programmer/analyst" may be a result of a general inability to communicate designs.

Professionals, designers, and programmer/analysts who cannot create appropriate abstractions are unlikely to create maintainable software, because maintenance requires that old programs be understood, and understanding requires that the code be organized into abstractions that are natural to its function. Lack of abstraction implies bad organization.

The good organization that arises from a use of abstraction in the design process helps in both maintenance and solving difficult programming problems and tends to carve the code into building blocks which can be reused in other situations.

This book is meant to provide an introduction to the controlled use of abstraction in planning and describing computer programs.

SUBJECT

Since programs are plans for performing actions on data, it is natural to abstract them by abstracting actions and abstracting data. A design language that deals with action and data abstractions is the central subject of this book.

There are three auxiliary subjects: how the design language aids in problem solving, how to create computer code that matches the designs, and what goals to keep in mind in the creation of designs.

Problem solving is a learn-by-doing activity. A book can only provide tools and show examples of their use. The design language of this book is a useful problem-solving tool, and Chapters 3 and 5 are devoted to examples of this usefulness.

Abstract designs are of no value unless their link to concrete programs is understood. Two appendixes are included to show how selected examples in the text can be implemented. One appendix is devoted to FORTRAN, the other to Pascal.

One chapter (Chapter 6) discusses goals which a designer should keep in mind. These goals are meant to aid in the creation of reliable and maintainable software. The material in this chapter is not the standard fare of software engineering texts. This book augments rather than replaces such texts.

The design language of this book is presented in three stages: Chapter 2 covers action abstractions, Chapter 4 covers data abstractions, and Chapter 7 discusses both types once again but with mathematical notation.

The guts of this book lie in Chapter 4, where the topic of data abstraction is introduced. This material serves as a link between code, on one hand, and the mathematics of Chapter 7, on the other.

The material in Chapter 4 is not just a link between concrete code and abstract mathematics. More than that, it combines the notions of data abstraction and information hiding in such a way as to explain how sequential computer programs and their designs can be organized into separate, cohesive modules. This material can be useful to many individuals who do not wish to pursue the more mathematical approach of Chapter 7. None of the problem-solving examples of the book depends on the more mathematical approach.

The kind of data abstraction emphasized here is a concept whose time has come. Versions of it have appeared in the Ada* programming language and in the iAPX 432 microcomputer by Intel.

I have tried for a readable progression from concrete examples to abstract examples. By placing this material in one coherent book that contains both code and axioms, I hope to make the abstractions come alive in a language for talking about real programs. While a computer science professor, I saw far too many students who could deal with concrete *and* abstract concepts but *not* both together. For these students, concrete constructs are created without coherent plans, and abstract constructs are merely an intellectual game which has no grounding in reality.

Abstraction for Programmers is about abstraction, and it is for programmers.

READER'S BACKGROUND

If this book appeals to you, there is a good chance you can read it. Mastering the abstract design language of this book requires the same skills that are required of a design-oriented programmer: an ability to work with simple mathematical abstractions and an ability to organize thoughts on paper so that others can understand them.

If you are a design-oriented programmer, you have these abilities. Unfortunately, it is possible to achieve a reputation as a good programmer without them.

Some people who have reputations as good programmers are hackers. They achieve their results by experimentation, and their programs provide little guidance to others who would understand them. If you are a hacker and you want to become a better hacker—maybe even a wizard, then this book is not for you.

A wizard is a person who solves all manner of programming problems by disappearing into a room with a direct link to a computer for a night or a week or whatever and then produces a miracle. Characteristics of wizards are that their activity is solitary and their work is incomprehensible to others—and they produce miracles. Wizards have been a valuable commodity because often the only way to get things done was to resort to black-box magic. This situation is changing because the teachers of wizards are getting their act together. It is possible to envision a day in which problems can be solved without recourse to black-box magic. When that judgment day comes, wizards

* Ada is a trademark of the U.S. government, Ada Joint Program Office.

will be found lacking because their inability to work in teams and to produce programs that other people can maintain will be the only characteristics that distinguish them from other programmers who can get things done. Like the wizards of olden times, the breed will die out.

If you are a design-oriented programmer and are willing to work at understanding this material, you can probably read this book even if you lack all the prerequisites listed below.

If you are not a design-oriented programmer but you wish to become one, this book can help—provided you have a relevant academic background. A good college programming course using FORTRAN or Pascal is suggested before reading any of this material. A second substantial programming course using some language that is at least similar to FORTRAN or Pascal is suggested before reading Chapters 4 and 5. Finally, a course in discrete structures, combinatorial analysis, abstract algebra, *or* mathematical logic is suggested before reading Chapter 7. (The material in this chapter is self-contained, but the mathematical maturity obtainable in one of these courses is desirable for complete understanding.)

INTEGRATION INTO THE CURRICULUM

Comments by individuals who have read prepublication drafts of this book (some of them were undergraduates) indicate many college-educated programmers can read much of, if not all, this material on their own. Even so, this book has been written to be used in the computer science curriculum, and this section provides some guidance to professors who would like to fit the material into a 4-year undergraduate program.

The material in this book is, by and large, self-contained. Anyone familiar with a standard procedural language or even with an assembly language that has been enhanced with constructs for selection and repetition will have the minimum knowledge for covering this material. Some of the examples in Chapter 2 are given—albeit with a different emphasis—in elementary programming courses. However, experience shows that students who lack a substantial programming background have difficulty seeing the need for this kind of material. Do not let the simplicity of the examples convince you that the average first- or second-year student will take readily to the concept of abstraction that is being explained. Further, most students will do well to have taken a course in mathematics beyond calculus before attempting Chapter 7.

The intended use for this text is a third-year course in data abstraction and problem solving. It could precede or succeed a course in data structures, but students who have taken data structures will get more from this material.

Since many colleges do not have such a course, the problem is one of where to insert this material.

Any third- or fourth-year course with a substantial nonnumeric programming content and some room for redefinition of that content is a possibility.

A course in software engineering is a possibility. If the software engineering part is taken from a book of readings such as [FRE] or a small, easy-to-read book such as [SOM], there would be room to discuss data abstraction as a method of design.

To make room for other material, any subset of the following can be omitted:

1 Section 2.4
2 Section 4.3
3 Section 5.3
4 Section 4.5 and Chapter 7 (or just Chapter 7)
5 Chapters 5 and 6 (or just Chapter 6)

Section 5.3 and Chapter 7 are the first omissions I would make.

Beginning graduate students from other disciplines can also benefit from a course in data abstraction based on this book. Others may benefit from the use of this book as a supplement in more advanced courses.

Although this material would seem to fit with the Ada programming language, experience in teaching Ada indicates that to combine a lot of Ada with a lot of this material would be a mistake. Subsets of each could be profitably combined into one course.

ACKNOWLEDGMENTS

A line from an old Chilliwack song goes, "If there ain't no audience, there just ain't no show." Ten people were my audience while I wrote this book. No one had time to read all the material, but together they provided me with necessary and valuable feedback. I remain grateful to Norm Delisle (Tektronix Inc.); Karen Zimmer (Yankee Atomic Electric); Steve Alpert, David Brown, James Coggins, and Ray Scott (Worcester Polytechnic Institute, faculty); and Jatin Desai, Dan Fretz, Todd Guay, and Stacey Marsella (Worcester Polytechnic Institute, students).

The last individual remains my wife—in spite of late nights, missed outings, low-priority house projects, and a mess of papers and books that seemed to spread from room to room.

Valuable feedback was also obtained from the reviewers, namely, Richard Andree (University of Oklahoma at Norman), Dean Arden (SUNY Albany), Moshe Augenstein (Brooklyn College), Richard Lorentz (Harvey Mudd College), Susan Rulon (North Texas State University), Mark Tuttle (University of California, Berkeley), and Peter Wegner (Brown University). I alone am responsible for the choice of material as well as any possible errors.

J. A. Zimmer

References for the Preface

[FRE]: Freeman, P., and Wasserman, A. I. *Tutorial on Software Design,* 4th ed., IEEE Computer Society, Los Angeles, 1983.
[PARI]: Parikh, G., and Zvegintzov, N. *Tutorial on Software Maintenance,* IEEE Computer Society, Los Angeles, 1983, p. 1.

[SOM]: Sommerville, I. *Software Engineering,* International Computer Science Series, Addison-Wesley, Reading, Mass., 1982.

[WIR]: Wirth, N. "On the Composition of Well-Structured Programs," ACM Computing Surveys, December 1974.

TERMINOLOGY

These terms are used throughout the book:

An *algorithm* is a finite set of rules which can be followed like a recipe to accomplish some well-defined task in a finite time. A correctly functioning computer program is an example of an algorithm. A correct design for a computer program is another.

Data coupling is the data shared between a metacode algorithm and a subset of that metacode. See Section 2.3.

FORTRAN refers to the dialect known as FORTRAN 77.

The symbol "iff" stands for "if and only if." For example, to say "X is greater than 10 iff L is true," is to say that "whenever X is greater than 10, it follows that L is true" *and* that "whenever L is true, it follows that X is greater than 10."

The symbol "mod" stands for "modulo" and represents an arithmetic function which is present in both Pascal and FORTRAN. For positive integer arguments it means the same thing in both languages. In this book it is written "I mod J" for positive integers I and J, and it means "the remainder of I divided by J." This remainder is the whole-number remainder we learned to find in elementary school.

Metacode is described in Sections 1.2 and 2.1.

Nondecreasing and *nonincreasing* are mathematical terms that are applied to sequences $X_1, X_2, \ldots, X_N$ of N real numbers. Nondecreasing means that $X_1 \leq X_2 \leq \ldots \leq X_N$, and nonincreasing means that $X_1 \geq X_2 \geq \ldots \geq X_N$. These terms appear to be a convoluted way of saying, respectively, "increasing" and "decreasing," but there is a difference. For example, a sequence in which the same value is repeated cannot in a strict sense be increasing; instead, it must be said to be nondecreasing.

Object modules are described in Sections 1.2 and 4.1.

There are many ways in which programs and subprograms are the same, so a single term, *program unit,* is used to describe both. Thus when something is said to be a program unit, you know it is a program, subroutine, procedure, or function, but you don't know which.

A *sequence* is a possibly infinite list of elements which may be empty. What is important about a sequence is that the elements, if any, come in a particular order: there is a first, a second, a third, and so on until the last element, if any, is reached.

A *vector* is a one-dimensional array. For example, the following declarations create a vector V of 10 integers and a vector C of 100-character strings in Pascal and then in FORTRAN:

```
type CharacterString = packed array[1 . . 35] of Char;
var V : array[1 . . 10] of Integer;
    C : array [1 . . 100] of CharacterString;
```

and

```
INTEGER V(10)
CHARACTER*35 C(100)
```

ABSTRACTION FOR PROGRAMMERS

CHAPTER 1

ABSTRACTION MAKES BETTER PROGRAMMERS

These drawings appear in a document created in India almost 1000 years ago [CAJ]:

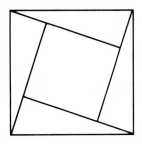 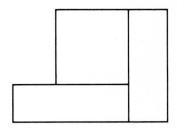

The word ''behold'' is all the explanation that is given. ''Beholding'' doesn't seem to be quite enough. It takes careful study to realize that these drawings contain a rather slick explanation of a mathematical fact which we in the West know as the Pythagorean theorem.

One of the first methods developed to explain a computer program was to draw a picture of it called a flowchart and say ''behold''!

Both these approaches involve an attempt to abstract the thing which is being described so that the beholder can understand what is really going on.

This book discusses how to do a better job of abstracting a computer program so that the beholder can understand what is really going on. Although the abstractions developed here could make good documentation tools, the book is not about a better way to document programs. Documentation is not usually done for the first beholder of any given program. The first beholder is the person who designs it. Documentation is usually for subsequent beholders. The concern here is mainly, but not exclusively, for the designer.

A design is an organized way of looking at a program-to-be. This organization must exist before the program is written. It determines the quality of the finished program. It provides the understanding of why the program works. Without it, debugging is without direction and unnecessarily frustrating.

A design is expressed at a more abstract level than the program is. If this were not the case, the program could probably be its own design. However, a design which is too abstract is an abdication of the designer's role. A designer must learn how to distinguish what is essential and what is not.

Computer programs consist of planned actions on data. Software designs must, therefore, abstract actions and data. Section 1.2 is an introduction to these kinds of abstraction and provides a quick overview of the book. To set the stage, Section 1.1 discusses the concept of abstraction itself.

1.1   ABSTRACTION IS FOR COMMUNICATING AND PLANNING

Most of our communication and planning involves abstractions. For example, when I explain to others how to find my house, I use concepts such as "intersection" and "left-hand rule." Both these concepts are abstractions. An intersection of streets can take on many forms; the concept stands for all of them. A left-hand rule is a procedure by which one turns left at every opportunity. The concept stands for a process of making decisions (about what the opportunities to turn left are) and carrying out actions (turning left and proceeding forward).

To use abstractions in communicating, the communicator and the communicatee must have a common understanding of what the abstractions actually represent. Without this common understanding, there is no communication; or worse, there is miscommunication. Achieving this common understanding is very difficult at times.

A plan is a form of communication that works forward in time. When we follow a plan, we are following a communication that was created for us in the past. When we make a plan, we act as if there will be somebody in the future who will pay attention to the plan.

Whether we are building skyscrapers or computers, whether we are expanding a business or merely avoiding bankruptcy, we use abstractions to construct and carry out our plans.

We learn these abstractions from others by seeing examples of their use. When we learn well, we can communicate with those who taught us and with others who have been similarly taught. When we don't, we can't.

Dealing with abstractions is natural for human beings. Anybody who has raised children has seen evidence of this. Try to teach an infant how to recognize a picture of a dog. Is it hard? Does the infant, almost without any effort on your part, recognize a real dog when presented with one? No, it is not hard. Yes, the infant does recognize a real dog. In fact, the main problem is that the infant overabstracts. Show that infant a picture of a horse, and what happens? "See dog." Show that infant a real horse, and what happens? "See dog."

We never outgrow our ability to deal with abstractions or our need for them. Computer programmers need abstractions to plan and to communicate. Unfortunately, the first couple of generations of programmers did not have any grown-ups around to correct those "dogs" of programs which were written! Slowly, much too slowly for comfort, we are learning appropriate abstractions for our profession.

The concept of *abstraction* is, itself, abstract, but it is an example of the kind of abstraction which cannot be used to describe something as precise as a computer program. Computer programs require precision even when abstraction is required to make them intelligible.

Although a precise definition of abstraction is beyond the pale of this book and although there may not even be a satisfactory definition, it is possible to list some principles that an abstraction for designing computer programs should satisfy:

It abbreviates, or is simpler than, the thing which it abstracts. The infant's concept of dog seems to be tied up with a visual thing that has a body, four legs on the bottom, a head at one end, and a tail at the other. This is a much simpler thing than a dog. Another way of making this point is to say that an abstraction omits irrelevant details.

There is more than one thing abstracted by a given abstraction. Dog, horse, and several creations of Dr. Seuss are abstracted by the view of dog described above. An abstraction characterizes a set of things. It can be said to *abstract* any element of the set.

It is precise. The description must be so exact that there could never be any doubt when the question is asked, Is this thing an example of that abstraction?

It is complete and accurate. If my software does everything your abstraction says, it had better do what you intended also! Another way of making this point is to say that the abstraction must contain all relevant details.

It may be hierarchical. An abstraction A is often stated in terms of abstractions B and C.

The ability to create abstractions which satisfy these requirements is not learned as easily as the mere use of abstractions. And simultaneous satisfaction of these requirements is necessary. Without abbreviation and simplification, a designer's plans and communications are difficult to understand because the general picture is missing. Without precision, the plans can go awry, and the communications can mislead.

An abstract design can be the means by which one person can conceive and direct a project that requires the work of many. It can be the glue that holds the project together. It can be the map that guides those who must find bugs and those who must find hooks onto which changes can be hung.

One design effort, which most people agree would be silly, is to "reinvent the wheel." Wheels are very useful things. That is part of the reason we all know of them. Another part is that the concept is simple. Were it complicated and hard to understand, it would not be well known. And if it were not well known, then it would be reinvented regularly. (The history of academic research demonstrates this point conclusively.)

Concepts exist for describing computer software which enable a complex program to appear as a combination of simple things. Programs that are so designed are more likely to produce "wheels" which can be used in other programs than are programs designed in a haphazard fashion.

But there is more: The process of creating an abstract design is an important part of the process of problem solving. When one begins to create a computer program, what comes to mind first is a vague generality. A *vague generality,* in this context, is a simplified answer which appears to be good enough, but is not. It is far too imprecise. Vague generalities are a part of our mental processes. To a large degree, abstractions are refinements of vague generalities. The trick of finding a solution to a problem is largely the trick of turning vague generalities into precise abstractions.

In theory, a proposed softward design D is an abstraction rather than a vague generality when it is always possible to answer with certainty, for a given program $P,$ the question, Is P an example of D? However, deciding whether this question will always be answerable is not easy. We learn to do it by comparing abstract designs with real programs. This book provides such comparisons. Two appendixes contain programs that match many of the designs in the text. One of the appendixes shows FORTRAN programs and the other Pascal programs.

An architect may deal with new building materials, or building codes, or lifestyles, but she seldom has to redefine such basic abstractions as "wall" and "room." A software designer is continually creating the basic abstractions behind her work. An architect's need to create her own abstract concepts to express her work is not as great as a software designers's. This is true of most other professions as well. Professionals in these fields are usually trained without ever reading an exposition of the difference between abstractions and vague generalities. However, because software designers often must deal with recently created or untested concepts, many need a clear understanding of the difference between an abstraction and a vague generality—hence the reason for this section.

Another goal of this book is to explain promising ideas for the "walls" and "rooms" of software design. These are the concepts of action abstraction and data abstraction. These concepts can be used to create design abstractions from vague generalities, but the concepts themselves are vague generalities.

If it seems that we, more than some of our other professional colleagues, live in a world of confused communications and paradoxical plans, the reason lies in the fact that the first couple of generations of programmers had nobody to correct them when they first began to distinguish between turkeys and swans. Not surprisingly, our first observations had to do with two legs and feathers. To distinguish between gobbling and gliding requires a better understanding of the nature of abstraction as it applies to our profession. This understanding is just now coming to us, and this book is meant to help.

1.2 ABSTRACTING ACTIONS AND DATA

Computer programs can be viewed as descriptions of actions on data. Designs of computer programs can be viewed as plans by which those descriptions will be written. Designs, too, deal with actions on data. Since designs are abstractions, many of the actions and data with which they deal must be abstract.

Designs of computer programs can, themselves, also be viewed as computer programs. A computer which executes them would be capable of handling abstract actions and data. If this computer really existed, we might do without computer programs and write only designs. Of course, this would allow us to make even more abstract designs of those designs. The advantage would be that we could handle even more complex problems than we do now. The cycle has no apparent ending.

The trick in establishing a design language is to create something which can (be need not) express concepts considerably more abstract than those which can be expressed in any present computer language and, at the same time, create something precise enough that those who know it can "play computer" and "execute" any abstract program written in it.

The language established in this book has no clean definition. It is learned, as English is learned, by means of example. And, with English, this language can express very precise or very imprecise ideas. But, unlike English, there is no room for imprecise communications.

Two basic concepts are the key to this language: abstracting actions with something called *metacode* and abstracting data with something called an *object module*.

Metacode is a cross between an imaginary computer language and English. (It is an abstract form of something called *pseudocode*.) The computer language parentage contributes the concept of executing actions, one at a time. Included are concepts similar to the if . . . then . . . and the loops of common computer languages. The English parentage contributes the ability to provide abstract descriptions of those actions.

Object modules are sets of actions which have been carefully defined to work together. This is achieved by defining a object module around some kind of data object. The glue which holds together the module's actions is their purpose for manipulating that data object. The object is considered to be contained by the module because it can be manipulated only through the actions of the module. (This concept is not to be confused with that of an *object code,* or machine language code that is ready to execute.)

As an example of metacode, consider Figure METACODE which contains an algorithm for reading this book:

Figure METACODE   How to Read This Book

```
repeat for chapters 1, 2, . . . , 7
    read the chapter
    if     Pascal implementation is interesting
        and Chapter is 2 or 4
        then
      read relevant parts of Appendix P
    elsif    FORTRAN implementation is interesting
        and Chapter is 2 or 4
        then
      read relevant parts of Appendix F
    fi
again
```

For those unfamiliar with the **elsif** construct, this reading procedure states that a reader should preferentially read Appendix P. Appendix F should be read only by readers who find FORTRAN but not Pascal implementation details interesting. Readers who find neither kind of implementation interesting should not read either appendix.

As an example of a object module, consider a multinational construction company which has inventory and bank accounts all over the world. The management procedures allow this inventory of goods and currency to be manipulated with commands such as the following:

move X (goods or currency) from country C to country D
use quantity Q of X (goods) on project P in country C
buy quantity Q of X (goods) in country C using local bank account

And the inventory can be examined with commands such as this:

What is the quantity Q of X (goods or currency) in country C?

These procedures abstract the physical and financial resources of the company. The abstraction is defined in terms of what can be done with those resources, not in terms of what they are. The company becomes an abstract object which management can *probe* for information or manipulate with *operations* that alter the disposition of the resources.[1]

These procedures should be complete enough to allow all necessary projects to be carried out so that management can restrict themselves to those management actions described in the procedures. In a sense, the company is contained in an abstraction that is manipulated with predefined probes and operations.

---

[1] This classification of management procedures into probes and operations fits the terminology of this book, not that of management science.

To be sure, this containment is something of a straitjacket. However, it is also a powerful tool. The predefined probes and operations provide a common language by which company plans can be drawn—plans which avoid details, but can be readily implemented because the machinery to carry them out has already been created. Execution of company projects can be audited because the auditors know how to trace the changes in resources through the predefined actions back to the plans.

In spite of these advantages, such a straitjacket is not an appealing or even, perhaps, an efficient way to manage human endeavors.

This book, however, is about the management of those resources available to a computer program, and such resources do not suffer from being placed in straitjackets. The opposite is true because the creation and use of object modules to manage input, output, and temporary data storage make those resources easier for the programmer to manage.

The design approach of this book involves two steps:

1 Make the problem easier by making the computer better for solving the problem. Do this by defining some object modules which perform data manipulations that are used for this particular problem.

2 Write metacode which uses those predefined data manipulations.

The concept of metacode is covered in Chapter 2. Metacode can be used without object modules and must be understood before object modules can be understood. It fits well with a kind of program development called *top-down*. This and related problem-solving ideas are described in Chapter 3.

The concept of object module is covered in Chapter 4. Probes and operations defined by an object module provide an ad hoc language in which plans can be drawn for the execution of a program—plans which avoid details, but can be readily implemented because the actions of the object module are (taken singly) not difficult to implement. Plans for related programs can be created by using the same object module. Execution of the planned program can be audited because the programmer knows how to trace execution time changes in the modularized objects back to the plans. This makes debugging easier.

Chapter 5 covers the above-mentioned two-step design method as well as related problem-solving approaches.

A fairly high level of abstraction can be obtained with metacode and object modules as described in Chapters 2 and 4. Descriptions at this level of abstraction are often easier if mathematics replaces English as the principal means of discourse. Chapter 7 introduces a form of mathematics that is suitably expressive.

Actually, creating abstract designs is not quite enough. The designs ought to have a number of properties mentioned in Chapter 6. Among these is the property of simplicity.

Designs of computer programs are not written for computers to read, and they are not written to document existing and presumably correct programs.

They are written to plan and communicate. Both goals are easier to attain with abstractions to help organize and simplify the various parts of a design and their interrelationships.

REFERENCES

[CAJ]: Cajori, Florian: *A History of Mathematics,* MacMillan & Co., 1895, p. 97.

CHAPTER 2

ACTION ABSTRACTION

Although the purpose of studying action abstractions is to learn a language in which to design computer programs, this chapter is not concerned with designing computer programs. Instead, it is concerned with the form of such designs and with the exact relationship between a program and its design. Emphasis on this relationship is necessary because a program designer who cannot see in advance the kind of program she has designed is like an architect who cannot see (and feel) the kind of building her plans document—both are buffoons.

In this chapter techniques of action abstraction are developed as if they were documentation tools; i.e., we proceed from detailed descriptions of algorithms to more abstract descriptions.

This is backward from what is done in designing. The purpose of this backward exposition is to teach the tools of design.

Computer science students can learn about their design tools by drafting designs of existing software in the same way that architecture students can learn about their design tools by drafting drawings of existing buildings.

Action abstractions are given in the form of *metacode,* a language whose mother is English and whose father is unknown but clearly was a computer programming language of some kind. The usual methods by which programming languages represent repetition and selection of actions are given metacode analogs in Section 2.1. They come from the father's side, and the father has the easy part. From the mother's side comes the use of English. Although all readers of this book know some English, using it correctly in metacode is something else.

Many readers will have seen metacode in its guise as pseudocode. Pseudocode is often introduced in a beginning programming book. One major purpose of a beginning text is to introduce a programming language. What better way than to give examples which contain a step-by-step account of what a program does? These accounts are often written in pseudocode. Such pseudocode is *not* more abstract than the code it explains; therefore, it has nothing to do with program design. We refer to such concrete pseudocode as *detailed metacode*. Our objective is to learn to write abstract metacode. But in so doing we study the relationship between the abstract and the concrete. This study is begun in Section 2.2 and resumes in later chapters.

Although this chapter concerns action abstractions, the abstracted actions have the purpose of manipulating data. Section 2.3 discusses how data should be dealt with when an action abstraction is written. This discussion provides some examples concerned with finding an appropriate, consistent level of abstraction.

When computer programs are viewed with some degree of abstraction, many deficiencies stand exposed. Section 2.4 shows an example of this. A procedure that has been written in detailed metacode is abstracted and then rewritten to obtain something better.

2.1 SELECTING AND REPEATING ACTIONS

In algorithmic computer languages, programmers exercise control over the way their programs respond to run-time conditions by means of special control statements that repeat and select actions. Since much of programming in these languages is the determination of these selections and repetitions, it is only natural to make some of this determination part of the design process.

Metacode-based design methods use constructs like the **if** and the looping statements of algorithmic languages. The basic forms used in this book are

```
if · · · then
    ·
    ·
    ·
else
    ·
    ·
    ·
fi
```

and

```
repeat
    ·
    ·
    ·
again
```

The first indicates that one of two possible finite sequences of actions will be chosen. The second indicates that a finite sequence of actions will be repeated forever. There are other ways of indicating the selection and the repetition of actions, but we make do with variants of these two.

A metacode segment defines the execution of a sequence of *metasteps* in much the same way as a code segment defines the execution of a sequence of statements in some computer language. The flow of execution is defined by the selection and repetition constructs. Metasteps are described in English but make use of the concepts of algebra and assignment to a variable. Variables, however, are not usually declared explicitly in metacode. Metacode assignments have no special syntax. Anything that a reader will not misinterpret is allowed.

A metacode segment is a plan by which a program segment will be built later. The presence of a selection or repetition construct in metacode requires that program segment to contain a matching selection or repetition. Thus where there are **if**'s and **repeat**'s in the metacode, there must be matching selections and repetitions in the program segment. However, there may be selections and repetitions in the program segment which do not correspond to **if**'s and **repeat**'s in the metacode segment.

The program segment should be written so that its selections and repetitions which match **if**'s and **repeat**'s in the metacode segment can be easily identified.

Every metastep should correspond to a sequence of statements in the program segment. Every metatest should correspond to a boolean expression in the program segment. Sometimes there will be extra statements in the program segment to set up the boolean expression so that it performs the desired test.

You can study the nature of the match between metacode segments and program segments by comparing the program segments in Appendixes P3, P4, F3, and F4 with the corresponding designs in this chapter and Chapter 4.

The metacode constructs for selection and repetition given above are skeletons which can be filled with English:

if it is raining **then**
   carry an umbrella
else
   forget the umbrella someplace
fi

or

repeat for one hundred times
   "I will not lose my umbrella."
again

In these cases "carry an umbrella", "forget the umbrella someplace", and "I will not lose my umbrella" are metasteps. Metasteps can also look far more like a programming language:

if $A > 0$ **then**
   $B \leftarrow A \times B$
else
   $B \leftarrow -A \times B$
fi

The **if** construct has a slightly different form when one of N actions is to be selected:

```
if P₁ then
   S₁
elsif P₂ then
   S₂
      .
      .
      .
else
   Sₙ
fi
```

Here the S_i's are sequences of metasteps. The P_i's are called *metatests*. They are analogous to the logical expressions of FORTRAN or the boolean expressions of Pascal and are used to determine which action the **if** construct will select. Execution of the construct shown here causes exactly one sequence from

$$S_1, S_2, \ldots, S_N$$

to be executed. Metasteps S_1 are chosen whenever metatest P_1 evaluates to true. Metatest P_2 is evaluated only if P_1 is false. If P_2 is found to be true, then metasteps S_2 are executed. And so on. Metasteps S_N are executed only if all the metatests evaluated to false.

As an example of the **if** construct, suppose we are writing a chess-playing program, and the method to be used in determining the computer's next move depends on two things. First, it depends on whether the game is in its beginning, middle, or end. Second, it depends on whether the game is to be played offensively or defensively. Figure CHESS_TABLE shows the possible play styles. There are six mutually exclusive cases. Metacode which says the same thing appears in Figure CHESS_METACODE.

There is no need here to go into either the methods of play or the classification schemes. The **else** clause, although not essential, can help the resulting program point out to the programmer any gross mistakes in the classification scheme. Even when the classification scheme is foolproof, this clause might be useful

Figure CHESS_TABLE   Table for Choice of Chess-Playing Method

Tactics	Game		
	Beginning	Middle	End
Offensive	A	C	E
Defensive	B	D	F

Figure CHESS_METACODE   Metacode for Choice of Chess-Playing Method

```
if beginning game and offensive play then
    choose move with method A
elsif beginning game and defensive play then
    choose move with method B
elsif middle game and offensive play then
    choose move with method C
elsif middle game and defensive play then
    choose move with method D
elsif end game and offensive play then
    choose move with method E
elsif end game and defensive play then
    choose move with method F
else
    (some serious classification error has occurred)
fi
```

because it could signal problems at a later time when the classification scheme is altered.

Although the **repeat** . . . **again** construct of metacode indicates no conditions for terminating the repetition, termination is almost always desired. A rule of structured programming (and hence of structured design) is that such a termination condition be placed at one single, specific place within the loop. Several forms may be used:

```
repeat while P
    S
again
```

or

```
repeat for· · ·
    S
again
```

or

```
repeat
    S
again until P
```

or, finally,

```
repeat
    S₁
exit when P
    S₂
again
```

In these forms, *P* stands for a metatest and *S* for a finite sequence of metasteps. These *P*'s are referred to as *repetition tests*. The second form is meant to be filled in with something like $I \leftarrow 1, \ldots, N$, and this, too, is called a repetition test. It is the same thing found in the DO loop of FORTRAN and the **for** loop of Pascal.

The first two forms show the repetition test at the beginning of the loop. Repetition of the statements in the loop continues until the repetition test provides a false value. If the test provides a false value the first time, then the statements in the loop are repeated 0 times, i.e., they are not executed.

In the last two of these forms, at least some statements of the loop are always executed at least once, and the loop is terminated when the test provides a true answer. In the third form, the repetition test is at the end of the loop. In this form, the statements in the loop are always executed at least once. In the last form, the repetition test is in the "middle" of the loop. Some of the statements are always executed at least once. The rest are not executed on the final repetition.

Appendixes F1 and P1 show how these repetitions are implemented in FORTRAN and Pascal, respectively.

The remainder of this section considers differences between these variants of **repeat . . . again** by showing how linear search looks with each variant.

Suppose that a value *X* is being sought in a vector *V* which has *V_SIZE* elements. A boolean variable *FOUND* is to be set equal to true iff (if and only if) *X* is present in *V*.

A **repeat for** version of the linear search is as follows:

```
FOUND ← false
repeat for I ← 1 to V_SIZE
    FOUND ← FOUND or V(I) = X
again
```

(Readers who find the boolean manipulations confusing are referred to the Tutorial on Boolean Expressions at the end of this section.)

The number of times this loop repeats is fixed before the repetition begins. For a linear search this is unattractive. If, for example, $V(1) = X$, then *X* can be found straight off, but a **repeat for** loop is repeated *V_SIZE* times anyway.

The **repeat while** version would seem to overcome this problem. Here is a linear search that uses it:

```
I ← 1
repeat while (I ≤ V_SIZE) and (V(I) ≠ X)
    I ← I + 1
again
FOUND ← I ≠ V_SIZE + 1
```

Unfortunately, this example cannot be coded into many dialects of FORTRAN or Pascal. The problem is that when X is not present, I will become V_SIZE + 1 and the last repetition test will be

$(V\_SIZE + 1 < V\_SIZE)$ AND $(V(V\_SIZE + 1) \neq X)$

The second part of this test can cause a subscript-out-of-range error.

A correct way to use a **repeat while** loop in a linear search is to handle the last element of V differently from the others:

```
I ← 1
repeat while I < V_SIZE and V(I) ≠ X
    I ← I + 1
again
FOUND ← V(I) = X
```

There are still two more forms of the **repeat . . . again** loop to consider. One of these produces the following:

```
I ← 0
repeat
    I ← I + 1
again until I = V_SIZE OR V(I) = X
FOUND ← V(I) = X
```

and the other form produces:

```
I ← 0
FOUND ← false
repeat
    I ← I + 1
exit when FOUND or I > V_SIZE
    FOUND ← V(I) = X
again
```

Some readers may wish to use two **exit when**'s: **exit when** $I > V\_SIZE$ and, in the same loop, **exit when** $V(I) = X$. This would not be acceptable because it creates two different repetition tests—a violation of a principle of structured programming. Similarly, a combination of the **exit when** form with one of the other looping forms is forbidden—again, because no loop is permitted multiple repetition tests.

This section has explained the basic building blocks of metacode: section and repetition. The flow of control of all metacode procedures is determined by these constructs and these constructs only.[1]

The free-form aspect of metacode depends on our common knowledge of English and mathematics. It is, of course, the more difficult aspect of metacode

---

[1] Function and subroutine invocations are handled informally. They are viewed as references to lower levels of abstraction and not as alternations in the flow of control.

to write properly. In this section, free-form statements have mimicked statements of Pascal and FORTRAN. More abstract free-form statements are the subject of the rest of this chapter.

Tutorial on Boolean Expressions

Boolean expressions are those things which are evaluated to determine the flow of metacode execution when **if, repeat while, again until,** or **exit when** is encountered. (They are called LOGICAL expressions by FORTRAN programmers.) For example, in the metacode segment

> **if** $X > 100.0$ **then** output *"X is large"* **fi**

the expression "$X > 100.0$" is a boolean expression. It generates a boolean value of true or false which is used to decide whether to execute the output statement.

There are other ways of generating a boolean value to control the flow of execution. For example, this metacode segment will always execute its output statement:

> **if** true **then** output *"X is large"* **fi**

And this metacode segment makes use of the boolean variable *XLARGE* to store a boolean value for the **if** construct:

> *XLARGE* ← $X > 100.0$;
> **if** *XLARGE* **then** output *"X is large"* **fi**

The assignment, of course, causes *XLARGE* to be true when $X > 100.0$ and *XLARGE* to be false when $X \leq 100.0$. In Pascal it is written

> XLARGE := $X > 100.0$

in FORTRAN it is written

> XLARGE = X .GT. 100.0

Of course, boolean expressions can be much more complex than $X > 100.0$, which consists only of three pieces—the relational operator $>$ and two arithmetic expressions on either side of it. Compound boolean expressions are built up from the simple ones by using the boolean operators *and, or,* and *not.* Some examples are

> not($(X > 100.0$ and *YSMALL*)

and

> $(X < 100.0)$ or (not *YSMALL*)

These are built up from three simple expressions: $X > 100.0$, $X \leq 100.0$, and *YSMALL*. The boolean variable *YSMALL* counts as a simple boolean expression—even though it doesn't consist of a relational operator and two arithmetic expressions—because it generates a true or false value and cannot be broken down into anything smaller that generates a true or false value.

When a boolean variable is required in metacode or in code (e.g., the variable *FOUND* of this section), a single statement such as

FOUND ← FOUND or (V(I) = X)

is preferred to the use of an **if** that accomplishes the same purpose.

Careful use of compound boolean expressions can help produce programs that are reliable and readable. To accomplish this, however, it is necessary to understand thoroughly how a true or false value is obtained during execution. You can test your understanding by trying to determine the difference between the two compound logical expressions involving *YSMALL* above.

A systematic method to make such a determination is to use a *truth table*. Figure AND_COMPOUND shows one for the first expression. The first two columns represent the two simple expressions. We must make our analysis under the assumption that either of these simple expressions could, at some time, evaluate to true or false. So all possible combinations of true and false have been listed in the first two columns. Each row represents a different combination of true and false, that is, a different situation which could affect the value of the compound expression. We want to find out the truth or falsity of the compound expression for each situation. Two additional columns aid in this. For each row, the third column shows the value of the expression

$(X > 100.0)$ and *YSMALL*

and the fourth column shows the value of the entire expression. The third column is filled in first. Since it is a combination of the first two that uses *and,* a true is placed only in that row for which both the first and second columns are true. The fourth column is filled in last. Since it is a negation of the third column, each row is just the logical opposite of the entry in the third column.

Figure AND_COMPOUND   Truth Table for not($(X > 100.0)$ and *YSMALL*)

$X > 100.0$	YSMALL	$(X > 100.0)$ and YSMALL	not($(X > 100.0)$ and YSMALL
true	true	true	false
true	false	false	true
false	true	false	true
false	false	false	true

Figure OR_COMPOUND   Truth Table for (X <= 100.0) or (not YSMALL)

X > 100.0	YSMALL	(X <= 100.0)	not YSMALL	(X <= 100.0) or (not YSMALL)
true	true	false	false	false
true	false	false	true	true
false	true	true	false	true
false	false	true	true	true

Figure OR_COMPOUND is a truth table for the second compound expression above. It is generated in the same manner. Note that the fifth column, being a combination of the second and fourth columns that uses *or,* has a false place only in that row for which both the first and the third columns are false.

A comparison of Figure AND_COMPOUND and Figure OR_COMPOUND shows the differences between the two compound boolean expressions. For each possible situation, the two expressions, as shown in the last column of each, evaluate to the same thing! Two boolean expressions which pass this test are said to be *logically equivalent.* They can be used interchangeably with a program design.

The truth table technique can be used to analyze any compound boolean expression. An expression that contained three different simple expressions would require rows that allow all possible combinations of three values of true and false. Eight rows are needed. Four different simple expressions would require sixteen rows, etc. Once all the situations of truth and falsity of the various simple expressions are known, the resulting truth or falsity of the compound expression can be systematically calculated in the manner of the previous examples.

It is not necessary to make a truth table each time there are two compound expressions to compare. Sometimes two rules known as *DeMorgan's laws* can be used to make the comparisons. These state that certain patterns of compound expressions are always equivalent to each other:

not (*P* and *Q*) ⇔ (not *P*) or (not *Q*)
not (*P* or *Q*) ⇔ (not *P*) and (not *Q*)

Here ⇔ means "is logically equivalent to," and the symbols *P* and *Q* stand for boolean expressions of any kind. If *P* stands for *X* > 100.0 and *Q* stands for *YSMALL,* then the first of DeMorgan's law tells us that the two compound boolean expressions given above are indeed equivalent. When they are applicable, DeMorgan's laws are much easier to apply than truth tables. They are applicable often enough to warrant memorization.

EXERCISES

2.1.1 Rewrite the following, using **elsif** and no **else:**

```
if P₁ then
  if P₂ then
    S₁
  else
    S₂
  fi
else
  if P₃ then
    S₃
  fi
fi
```

The same P_i's and S_i's should be visible in your version as in the original.

2.1.2 What would be output by each of the following?

```
a  N ← 3
   repeat for I ← 4, 5, . . ., N
     output I
   again
b  I ← 3
   J ← 7
   repeat while not ( I < 3 or J < 3 )
     I ← I + 1
     J ← J − 1
     output I and J
   again
c  N ← 3
   I ← 4
   repeat
     output I
     I ← I + 1
   until I > N
d  I ← 3
   J ← 7
   repeat
     J ← J − 1
     exit when I < 3 or J < 3
     I ← I + 1
     output I and J
   again
```

2.1.3 Write a metacode segment which searches a vector V for a value X, returns 0 if X isn't there and returns the largest I such that $V(I) = X$ if it is. Adapt the **repeat while** search technique shown in this section.

2.1.4 Use a truth table argument to show that the following metacode segments will produce the same output:

```
a input I
  repeat while 1 ≤ I and I ≤ 5
    output I
    input I
b again
  repeat
    input I
  exit when > I or I > 5
    output I
  again
```

2.1.5 Write a metacode segment and a matching program segment which reads in N numbers and prints them in reverse order. Test your program on data with $N = 1$ and with $N = 10$.

2.1.6 Write a metacode segment and a matching program segment which reads in an unknown number of integers and prints them out "rotated." That is, the second number to be read in—it there is one—should be printed first, the third number to be read in should be printed second, etc. Finally, the first number to be read in should be printed last. Test your program 3 times—once with ten numbers, once with one number, and once with zero numbers.

2.1.7 Write a metacode segment and a matching program segment for a subprogram which updates three real variables so that they are arranged in nondecreasing order. Then write a metacode which reads in three real numbers, prints them out in nondecreasing order, and does this 6 different times. The metacode should have one metastep which rearranges the numbers. Write a matching code in which this metastep appears as a subprogram invocation. Test your program with six sets of numbers representing all possible arrangements of -1.0, 2.0, and 3.0.

2.1.8 Write a metacode segment and a matching program segment which reads in three real numbers and either prints "These numbers do not represent the lengths of the sides of a right triangle" or "These numbers probably represent the sides of a right triangle with hypotenuse. . . ." Of course, the length of the hypotenuse should be filled in. Your metacode should use the metastep developed in exercise 2.1.7. Your metatest of "equality" between the square of the hypotenuse and the sum of the squares of the legs should accept lengths in which equality is missed by less than 0.0001. Make up test data yourself. Try to get one set in which the test produces exact equality, one in which the test is "close enough," one in which the test is not quite close enough, and one in which the test is nowhere near close. You will need to have your code do extra writing during the test so that you can see if your test data is what you expect.

2.2 CONDENSING ACTIONS

Metacode which matches code on a statement-by-statement basis, as in Section 2.1, is worthless for design purposes. To write such metacode before building a program would essentially require that the program be coded twice—once in the matacode and once again in the real code. A metacode-based design must involve abstract metasteps. Their abstraction must be achieved without losing precision, and their relationship to the things which they abstract must be clear to their creator and to anybody else who must read the design.

In this section, metacode abstractions are introduced by creating them from existing detailed metacode.

Anybody who creates an abstraction must choose its level carefully. If it is too abstract, the readers will perceive it as a vague generality. If it is too concrete, the readers will perceive it as overly informative or simply as boring.

A metastep which is written at a carefully chosen level of abstraction may not necessarily represent an action whose implementation is obvious. The effect of the action, of course, must be clear, or else the metastep is not an abstraction. However, to know what must be done isn't necessarily to know how to do it.

Metasteps which do not have clear implementations can be given metacode designs of their own. A design, therefore, may consist of a hierarchy of metacode procedures. The top-level metacode procedure describes an action which solves the problem. Lower-level metacode procedures describe actions which are metasteps in other metacode procedures.

The correct level of abstraction for any given metacode procedure depends on the set of concepts which the author and the readers of the abstraction share. The correct level for this book varies by chapter. In Section 2.1 it was no more abstract than the code itself would be. Now is the time for a small jump upward. There will be another jump upward in Chapters 4 and 7.

To begin, consider Figure COUNT_DETAIL which shows detailed metacode for a procedure that imports a vector of characters S and exports a vector of integers $LETTER\_COUNT$ such that the first element of $LETTER\_COUNT$ is the number of A's in S, the second is the number of B's in S, and so on. Only uppercase letters are considered.

The "numeric value of" a character is the unsigned integer code that represents the character within the computer.

Code that matches Figure COUNT_DETAIL appears in appendixes F3 and P3.

Figure COUNT_DETAIL   Counting Letters of the Alphabet which Occur in a String

```
repeat for I ← 1, . . . , 26
   LETTER_COUNT(I) ← 0
again
I ← 1
repeat while I ≤ S_LENGTH
   ILETTER − (numeric value of S(I) − (numeric value of "A") + 1
   LETTER_COUNT(ILETTER) ← LETTER_COUNT(ILETTER) + 1
   I ← I + 1
again
```

Figures COUNT and COUNT_ABS show abstractions of Figure COUNT_DETAIL. Which is better?

Figure COUNT   Low-Level Abstraction of Figure COUNT_DETAIL

```
LETTER_COUNT ← 0s
I ← 1
repeat while I ≤ length of S
   LETTER_COUNT(Position of S(I) in alphabet) ←
      LETTER_COUNT(position of S(I) in alphabet) + 1
   I ← I + 1
again
```

Figure COUNT_ABS   Abstraction of Figure COUNT_DETAIL

```
LETTER_COUNT ← a vector whose Ith element counts the number of
   occurrences in S of the Ith letter of the alphabet
```

Clearly Figure COUNT_ABS is the more abstract. Its level of abstraction gives no information about how the counting is to be done. Such a level of abstraction is appropriate when the designer knows the implementor will write satisfactory code without any further specification.

The abstractions in Figure COUNT involve the way in which both *LETTER_COUNT* is initialized and the position of a letter in the alphabet is found.

Figure COUNT does not describe much of an abstraction, but then the problem statement does not describe much of a problem. In some situations an implementor should be given more guidance than is available from Figure COUNT_ABS. Then the kind of low-level abstraction represented by Figure COUNT is a good way to provide that guidance.

Thus neither Figure COUNT nor Figure COUNT_ABS is better. Both are abstractions. The requirements of the day regulate which would be chosen.

The problem of sorting a vector *V* of integers into nondecreasing order is a source of examples for showing useful abstraction.

Some of the integers to be sorted may be duplicated. This is the reason why the term "nondecreasing" rather than "increasing" is used. (Similarly, when sorting into decreasing order but allowing duplications, we use the term "nonincreasing.")

As was the case with the letter-counting example, a high level of abstraction is possible that says simply:

```
V ← V rearranged into nondecreasing order
```

But such a level of abstraction would make it impossible to distinguish between two sorting techniques. We will aim toward a lower level of abstraction—one in which a designer who knew a particular sorting technique could explain it to an implementor who did not.

The first sorting technique is called *selection sort*. The basic plan is to find a smallest element of *V* and exchange its value with the value in *V*(1). Then we wish to find a smallest remaining element and trade its value with the value in *V*(2). And so on. A detailed version of the procedure is shown in Figure SELECT_DETAIL. It assumes there are *V_SIZE* elements to sort.

Figure SELECT_DETAIL   Selection Sort (Detailed Version)
```
repeat for I ← 1, . . . , V_SIZE − 1
   LO ← I
   repeat for J ← I + 1, . . . , V_SIZE
      if V(LO) > V(J) then LO ← J fi
   again
   T ← V(LO)
   V(LO) ← V(I)
   V(I) ← T
again
```

An abstract version of Figure SELECT_DETAIL is obtained by breaking it into its constituent actions. These were described in the last paragraph. One action finds where the smallest remaining unsorted value is. Another trades this value with the next value of $V(I)$. Figure SELECT_SORT shows the abstraction.

Figure SELECT_SORT   Selection Sort
```
repeat for I ← 1, . . . , (length of V) − 1
   LO ← index of a smallest value in V(I), . . . , V(length of V)
   interchange V(I) and V(LO)
again
```

Figure SELECT_SORT represents a more useful abstraction than Figure COUNT because it breaks the action into simpler constituent actions, showing how they fit together.

The second sorting technique is called *insertion sort*. As seen, selection sort builds a sorted vector from the left by searching V for the correct value to put in $V(1)$, then $V(2)$, . . . ,$V(N)$ for the correct value to put into $V(2)$, etc. Insertion sort builds a sorted vector from the left by placing $V(1)$, $V(2)$ into order; then $V(1)$, $V(2)$, $V(3)$; and so on. Each stage involves an insertion of the next element into the sorted part that has been built from the left. In selection sort, the emphasis is on selecting a final value; in insertion sort, it is on inserting whatever value comes next.

Let's dispense with a detailed version of insertion sort. You can see what it does from the abstract metacode in Figure INSERT_SORT. Some comments have been placed in the metacode to explain why the method works.

Figure INSERT_SORT   Insertion Sort
```
repeat for I ← 1, . . . (length of V) − 1
   {note that V(1), . . . , V(I) are in nondecreasing order}
   insert V(I+1) into V(1), . . . , V(I) so that the resulting I+1 elements are in
      nondecreasing order
again
{note that V(1), . . . , V(length of V) are in nondecreasing order}
```

You saw the details for selection sort first and then the design. This was consistent with the goal of learning to describe detailed metacode with abstract metacode, but would it be a good way to learn a new sorting technique?

You saw abstract metacode for insertion sort but no detailed metacode. Isn't it easier to understand with the abstract metacode than it would be if you only had the detailed metacode to read?

Although the ultimate goal is to learn to write abstract metacode, we continue in this chapter to look at detailed metacode first. The relationship between abstractions and the code or detailed metacode which they abstract must be studied before we can write good abstractions.

Consider, as a final example, a function which determines whether a string *PATTERN* is present in a string *TEXT*. If *PATTERN* is present, the function returns the index of *TEXT* where *PATTERN* begins; otherwise, 0 is returned. Once again we consider first a detailed version of the algorithm and then how to form a more abstract version.

Figure PATTERN_DETAIL shows detailed metacode for the pattern-matching function. The *I*th character of a string *X* is denoted by *X(I)*. The approach is to check successive values of *I* for a match from the *I*th place in *TEXT* onward, i.e., for the following:

PATTERN(1), ..., *PATTERN*(*PATTERN_SIZE*) =
TEXT(*I*), ..., *TEXT*(*I* + *PATTERN_SIZE* − 1)

Good metacode for this problem should represent this approach and outline the detailed metacode given in Figure PATTERN_DETAIL. Such metacode is rather easy to write because all but one of the statements inside the outer loop are directed toward finding whether a match exists from *I* onward. Replacing these statements with a metastep that expresses their purpose gives us the metacode in Figure PATTERN. The variable MATCH_FOUND is removed because its purpose can be expressed with a more expressive English phrase.

Figure PATTERN_DETAIL   Pattern-Matching Function

```
I ← 1
MATCH_FOUND ← false
repeat while not MATCH_FOUND and I + PATTERN_SIZE − 1 ≤ TEXT_SIZE
  T ← I
  P ← 1
  MATCH_FOUND ← false
  repeat while not MATCH_FOUND and P ≤ PATTERN_SIZE
    MATCH_FOUND ← PATTERN(P) = TEXT(T)
    P ← P + 1
    T ← 1
  again
  I ← I + 1
again
if MATCH_FOUND then
  return I − 1
else
  return 0
fi
```

Figure PATTERN   Design for Pattern-Matching Function

```
I ← 1
repeat while matching substring not found and
              I + (length of PATTERN) − 1 ≤ (length of TEXT)
    check match, i.e., whether PATTERN(1), . . . , PATTERN(length of PATTERN)
        = TEXT(I), . . . , TEXT(I + (length of PATTERN) − 1)
    I ← I + 1
again
if matching substring found then
    return I − 1
else
    return 0
fi
```

The relationship between a design and the code which implements it can be further exemplified by comparing Figure PATTERN with a second detailed metacode implementation, given in Figure PATTERN_DETAIL_2. Notice that the Figures PATTERN_DETAIL, PATTERN, and PATTERN_DE-TAIL_2 have a lot of metacode in common. Figure PATTERN has one metastep that is an abstraction of several metasteps in *PATTERN_DETAIL* and in *PATTERN_DETAIL_2*. With the exception of this metastep and the metasteps it abstracts, there are no differences between these figures. This is how abstract metacode should be related to the code which it abstracts. The detailed version is obtained from the abstract version by replacing the abstract steps with several detailed steps and leaving the rest untouched.

Figure PATTERN_DETAIL_2   Another Pattern-Matching Function

```
I ← 1
MATCH_FOUND ← false
repeat while not MATCH_FOUND and I + PATTERN_SIZE − 1 ≤ TEXT_SIZE
    D ← 1
    repeat while    PATTERN(D) = TEXT(D + I − 1)
                  and D < PATTERN_SIZE
        D ← D + 1
    again
    MATCH_FOUND ← PATTERN(D) = TEXT(D + I − 1)
    I ← I + 1
again
if MATCH_FOUND then
    return I − 1
else
    return 0
fi
```

This section introduces the writing of abstract metacode. Emphasis has been placed on low-level abstractions so that their relationship with the code they abstract can be well understood. Emphasis has also been on the use of abstraction in explaining existing algorithms. This is not the way to design programs, but for many people it is the way to begin understanding abstractions and the degree of precision which they require.

EXERCISES

2.2.1 The Pascal code in Figure COUNT_P of Appendix P3 and the FORTRAN code in Figure COUNT_F of Appendix F3 are implementations of the design in Figure COUNT. If the letter-counting goal were changed to count lowercase letters along with their uppercase counterparts, Figure COUNT would still be a correct design, but neither COUNT_P nor COUNT_F would be a correct implementation. Write a correct Pascal or FORTRAN program that matches Figure COUNT for the changed goal.

2.2.2 It is possible to trace the execution of metacode algorithms for given data in the same way that it is possible to trace the execution of code algorithms. Such tracing helps to understand the metatests and metasteps and find any ambiguities that may be lurking within.

Each row of the following incomplete trace table should indicate the contents of V and LO at the beginnings of successive iterations of the outer loop of SE-LECT_DETAIL. Because this loop appears in SELECT_SORT as well as in SELECT_DETAIL, this trace table shows the effect of an "execution" of the abstract version as well as of the detailed version. Complete the table.

V(1)	V(2)	V(3)	V(4)	V(5)	LO	Iteration number
6	−1	4	3	2	?	1
−1	6	4	3	2	2	2

2.2.3 The following incomplete trace table begins a trace of the metacode in Figure IN-SERT_SORT. Complete it.

V(1)	V(2)	V(3)	V(4)	V(5)	Iteration number
6	−1	4	3	2	1

2.2.4 Write detailed metacode that matches Figure INSERT_SORT.

2.2.5 Compare the inner loops of Figure PATTERN_DETAIL and PATTERN_DE-TAIL_2. Which best fits the form for searching a vector as shown in Section 2.1? Explain.

2.2.6 Will the metacode in Figures PATTERN and PATTERN_DETAIL_3 perform the same task? Is Figure PATTERN an abstraction of the metacode given in Figure PATTERN_DETAIL_3? Before answering the second question, review the paragraph in the first part of Section 2.1 about the relationship between a metacode segment and a matching program segment. This paragraph applies if the abstract metacode in Figure PATTERN is considered to be the metacode segment and the detailed metacode in Figure PATTERN_DETAIL_3 is considered to be the program segment.

2.2.7 Write metacode for a program that inputs twenty integers, sorts them into nonincreasing order, and then prints them. The sorting algorithm should be selection sort. The level of abstraction of your metacode should be that of Figure SELECT_SORT. The input and output should, if possible, be done "on

Figure PATTERN_DETAIL_3 **Pattern-Matching Function**

```
I ← 1
MATCH_FOUND ← false
repeat
    T ← I
    P ← 1
    MATCH_FOUND ← false
    repeat while    not MATCH_FOUND and P ≤ PATTERN_SIZE
                and I + PATTERN_SIZE – 1 ≤ TEXT_SIZE
        MATCH_FOUND ≤ PATTERN(P) = TEXT(T)
        P ← P + 1
        T ← T + 1
    again
    I ← I + 1
again until MATCH_FOUND or I + PATTERN_SIZE – 1 > TEXT_SIZE
if MATCH_FOUND then
    return I – 1
else
    return 0
fi
```

the fly,'' within the loop of Figure SELECT_SORT. Test it on input that is already in decreasing order, on input that is in nondecreasing order (with some duplications), and on input in which the even-numbered items are in decreasing order while the odd-numbered items are in nondecreasing order.

2.2.8 Repeat exercise 2.2.7 for sorting character strings of ten characters each with insertion sort. The input file should consist of names typed in fields of ten characters.

2.2.9 Write abstract metacode for a version of insertion sort that builds a sorted vector from the right. Your level of abstraction should be the same as in Figure INSERT_SORT.

2.2.10 Implement and test a subprogram which imports character strings *TEXT* and *PATTERN* and returns 0 if *PATTERN* is not present in *TEXT* or *I* if *PATTERN* is present and its first occurrence begins in *TEXT(I)*. Your implementation should fit the metacode in Figure PATTERN but be different from that in Figures PATTERN_DETAIL and PATTERN_DETAIL_2. Changing variable names or adding extra statements which have no effect will not produce an implementation that is considered different. Arrange to test your implementation on these strings:

```
TEXT = 'HEEHEEHEE' PATTERN = 'HE'
TEXT = 'HEEHEEHEE' PATTERN = 'HEEE'
TEXT = 'HE'          PATTERN = 'HEEHEEHEE'
TEXT = 'H HHHHHHH' PATTERN = 'HH'
```

2.3 DEALING WITH DATA

Removing variables, or references to variables, can be an important aspect of action abstraction. When to remove them and how to be honest about it are the subject matter of this section.

Data-Type Dictionaries

The easiest way to remove variables is to use one word, phrase, or symbol to represent a whole slew of data. Manual filing systems have involved such "abstractions" for a very long time. The phrase "student record," for example, represents a lot of information that may be filed for a given student. Exactly which information is filed will vary from school to school. Whatever it is, "student record" describes it.

The fuzziness of the idea of "student record" can be firmed up by giving some details about what is to be included in a student record or, as is seen in Chapters 4 and 7, by giving a precise functional description. Although the first method isn't, strictly speaking, a use of abstraction, it can be done in a way that removes the details from the metacode, and removal of details from metacode is usually a good idea. The approach to removing details from metacode is to put some of the details in a document called the *data-type dictionary*.

A data-type dictionary contains descriptions of the kinds of data that are used in the metacode—except for numeric, string, character, or boolean data. The dictionary is written before the metacode, and it does not contain descriptions of variables. Each kind of data is given a name, and the names are arranged alphabetically.

What is involved is a two-step approach to the definition of data variables. In the first step (taken in the data dictionary), the general form and content of the data are defined. Such a definition describes a *data type*. In the second step (taken, as necessary, in the metacode or the code), variables having the predefined data type are introduced. Some programming languages, such as Pascal, permit this two-step approach within the code itself. Others, such as FORTRAN, do not. Regardless of the language used for coding, the two-step approach and the concomitant use of a data dictionary should be followed.

Figure DATA_DICTIONARY shows a sample data-type dictionary which defines four data types: *Account Record, Account Type, Address Information,* and *Customer Record.*

The data types in Figure DATA_DICTIONARY consist of groupings, called *data records,* of different kinds of information. An *Account Record* consists of four other things. A *Customer Record* consists of five things. One of the parts of a *Customer Record* (the one within curly brackets) is a set of account records. There may be 0, or 100, or more. The number of accounts varies from customer to customer or for the same customer from time to time. An implementation may impose a maximum number of *Account Records,* but if so, that maximum number must be given in the problem statement.

The *Account Type* data type is somewhat different from the rest. It consists of only one thing. That thing denotes the kind of bank account. The possibilities are listed: savings, checking, and NOW. (FORTRAN programmers should see

Figure DATA_DICTIONARY   A Data-Type Dictionary

Account Record
    Account Type
    Account Number
    Present Balance
    Date Last Transaction
Account Type
    (savings, checking, NOW)
Address Information
    Telephone Number
    Street Address
    Town Address
    Zip Code
Customer Record
    Name
    Social Security Number
    Address Information
    Number of Accounts
    {*Account Record*}

the implementation of FILE_MERGE in Appendix F3 for an implementation technique.)

A data-type dictionary intentionally contains only enough information for the metacode to make sense. It does not determine the exact form of the data items to be handled. In Figure DATA_DICTIONARY, for example, there is no indication of whether telelphone numbers are complete with area codes, and there is no indication of the maximum number, if any, of bank accounts which a customer can have. This missing information should be available in the problem statement. By leaving such details out of the data-type dictionary, the designer ensures that changes in details will not require revisions in the dictionary. And, more importantly, the designer can get on with the business of planning without becoming bogged down in details.

When a large team of programmers is needed to accomplish the implementation, it is too much to expect each programmer to read the problem specification. In these cases, after the design is finished and before the implementation is begun, the data-type dictionary should be augmented with the detailed information needed to implement variables of the specified types.

The data-type dictionary of Figure DATA_DICTIONARY can be used for many different procedures. Some may make use of a customer record without needing very many of its details. Suppose, for example, that a bank keeps its customer records by branch. That is, there is a separate file of customer records for each branch, and each file is kept in alphabetical order by customer name. If one branch were to close and all its customers were to be transferred to another branch, some procedure would be needed to combine two customer files into one. One such procedure is given in Figure FILE_MERGE.

Figure FILE_MERGE Merging Customer Files

input first customer records, if any, from branches *A* and *B*
repeat while unprocessed customers exist for both branches
   if customer *A*'s name precedes customer *B*'s name **then**
     output customer *A*'s record onto combined branch file
     input another customer record, if any, from branch *A*
   else
     output customer *B*'s record onto combined branch file
     input another customer record, if any, from branch *B*
  fi
again
finish copying any remaining branch *A* records onto combined file
finish copying any remaining branch *B* records onto combined file

This file-merging example shows how a data-type dictionary can be used to remove detail from the metacode. Although the references to the data types of Figure DATA_DICTIONARY are casual, they are clear. This is often a good way to write metacode. It leaves the choosing of variables for a later time when more of the requirements for that choice are understood.

Figure FILE_MERGE is implemented in Appendixes F and P.

Data Coupling

The concept of *data coupling* is important to this book. It is the data shared between a metacode segment and a part of that metacode segment.

For example, the data coupling of the first four statements of the following metacode segment is *A* and *C*:

$A \leftarrow 2$
$B \leftarrow 3$
$C \leftarrow A + B$
$A \leftarrow 2 \times C$
output *A* and *C*

Suppose *M* is a metacode segment and *S* is any set of its metasteps and metatests. Let $-S$ be the metasteps and metatests of *M* which do not appear in *S*. (Neither the metasteps in *S* nor those of $-S$ need form a contiguous segment of *M*.) A data object appearing in both *S* and $-S$ which is given a value in *S* that is used in $-S$ is said to be an *export*. A data object in *S* and $-S$ which is given a value in $-S$ that is used in *S* is said to be an *import*. A data object which is both an import and an export is said to be an *update*. A data object in *S* which is an import, export, or update is said to be in the *data coupling* of *S*. A data object in *S* which is not an import, export, or update is said to be *local* to *S*.

These concepts are shown pictorially in Figure DATA_COUPLING.

Applying these definitions to the metacode given above, we see that *B* is local to the first four statements, whereas *A* and *C* are exported. Also *A* and *C* are imported by the last step. (Do not confuse "import" with "input" or "export" with "output.")

**Figure DATA_COUPLING   Data Coupling of Steps *S* within
Program *M***
Arrows indicate data coupling. *M* is represented by the whole
picture.

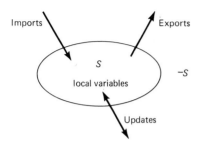

The data coupling of the third and fourth metasteps consists of A, B, and
C, of which B is imported, A is updated, and C is exported.
   Now consider these metasteps

$$T \leftarrow A$$
$$A \leftarrow B$$
$$B \leftarrow T$$

as a subset S of some metacode segment M. It is likely that their use in M
would be to interchange A and B. With this purpose, T would be local, and
both A and B would be updated. If these metasteps represented a subprogram,
their data coupling would be different for each invocation of the subprogram,
but it would always consist of two updated data objects—which two would
depend on the actual parameters or arguments used in the invocation.
   When we write metacode, we often write metasteps such as "interchange
X and Y" which may or may not be implemented as subprograms. The choice
of whether to write a subprogram often belongs to the implementor rather
than the designer. One reason that the notion of subprogram can be avoided
in metacode is that the data coupling of metasteps, such as "interchange . . .,"
would be the same regardless of the method of implementation.
   Designs that involve data abstractions deal with discontiguous sets of
metasteps and metatests that all belong to the same object module. The data
coupling of object modules is discussed in Section 4.2. For now, it is enough
to mention that a set S of metasteps and metatests whose coupling interests
us will not always represent a contiguous part of the metacode.
   As a different kind of example, consider the metacode segment in Figure
COUPLING. Never mind what it does—look at the data coupling of the
metasteps inside the loop. This data coupling is X, I, and $SWITCHING$, all of
which are updates. Notice that all of X is said to be updated, although it will
never be true that each element of X is changed and, in some instances, none
of X may be changed.

Figure COUPLING An Example of Data Coupling

```
SWITCHING ← true
I ← N
repeat while SWITCHING and I > 1
    P ← greatest integer in I/2
    if X(I) < X(P) then
        interchange X(I) and X(P)
        SWITCHING ← true
        I ← PO
    else
        SWITCHING ← false
    fi
again
```

Rules For Using Variables In Metacode

Two rules should be applied when you consider the way metacode uses data:

1 The data coupling between a metastep or metatest and the metacode where it is used should be readily apparent.

2 There should be no extraneous variables in the metacode.

The first rule is to write metasteps in such a way as to make their data coupling apparent. For example, the metastep

    A ← revised estimate

does not say very much about its data coupling. The calculation to revise A almost certainly requires some data. If that data comes from an input file, the metastep correctly reflects the data coupling but is probably badly worded. If that data comes from the metacode that uses this metastep, it is part of the coupling. To make this coupling apparent, the metacode should read something similar to the following:

    update A

if only A is required to do the revision, or

    A ← updated estimate based upon A and X

if also X is required to do the revision, or

    A ← revised estimate based on X and Y

if X and Y are imported and A is exported.

Variables local to the calculation that revises A are not a part of the coupling and should not appear in the metastep. In fact, as seen below, such variables are considered extraneous.

It is, of course, not necessary that the data coupling be indicated with actual variables. For example, a metastep which updates a customer record might be as follows;

pay customer's savings balance X% interest

This metastep could appear in a metacode procedure that first obtains the customer record and later places it back into permanent storage. (An entry for "customer record" in the data-type dictionary would be required.) The customer's savings balance (or balances) is updated, and a rate of interest is imported.

The second rule is that there should be no extraneous variables in the metacode. What is an extraneous variable? It is a variable that would be necessary for the code to work properly, but which isn't really necessary to describe what that code does. It is not necessarily extraneous to the code—only to the design. Further, in situations where the design is expressed with multiple levels of metacode, it need not be extraneous to the design—only to the abstraction level under consideration.

For example, in the following code, which interchanges the values of variables X and Y, the variable T is extraneous:

```
T ← X
X ← Y
Y ← T
```

A metastep which says "interchange X and Y" is preferable to any description that involves T.

Often, extraneous variables are *temporary* variables, such as T. Temporary variables are avoided by choosing metasteps which perform the whole action that requires them. They become local to the chosen metastep and so need not be mentioned. Temporary variables are recognized by short lifespans and purposes which are inconsequential in the scheme of things.

Although temporary variables are almost always extraneous, sometimes they enhance clarity and should be kept.

Another kind of extraneous variable is one which has been inserted because the computer language, not the logic of the problem, requires it. For example, in some dialects of FORTRAN, the statement

```
DO 10 I = J+1,N−1
```

would have to be written this way:

```
IUP = I+1
NDOWN = N−1
DO 10 I = IUP,NDOWN
```

Both variables *IUP* and *NDOWN* are extraneous. They are there because of peculiarities of the language. Although neither FORTRAN nor Pascal has this problem with its loop control, both do suffer from another peculiarity which forces the use of extraneous variables: Functions cannot return array values— the value returned is restricted to be an integer, real, character, or boolean.[2] This means that, for example, a subprogram which reverses the order of the elements in a vector, without changing the vector, could not be written as a function which imports the original vector and returns the reversed one. Instead, it would have to be written as a procedure with two arguments—one for the vector to be reversed and one for the reversed version. Metacode reflecting this restriction might look like this:

```
let U be V in reverse order
output U
```

The variable *U* is extraneous. The metacode should be written this way:

```
output the elements of V in reverse order
```

And in some programming languages (notably APL and Ada,[3] it would be coded in essentially that way, for example,

```
output_vector(reverse_vector(V))
```

A final reason for extraneous variables is the wish to optimize the speed of execution. A programmer says to herself, "Why make the machine calculate *V/PI* in all those places? Instead put the value in a new variable *VBYPI*." The new variable is extraneous to the design. Often it is even extraneous to the code because the extra speed it obtains isn't necessary or because the compiler can take care of such optimizations without any help from the programmer.

Whatever the case may be, remember that what is good for code is not always good for design. At the design level there is no machine to worry about—not directly anyway. There are readers of the design to worry about. Those readers will usually understand better if they don't have to memorize the meaning of a new variable every few statements. The variable *VBYPI* is extraneous.

The last paragraphs are not an apology for designs that utilize inefficient algorithms. The choice of an appropriate algorithm is very much a design-level activity, and it is best carried out without consideration of special machine-level tricks to achieve faster execution.

Examples

As an example of explicit data coupling, consider a program which calculates the root of a continuous function *f*; i.e., it calculates an *X* such that *f(X)* is 0 (or at least very close). This metacode works by generating an approximate

---

[2] FORTRAN doesn't allow character data to be returned.
[3] Ada is a trademark of the U.S. government, Ada Joint Program Office.

answer and improving the approximation, over and over, until it is close enough or cannot be significantly improved. Suggested metacode is shown in Figure VAGUE_ROOT.

The exact algorithm is not specified in this figure. The intent would be to provide more detailed explanations of the metasteps at a later time—perhaps by means of additional metacode procedures. However, even without this added explanation, it is possible to be quite skeptical as to the degree to which this metacode follows the rule about making all data coupling apparent. The metatest "it is possible to improve X significantly" is pretty strange. What constitutes an improvement? Won't the answer require data beyond the current value of X?

Suppose, now, that the metastep "$X \leftarrow$ first approximation" actually produces two estimates X and Y for which $f(Y) \leq 0 \leq f(X)$ and that the metastep "$X \leftarrow$ next approximation", in fact, diddles with both estimates so that the interval between Y and X becomes smaller. This is a common technique. Figure VAGUE_ROOT, however, is not metacode which abstracts it. To do that, the coupling must be correctly shown, as in Figure ROOT.

This is the most abstract example we've seen so far. A lot of detail is missing, but note that a reader of Figure ROOT can understand why the loop will terminate with an approximate root.

Figure VAGUE_ROOT   Finding a Root X Such That f(X) = 0

```
X ← first approximation
repeat while   it is possible to improve X significantly
               and f(X) is not close enough to 0
   X ← next approximation
again
```

Figure ROOT   A Possible Abstraction of a Program to Find a Root

```
X,Y ← estimated roots such that f(Y) ≤ 0 f(X)
repeat while | X − Y | > A and | f(X) | > B
   X,Y ← update of X,Y with | X − Y | less than ¾ its
          original value and f(X) ≤ f(Y)
again
```

As an example concerned with extraneous variables, reconsider the letter-counting algorithm in Figure COUNT of Section 2.2, and compare it with the same algorithm represented without variables in Figure NO_VARIABLES. The algorithm is for counting the occurrences of each letter of the alphabet that appear a given string S. The question is, Is Figure NO_VARIABLES an improvement?

Figure NO_VARIABLES   Abstraction of Figure COUNT

```
get first letter
repeat while a letter was obtainable
   increment count for this letter by 1
   get next letter
again
```

An implementor of the metacode in Figure NO_VARIABLES has much more freedom to choose her own data structures than an implementor of the metacode in Figure COUNT. There is nothing in Figure NO_VARIABLES that requires the original text to be located in a string variable. The phrase "get the first letter", for example, *could* refer to something like "*I*← 1" as the corresponding metastep of Figure COUNT states. But it need not. It could also refer to the input of the first letter from a text file. Likewise, the phrase "a letter was obtainable" could mean either "*I* ≤ *S_LENGTH*" or "another letter has been input".

In an important sense, therefore, Figure NO_VARIABLES is more abstract than Figure COUNT. It captures the essence of the counting process without describing peripheral issues such as the location of the data to be counted.

However, the problem statement is to count the occurrences of letters in a string *S*. With such a problem statement, the variable *S* is not extraneous to the design; it is required. Figure NO_VARIABLES is an example of a misapplication of the rule that extraneous variables should be eliminated. As mentioned in Section 2.2, this problem is so simple that it hardly needs metacode which is more detailed than the problem statement itself. However, if such metacode is to be written, then the detail of Figure COUNT is the right level of abstraction for explaining how the counting is to be done.

An example concerning both coupling and extraneous variables is a program to print a table of declining-balance depreciation. Declining balance is a method used sometimes by businesses to keep a record of the value of their possessions. The purchase price, a salvage value, and a lifetime (some number of years) are input. Each year, the book value is to be depreciated by twice last year's book value divided by the lifetime; and when the book value reaches the salvage value or when the lifetime is over, the depreciation stops. Figure DECLINE_DETAIL shows detailed metacode for accomplishing this task.

Figure DECLINE_DETAIL   Declining-Balance Depreciation

```
AGE, ANNUAL_DEP and ACCUMULATED_DEP ← 0
input BOOK_VALUE {i.e. the purchase price}, SALVAGE_VALUE, LIFETIME
RATE ← 2/LIFETIME
output a header for the table
output AGE, ANNUAL_DEP, ACCUMULATED_DEP, and BOOK_VALUE
repeat while AGE < LIFETIME and BOOK_VALUE > SALVAGE_VALUE
   AGE ← AGE + 1
   ANNUAL_DEP ← RATE × BOOK_VALUE
   if BOOK_VALUE − ANNUAL_DEP > SALVAGE_VALUE then
      BOOK_VALUE ← BOOK_VALUE − ANNUAL_DEP
   else
      ANNUAL_DEP ← BOOK_VALUE − SALVAGE_VALUE
      BOOK_VALUE ← SALVAGE_VALUE
   fi
   ACCUMULATED_DEP ← ANNUAL_DEP + ACCUMULATED_DEP
   output AGE, ANNUAL_DEP, ACCUMULATED_DEP, and BOOK_VALUE
again
```

Figures DECLINE_ABS_1, DECLINE_ABS_2, and DECLINE_ABS_3 contain abstracted versions of the depreciation metacode in Figure DE-CLINE_DETAIL. Which is best? For that matter, which is worst?

All have the *RATE* variable removed. It is extraneous because it stands for 2/*LIFETIME*.

Figure DECLINE_ABS_1 has the fewest statements. That might be an indication that it is most abstract. However, it achieves its brevity by being inaccurate and vague. The *AGE* variable is initialized and used in the repetition test, but is never updated. Perhaps the step "*AGE ← AGE* + 1" has been forgotten, or perhaps it is supposed to be included in the "calculate . . . *ANNUAL_DEP*, *ACCUMULATED_DEP*, and new *BOOK_VALUE*" step. If the latter is true, then the coupling of the "calculate" step should include *AGE*. Either way, the metacode is vague and unacceptable. Figure DE-CLINE_ABS_1 is the worst.

Because of the rule about explicitly stating all data coupling, it is possible to read the algorithm in Figure DECLINE_ABS_1 and know that the variable *AGE* is never updated. Without this rule, it would not be possible to see from the metasteps of an algorithm where or if variables are altered.

Figure DECLINE_ABS_1   An Abstracted Depreciation Program

```
AGE, ANNUAL_DEP, and ACCUMULATED_DEP ← 0
input BOOK_VALUE, SALVAGE_VALUE, LIFETIME
output a header for the table
output AGE, ANNUAL_DEP, ACCUMULATED_DEP, and BOOK_VALUE
repeat while AGE < LIFETIME and BOOK_VALUE > SALVAGE_VALUE
   calculate ANNUAL_DEP, ACCUMULATED_DEP, and new BOOK_VALUE
      according to declining-balance method
   output AGE, ANNUAL_DEP, ACCUMULATED_DEP, and BOOK_VALUE
again
```

Figure DECLINE_ABS_2   An Abstracted Depreciation Program

```
AGE, ANNUAL_DEP, and ACCUMULATED_DEP ← 0
input BOOK_VALUE, SALVAGE_VALUE, LIFETIME
output a header for the table
output AGE, ANNUAL_DEP, ACCUMULATED_DEP, and BOOK_VALUE
repeat while AGE < LIFETIME and BOOK_VALUE > SALVAGE_VALUE
   AGE ← AGE + 1
   calculate ANNUAL_DEP and update ACCUMULATED_DEP and BOOK_VALUE
      with help from SALVAGE_VALUE and LIFETIME
      using declining-balance method
   output AGE, ANNUAL_DEP, ACCUMULATED_DEP, and BOOK_VALUE
again
```

In Figure DECLINE_ABS_2, the coupling of the metasteps is clearly indicated. Since the extraneous variables have also been removed, it follows the rules. Since it makes sense and accurately describes the metacode in Figure DECLINE_DETAIL, it is an adequate abstraction.

Figure DECLINE_ABS_3   An Abstracted Depreciation Program

set initial values for *AGE* and the yearly depreciation information
input *BOOK_VALUE, SALVAGE_VALUE, LIFETIME*
output a header for the table
output *AGE*, the yearly depreciation information, and *BOOK_VALUE*
repeat while *AGE* < *LIFETIME* and *BOOK_VALUE* > *SALVAGE_VALUE*
  AGE ← *AGE* + 1
  update the yearly depreciation information and *BOOK_VALUE*
    with help from *SALVAGE_VALUE* and *LIFETIME*
    using declining-balance method
  output *AGE*, the yearly depreciation information, and *BOOK_VALUE*
again

Figure DECLINE_ABS_3 requires a data-type dictionary that defines "yearly depreciation information" as the years' depreciation and the accumulated depreciation by year end. In a context where these concepts are known and they apply to declining-balance depreciation, Figure DECLINE_ABS_3 is not too abstract for the problem. In another context, it is too abstract. Once again, we see that what constitutes an abstraction depends on the concepts which the communicator and the communicatee share. Figure DECLINE_ABS_3 is accurate, in context, and more abstract than Figure DECLINE_ABS_2. Accordingly, Figure DECLINE_ABS_3 is the best.

This section has discussed ways in which abstract metacode can have fewer variables than the code which it abstracts. To omit details without losing precision is difficult. Two aids have been provided: the data-type dictionary and rules for the usage of variables. With a data-type dictionary, metacode can refer to kinds of data without stating the details. The rules for variable usage help to decide which variables are unimportant to the metacode and to ensure that the metacode is honest about the usage of those variables which remain.

EXERCISES

2.3.1 Rewrite the metacode in Figure INSERT_SORT of Section 2.2 so that it applies to customer records of the kind in Figure DATA_DICTIONARY.

2.3.2 Choose one of your old programs and make a data-type dictionary for it. Try to choose a program whose data-type dictionary isn't too simple.

2.3.3 Read Appendix P2 or F2. Implement the code in Figure ADD_CONTEXT on your computer, and use it in a program that inputs an unknown number of integers and outputs the largest.

2.3.4 Read Appendix P2 or F2. Consider the program shown in Figures USE_DIFF and DIFF_CONTEXT. Suppose that the processing step in Figure USE_DIFF is merely to output the current difference. Each of the following contains a change to the problem solved by that program and suggests a change to the code which will solve the new problem. In all cases, the suggestion violates one of the rules for input module style. Explain the rule that is violated, and suggest another solution that keeps the input module style and violates no rules.

a The first ten integers in the input are to be skipped; then the program proceeds as originally. Accomplish this by adding a line to the code in Figure USE_DIFF which inputs ten integers but does nothing with them.

b The processing step in Figure USE_DIFF is changed to output both the current difference and the most recently input integer. Accomplish this in Pascal merely by writing "difState.New" and in FORTRAN by adding

COMMON/DFSTATE/OLD,NEW

to the declarations in USE_DIFF so that NEW can be written.

c The processing loop of USE_DIFF is altered so that the program will stop when a zero difference has been output. Accomplish this in Pascal by assigning false to difHas in the processing step after a zero difference has been output and in FORTRAN by assigning .FALSE. to DIFHAS after a zero difference has been output. (FORTRAN programmers: your correction may not use a STOP statement.)

2.3.5 Consider Figure MERGE and its implementation in Appendix P3 or F3. The example of this figure demonstrates the use of data-type dictionary and the use of an input module when there are dual input files. As a result, the implementation is rather long. Test your understanding by adapting the essential features to a simpler problem:

Write a design for a program which merges two files of integers that are in nondecreasing order and merges them into an output file that is in nondecreasing order. The integers appear one per line on all three files. Implement and test your design.

2.3.6 What is the data coupling of "interchange $X(I)$ and $X(P)$" in Figure COUPLING?

2.3.7 Choose one of your old programs, and write abstract metacode to describe it. Be sure that the rules of this section are followed. Also the level of abstraction should be high enough to make your algorithm appear much simpler but not so high as to gloss over its essential features.

Figure TRIG_EXERCISE Printing a Table of Sines and Cosines

```
ANGLE ← 0.0
PAGE ← 1
RADIAN_CONVERTER ← 3.1415/180.0
repeat while ANGLE ≤ 360.0
  output header with page number, PAGE
  PAGE ← PAGE + 1
  PAGE_LIMIT ← ANGLE + 25.5
  if PAGE_LIMIT > 360.0 then
    PAGE_LIMIT ← 360.0
  fi
  repeat while ANGLE ≤ PAGE_LIMIT
    ANGLE_IN_RADIANS ← RADIAN_CONVERTER × ANGLE
    SINE ← sin(ANGLE_IN_RADIANS)
    COSINE ← cos(ANGLE_IN_RADIANS)
    output ANGLE, SINE, COSINE
    ANGLE ← ANGLE + 0.5
  again
again
```

2.3.8 Consider the metacode in Figure TRIG_EXERCISE whose purpose is to print a table of sines and cosines (fifty-two lines per page and with angles in degrees incremented by 0.1).

a Which variables are extraneous?

b It happens that *PAGE_LIMIT* is one of the extraneous variables. Demonstrate this by rewriting the metatest "*ANGLE ≤ PAGE_LIMIT*" with an English phrase that will have the same effect without referencing *PAGE_LIMIT*.

c Write abstract metacode to accomplish the same task. (*Hint*: None of the metasteps creating *PAGE_LIMIT* need have any counterpart in the metacode.)

2.3.9 Write and test a program in Pascal or FORTRAN which implements your design of exercise 2.3.8 but does not match the metacode in Figure TRIG_EXERCISE.

2.4 SIMPLIFYING ALGORITHMS

Sometimes it is impossible to write a good design of a preexisting computer program or algorithm because the program or the algorithm is flawed. In such situations the program or algorithm should be redesigned. We study such a situation in this section. Besides showing how programs can be redesigned, the study is a continuation of our efforts to understand the relationship between a design and the program which it represents.

Our method is to create a design for a given flawed program, improve the design, and then recode the program from the improved design. The flawed program was originally written by a person who has been responsible for teaching structured programming to many students. Its flaw becomes apparent when a design is written—not before.

Figure PRICE_DETAIL shows detailed metacode for calculating the purchase price of an item from the quantity purchased and the unit price. The unit price is looked up in a vector of (item number, unit price) pairs at the beginning. The input for the program contains 1000 pairs of numbers, representing an item number and the corresponding unit price, and then an unknown number of transactions requiring a price calculation. Each transaction is represented with an item number and a quantity. The total price of a transaction is the quantity times the unit price for that item number. When the price cannot be calculated, the reason is that the transaction involved an item number which is not one of the 1000 pairs. In that case a message about a missing unit price is output.

A data-type dictionary should show that a unit price record consists of an item number and a unit price.

The introduction of abstraction requires that suitable metasteps be identified. The comment in Figure PRICE_DETAIL makes an obvious metastep that promises certain actions. Several variables of rather temporary significance are found in the steps that help to carry out the promise. The data coupling between those steps and the top level consists of *ITEM_NUMBER, QUANTITY,* and *UPR,* which is not excessive. The abstract design obtained by introducing this one metastep is shown in Figure PRICE_ABS.

Figure PRICE_DETAIL   Price Calculations
This metacode uses a variable *UPR* which is a vector of 1000 unit
price records.

```
input values for UPR
input first ITEM_NUMBER and QUANTITY
repeat while was an item to price
   { calculate and print the price from the QUANTITY by looking  }
   { up the unit price in UPR corresponding to ITEM_NUMBER—     }
   { if look up fails, output a message that there is no unit      }
   { price for ITEM_NUMBER                                        }
      I ← 1
      LOOKUP ← true
      repeat while LOOKUP
         if ITEM_NUMBER matches item number part of UPR(I) then
            P ← (unit price part of UPR(I) ) × QUANTITY
            output ITEM_NUMBER, QUANTITY, and P
            LOOKUP ← false
         else
            I ← I + 1
            if I > number of UPR's then
               output that unit price for ITEM_NUMBER is available
               LOOKUP ← false
            fi
         fi
      again
   input next ITEM_NUMBER and QUANTITY
again
```

Figure PRICE_ABS   Price Calculations Abstracted
This metacode uses a variable *UPR* which is a vector of 1000 unit
price records.

```
input values for UPR
input first ITEM_NUMBER and QUANTITY
repeat while there was an item to price
   calculate and print the price from the QUANTITY by looking up the
      unit price in UPR corresponding to ITEM_NUMBER—if look up
      fails, output a message that there is no unit price for
      ITEM_NUMBER
   input next ITEM_NUMBER and QUANTITY
again
```

Metasteps, as a rule, ought to bury complexity, not expose it. The metastep of Figure PRICE_ABS is the longest and most complex yet to appear in this book. For such a simple problem it seems out of place. A designer should suspect that it is a bad metastep. But is it bad because it is a poor choice of metastep for a basically good algorithm or because the underlying algorithm is flawed?

As indicated at the beginning of the section, the difficulty—in this case!—lies with the algorithm. There is no compelling reason why the actions of looking up a unit price and calculating the total price need to be combined. If

Figure PRICE_REVISED   Price Calculations Revisited
This metacode uses a variable *UPR* which is a vector of 1000 unit
price records.

```
input values for UPR
input first ITEM_NUMBER and QUANTITY
repeat while there was an item to price
   search for I such that the item number of UPR(I) = ITEM_NUMBER
   if I was found then
      output ITEM_NUMBER, QUANTITY, and total price
         (QUANTITY × unit price of UPR(I))
   else
      output that a unit price for ITEM_NUMBER is unavailable
   fi
   input next ITEM_NUMBER and QUANTITY
again
```

they are separated, then the metastep of Figure PRICE_ABS becomes two simpler metasteps as in Figure PRICE_REVISED.

It is reasonable to ask why Figure PRICE_REVISED represents a better algorithm than Figure PRICE_ABS. Three reasons, in order of importance, are that it is easier to understand, it is more flexible, and it can be made faster. It is easier to understand because there is no complicated single step to understand. It is more flexible because the searching is a step of its own, and so the search technique can be changed more easily. It is faster because the original required a linear search through *UPR* with three metatests to be checked each time *I* was incremented. A linear search may not be necessary. If it is, it can be done with fewer metatests by using the techniques of Section 2.1.

It is reasonable to question whether Figure PRICE_REVISED represents a better design than Figure PRICE_ABS. After all, isn't the complexity of the algorithm more apparent in Figure PRICE_REVISED? Aren't the metasteps supposed to bury this complexity?

The goal of burying complexity is an oversimplification. If that were all we wanted from our metacode, then every program would be designed with one metastep:

perform the job described in the problem statement

This metastep is as accurate as the problem itself. There is no data coupling to worry about, and all extraneous variables are missing. By the rules, it should be a perfect metastep. Obviously, something more is wanted than burying complexity.

The major goal of design has been forgotten. It is to explain a solution to the problem. That goal is accomplished by explaining some of the design with top-level metacode and burying the rest in the metasteps and metatests of that metacode. The difficulty with PRICE_ABS is that not enough is explained at the top level.

A comparison of the designs shown in Figures PRICE_ABS and PRICE_ REVISED must take into account the fact that Figure PRICE_REVISED explains more of its solution than does Figure PRICE_ABS. To achieve the same kind of detail from Figure PRICE_ABS, another level of metacode is needed. This is provided in Figure SEARCH_CALC.

Figure SEARCH_CALC   Search and Calculate
Further detail about the long metastep in Figure PRICE_ABS:
Calculate and print the price from the *QUANTITY* by looking up the
unit price in *UPR* corresponding to *ITEM_NUMBER*. If look-up fails,
output a message that there is no unit price for *ITEM_NUMBER*.

```
 I ← 1
repeat while search for ITEM_NUMBER is unfinished
   if ITEM_NUMBER = the item number part of UPR(I) then
      calculate total price from the QUANTITY and the unit price
         of UPR(I) and print the results (including ITEM_NUMBER)
   else
      I ← I + 1
      if I > number of UPR's then
         output a message that a unit price for ITEM_NUMBER is
            unavailable
      fi
   fi
again
```

Figure SEARCH_CALC must be added to Figure PRICE_ABS before a comparison of the original algorithm with that of Figure PRICE_REVISED can be made. When this is done, the revised algorithm is seen to be cleaner.

This section has shown one of the pitfalls of building a program before designing it. Without the perspective that a design gives, a program is likely to lack a clean, flexible organization.

Having looked in this chapter at the design of existing programs and at the relationship between a program (as represented by detailed metacode) and a design (as represented by abstract metacode), we are ready to turn our attention to the creation of new designs—at least for problems whose solutions can be described by using action abstractions.

EXERCISES

2.4.1 Explain how the detailed metacode in Figure PRICE_DETAIL does not match the metacode in Figure PRICE_REVISED.

2.4.2 It is likely that a unit price should be looked up from a data file rather than from an array. Write a more abstract version of Figure PRICE_REVISED that allows a unit price to be stored in an array or in a data file.

2.4.3 Redesign the metacode you created in exercise 2.3.8 so that the trigonometric tables are printed with 104 angles, sines, and cosines per page. The 104 items are to be printed in 52 rows. The first 52 angles, sines, and cosines appear on the left half of a page, and the second 52 angles, sines, and cosines appear on the right half.

2.4.4 Redesign the metacode in Figure FILE_MERGE of Section 2.3 so that the program halts and prints a message if one of the input files is found to be unsorted. Implement and test your design, using the data dictionary in Figure DATA_DICTIONARY. (You can borrow implementation ideas from Appendix P3 or F3.)

2.4.5 Choose one of your old programs—perhaps the same one you used in exercise 2.3.7. Write abstract metacode which describes it, rewrite the abstract metacode so that a cleaner algorithm is described, and then implement your new design. Run the new and old versions of the program on the same test data, and compare results. If there are errors, they had better be in the old version!

CHAPTER 3

PROBLEM SOLVING WITH ACTION ABSTRACTION

"I have been with you for quite a while, but I have received no instruction. Why so? Please be good enough to advise me." That is a student of Zen speaking to a master in one of my favorite stories; see [SUZ]. Some readers who have reached this far will be asked a similar question.

Abstraction, you may recall from Section 1.1, is for communicating and planning. It cannot be accomplished without a common understanding between the communicator and the communicatee. Before this chapter, you and I haven't had much of a common understanding.

At this point we can discuss some real examples because we have in common a notion of metacode and of how to make it precise. The problem-solving approach illustrated in this chapter involves writing a solution in a vague generality and then rewriting it as an abstraction. Until further concepts have been covered, this process of rewriting will lower the level of abstraction. In later chapters that will not always be the case.

Three approaches are useful in guiding the development of the vague metacode: bottom-up, top-down, and side-to-side. The bottom-up approach, considered and rejected in Section 3.1, is to settle details at the beginning so that the first metacode need not be so vague. The top-down approach, extolled in Section 3.2, is to write the vague abstract design first and then consider how the details must fit together. The side-to-side approach, explained in Section 3.3, is to tweak a known solution to a similar problem so that it works on the present problem.

The student of Zen had some misconceptions about what should be learned. Similarly, many who read a chapter about problem solving will have misconceptions about what problem solving is. In particular, they expect to be programmed with techniques that will solve lots of problems. It doesn't work that way. This chapter is not a program which can be read and then executed for purposes of seeing through a problem with X-ray eyes and making incredible intuitive leaps to a well-constructed solution. Nor does it describe a meat grinder which takes tough problems and produces suitable chunks (called metasteps) that can be patted together into an abstract design.

What does appear here is the exposition of several examples in which solutions are found by using the metacode developed in Chapter 2. The tricks of thinking from the top or from one side are useful, but you will find them very vague and amorphous when it comes to the crunch and you are solving your own problems. What will count then is your ability to express your own solution as a vague generality and then rewrite it as an abstraction.

Everybody seems to understand that problem solving is 10 percent inspiration and 90 percent perspiration. Few people seem to understand that much of the perspiration comes from writing false starts before the inspiration hits. When the problem has been solved, those false starts seem like wasted time. They aren't. They're the source of the inspriation.

More than anything else, what this book has to offer is guidance in writing down your ideas. If you practice the technique only when you know what you are doing, you will lose a rich source of inspiration.

3.1 BOTTOM-UP VERSUS TOP-DOWN

The controversy implicit in the title of this section is rather like the controversy of who runs the army, the generals or the sergeants. It cannot be answered by saying simply that the generals run the sergeants because there is no general present when the sergeants carry out those orders. In fact, when orders don't quite fit the situation, a sergeant may interpret them in a way that works.

This last observation points to one of the prongs of a dilemma. If you spend your time in the heights of strategic planning, you may create a plan whose parts can't be implemented. The other prong involves the possibility of the sergeants running the army. If you spend your time in the various trenches, your plans will probably fit together like one of those crazy machines whose only function is to impress its audience.

In this section a problem is worked from the bottom and from the top. Comparison of the results gives a clear indication that, in spite of all the sergeants' savvy, it is the generals who ought to run the army. Ways of incorporating the sergeants' point of view are discussed in Chapter 5.

We consider the problem of updating a date (month, day, year) from one day to the next. To work from the bottom up, we begin by considering the details of what must be done. The act of finding the next calendar date must be tailored to the day, month, and year of the present calendar date. There are two kinds of year: normal and leap. There are three possible ways that a date must be updated. These are indicated at the bottom of Figure MONTH_ END. A fourth action of reporting erroneous input is included for completeness.

Figure MONTH_END   What Day Is It Tomorrow?

Month	<28	28	29	30	31
			Day		
1	D	D	D	D	M
2	D	M*	E*	E	E
3	D	D	D	D	M
4	D	D	D	M	E
5	D	D	D	D	M
6	D	D	D	M	E
7	D	D	D	D	M
8	D	D	D	D	M
9	D	D	D	M	E
10	D	D	D	D	M
11	D	D	D	M	E
12	D	D	D	D	Y

Where the indicated actions are
D: increase day of month
M: set day to 1 and increase month of year
Y: set day and month to 1 and increase year
E: report erroneous input
*Two places where table must be changed for leap year are indicated with asterisks.

The top of the figure contains a table that indicates when these actions are applicable.

Detailed metacode that follows the plan of this chart appears in Figure BOTTOM_TOMORROW. (A companion chart for leap years is easily imagined

Figure BOTTOM_TOMORROW   Obtaining Tomorrow
This detailed metacode updates a date (*MONTH, DAY, YEAR*) by
making it into the next calendar date.

```
if      1 ≤ DAY < 28
        or DAY = 28 and MONTH = 2 and YEAR is leap
        or DAY = 28 and MONTH ≠ 2
        or DAY = 29 and MONTH ≠ 2
        or DAY = 30 and MONTH is 1,3,5,7,8,10, or 12
        then
        DAY ← DAY + 1
elsif   DAY = 28 and MONTH = 2 and YEAR is not leap
        or DAY = 29 and MONTH = 2 and YEAR is leap
        or DAY = 30 and MONTH is 4,6,9, or 11
        or DAY = 31 and MONTH is 1,3,5,7,8, or 10
        then
        DAY ←
        MONTH ← MONTH + 1
elsif   DAY = 31 and MONTH = 12
           then
        DAY ← MONTH ← 1
        YEAR ← YEAR + 1
else
        report error
fi
```

and so does not appear here.) The metacode uses metatests "year is leap" and "year is not leap." A year is leap if it is divisible by 400 or if it is divisible by 4 but not by 100.

The bottom-up method works in this case to produce a detailed solution to the whole problem. In another case there might be a need to solve the problem for several "bottoms" and then put the pieces together. Such a case would be less likely to work so smoothly. Without some substantial guidance, this approach can deteriorate to a situation analogous to making a jigsaw puzzle by cutting out the pieces individually and then attempting to put them together.

Even in the present, easy case, the bottom-up design techniques has led to an unnecessarily messy result. To see this, we need a less messy design to compare with. That can be found by applying a top-down design technique.

A top-level view of this procedure could have been produced without a chart, such as Figure MONTH_END, to guide the way. Figure VAGUE_TOMORROW shows such a view. It is a vague generality. The top-down approach is to fill in the details.

Figure VAGUE_TOMORROW   Obtaining Tomorrow: A Vague Guide

```
if DAY is not last day of MONTH then
    update DAY only
elsif DAY is last day of MONTH which isn't 12 then
    update DAY and MONTH
elsif DAY is last day of YEAR then
    update DAY, MONTH, and YEAR
else
    report erroneous input
fi
```

The most vague aspect of this metacode is the treatment of leap year. As it is presently worded, the test "*DAY* is last day of *MONTH*" implies that the last day is known and that it is easy to compare *DAY* with this last day. A comparison such as

$$DAY < LAST\_DAY(MONTH)$$

is the kind of thing you would expect such a metatest to mean. The problem, of course, is that the last day of the second month is not fixed. The coupling of this metatest with the top-level metacode must involve *YEAR* as well as *DAY* and *MONTH*. Unless. . .

It is possible to determine the last day of each month once at the beginning of the metacode procedure. Such a determination is not hard to make; it requires only a knowledge of the numbers of days each month has and a knowledge of what constitutes a leap year. Figure TOP_TOMORROW shows a design based on this approach.

Figure TOP_TOMORROW   Obtaining Tomorrow Again

LAST_DAY ← a vector whose *l*th element is the number of days in the *l*th month
                (depends on *YEAR*)
if *DAY* < *LAST_DAY* (*MONTH*) **then**
   DAY + 1
elsif *DAY* = *LAST_DAY*(*MONTH*) and *MONTH* ≠ 12 **then**
   DAY ← 1
   MONTH ← *MONTH* + 1
elsif *MONTH* = 12 and *DAY* = *LAST_DAY*(12) **then**
   DAY ← *MONTH* ← 1
   YEAR ← *YEAR* + 1
else
   report error
fi

The trick to the design in Figure TOP_TOMORROW is, of course, the use of the vector *LAST_DAY*. The point of this section is that this trick was harder to discover while mucking around in the trenches of the problem. It was the creation of a top level, and a vague one at that, which made the trick clearly visible to the designer.

EXERCISES

3.1.1 Write metacode that imports a year (four digits between 1900 and 2100, exclusive) and exports the day of the week on which the imported year will begin. Implement your metacode as a function, and test it for these years: 1901, 1948, 1995, 2001, and 2020. The results should be, respectively, Tuesday, Thursday, Sunday, Monday, and Wednesday.

3.1.2 Write metacode that imports a year (four digits between 1900 and 2100, exclusive) and prints a calendar for that year, one month per page. Your metacode should use the metasteps of exercise 3.1.1 and Figure TOP_TOMORROW. Implement your calendar generator.

3.1.3 Exercise 3.1.2 was a bottom-up exercise in that two metasteps were created before the top-level design. Do it again, top-down. Compare this version with the last. Which is better and why? Implement this version as well.

3.1.4 What is the main point of this section? Does it teach a technique or recommend avoidance of a technique?

3.2 TOP-DOWN

Top-down design is done this way: Write metacode which looks abstract but is vague; then rewrite it so that it is precise enough to be a design. Since the design is abstract, it may contain metasteps whose function is well defined but for which a method of implementation is not readily apparent. The vague-to-precise design method is reapplied to each of these, resulting in lower-level metacode for those top-level metasteps requiring some implementation detail. Although this process can go on for a long time, it won't in this section. The designing of solutions to larger problems works better when the methods of Chapter 4 are understood.

Two examples of top-down solutions are shown in this section. One explains a technique which every computer scientist must learn and which most readers will have already seen. The other has more of a real-world flavor.

The problem-solving technique shown here should help readers who have already seen the first example to reconstruct it for themselves when they need to use it, even if years intervene between the explanation and the need.

This example concerns the problem of searching for a value X in a vector V. The methods of Section 2.1 were linear searches; i.e., the elements of V are compared with X, one by one in a linear order. If the elements of V are in no special order, then a linear search is as good as can be done. If, however, the elements of V have been sorted, then there are better ways to look for X.

These better methods are based on the trivial fact that if V is in nondecreasing order, then for any index I these inequalities hold:

$$V(1) \leq V(2) \leq \cdots \leq V(I)$$

and

$$V(I) \leq V(I+1) \leq V(I+2) \leq \cdots \leq V(\text{length of } V)$$

These inequalities mean that if $X > V(I)$, then X is not in $\{X(1), V(2), \cdots, V(I)\}$ and that if $X < V(I)$, then X is not in $\{V(I), V(I+1), \cdots, V(\text{length of } V)\}$. The search method considered here, called the *binary search*, makes use of this observation: One quick look for X in the middle of V will, if we are lucky, reveal X without further ado and will, more likely, eliminate about half the possibilities.

To illustrate the point, consider this vector:

$V(1)$	$V(2)$	$V(3)$	$V(4)$	$V(5)$	$V(6)$	$V(7)$	$V(8)$	$V(9)$	$V(10)$
40	45	45	50	54	58	60	85	88	89

Let's begin a search for the value $X = 58$. Check $V(5)$. It is smaller than X. Thus everything to the left of $V(5)$ is smaller than X. Only $V(6)$, $V(7)$, $V(8)$, $V(9)$, and $V(10)$ remain to be checked out. Here $V(8)$ is in the middle of this list, so check it. It is larger than X. That means everything to the right of $V(8)$ is larger than X, and so only $V(6)$ and $V(7)$ remain to be checked out. Check $V(6)$. Jackpot! The value X is found at index position 6.

A linear search from the front would have required six checks of the type $V(I) = X$. The binary search made it in three. That is not much of a savings, but it gets better. If V consists of 1000 elements, then it can be shown that the binary search method will require at most ten checks to find X or determine that X is not there. The linear search, of course, could require as many as 1000 checks.

Figure VAGUE_SEARCH shows this basic idea. A binary search algorithm is described which imports a vector whose elements are in nondecreasing order and a value to seek. If the value is present in the vector, the algorithm exports its index—or the index of one of the value's occurrences. If the value is not present, the algorithm exports 0.

Figure VAGUE_SEARCH   Vague Binary Search

```
I ← a middle index of the indices of V
repeat
   if V(I) > X then
      {X cannot appear to the right of V(I)}
      I ← middle index of remaining indices to the left of V(I)
   elsif V(I) < X then
      {X cannot appear to the left of V(I)}
      I ← middle value of remaining indices to the right of V(I)
   fi
again until V(I) = X or there are no more indices to consider
if V(I) ≠ X then I ← 0 fi
```

What remains is to make Figure VAGUE_SEARCH precise. Expressions like "middle index of remaining indices to the left of $V(I)$" and "there are no more indices to consider" must be given a firm meaning. We have, as yet, no precise way to refer to the remaining indices. In the numeric example above, they were referenced by listing the remaining V's. That won't quite work, but it is a start. The remaining V's must have this form:

$$V(\text{low index}), \cdots, V(\text{high index})$$

Since the metacode must deal with indices, we need some concept of *search interval* that is defined in terms of indices, not V's. Let a search interval be a contiguous sequence of indices. It is characterized by a low index and a high index. It consists of all the integers between these two. It may be empty, in which case the high index will actually be lower than the low index. If the search interval is not empty, it has a midpoint which can be calculated thus:

$$\frac{\text{low index} + \text{high index}}{2}$$

Here the division is the integer division of FORTRAN or the **div** operation of Pascal.

These definitions are somewhat arbitrary. We could have picked different names or expressed the ideas slightly differently. No matter, for they are sufficient to the job which is now accomplished in Figure BINARY_SEARCH.

Consider, now, a somewhat less familiar and more applications-oriented example. An input file has been prepared with the daily readings of the New York Stock Exchange (N.Y.S.E.) composite index on it. A program is to be designed that reads this file and outputs the average daily increase (for those days that show increases), the average daily decrease (for those days that

Figure BINARY_SEARCH   A Binary Search
This design uses terms defined in the text.

```
search interval ← all the indices of V
repeat
    M ← midpoint of search interval
    if V(M) > X then
        {X cannot appear to the right of V(M)}
        search interval ← part of search interval strictly to left of M
    elsif V(M) < X then
        {X cannot appear to the left of V(M)}
        search interval ← part of search interval strictly to right of M
    fi
again until V(M) = X or search interval is empty
if V(M) ≠ X then M ← 0 fi
```

show decreases), the average length of a bull market, and the average length of a bear market.

For our purposes, the definition of a bull market is simplified: It is a sequence of N.Y.S.E. index readings which satisfies these properties:

1 The first reading is higher than the reading for the last day preceding the bull market, if any.

2 Each subsequent reading of the bull market is no less than the reading from the day before.

3 If the last reading of the bull market is not the last reading of the input file, then a smaller reading comes after it.

A bear market is defined similarly.

The length of a bull or bear market is the number of readings in it.

The description of top-down design began this way: "Write metacode that looks abstract, but is vague. . . ." This is shorthand for what top-down design really is. It omits a feature that is common to all approaches to design: understand the problem. Often, understanding does not come by being vague. To understand this problem, let's do what we did with the last problem and push some numbers around. Possible input data for this problem appears on the first line:

67.15	67.85	68.06	68.06	67.99	67.85	68.01	67.96	67.92
	+.70	+.21	0	−.07	−.14	+.16	−.05	−.04

For each input of a N.Y.S.E. index—other than the first—it is helpful to know whether a gain or loss from the previous input has been recorded. This information is recorded in an extra line just below the line of N.Y.S.E. indices.

One bull market of length 3 and another of length 1 are seen. Two bear markets of length 2 each are seen. The average length of either kind of market is, therefore, 2.0.

The average daily increase is the average of the positive differences; it is

0.357. The average daily decrease is the average of the negative differences, or 0.075.

Now we begin a vague metacode description of how those numbers were obtained. We make use of one fact that became glaringly apparent while pushing the numbers around: It is not the successive N.Y.S.E. readings which are important to this problem; rather, it is the successive differences in those readings.

Another helpful consideration before we write the vague metacode is to think about the kind of information which will need to be recorded before the averages can be found. There are, of course, eight numbers involved: total amount and number of increases, total amount and number of decreases, total number of bull days and runs, and total number of bear days and runs.

Figure VAGUE_NYSE shows the first attempt at this design. The major unsolved problems involve the recording of bull and bear market information. This recording is not simply a matter of updating a few variables. There is the problem of when to update them. The count of the number of bull markets, for example, should be updated only once per bull market. When is that? The phrase "as appropriate" in the last metastep say effectively, "sometimes this is a bull market and sometimes a bear market—the timing isn't known yet."

Figure VAGUE_NYSE   Vague N.Y.S.E. Statistics Gatherer

```
get first difference between N.Y.S.E. readings
repeat while there is more data
    if difference > 0 then
        record information for average daily increase
        record information for bull market length
    elsif difference < 0 then
        record information for average daily decrease
        record information for bear market length
    else
        record information for bull or bear market length as appropriate
    fi
    get next difference between N.Y.S.E. readings
again
calculate and print averages
```

The timing depends on knowing when a positive difference indicates the beginning of a bull market and when a zero difference indicates the continuation of one. Neither is hard to answer: A positive difference begins a bull market iff (if and only if) the previous reading was not in a bull market, and a zero continues a bull market iff the previous reading was in a bull market. For these questions to be answered during execution, the present market status must be kept current.

We could continue with our development of a precise version of VAGUE_ NYSE, but to do so would be to ignore some of the value of the top-down design. Top-down design allows different general approaches to be compared early. To achieve this, it is only necessary to write different approaches in vague metacode. What might be a different approach to the present problem?

VAGUE_NYSE can be characterized as a choose-an-action-depending-on-the-input approach. So the question is: What other way is there to choose an action? Figure VAGUE_NYSE_2 shows vague metacode that is based on a choose-an-action-depending-on-market-status approach.

**Figure VAGUE_NYSE_2   Status-Based Vague N.Y.S.E.
Statistics Gatherer**

```
get first difference between N.Y.S.E. readings
repeat while there was another difference
  if bull market then
    record beginning of bull market
    repeat
      record information for average daily increase
      record another bull market day
      get next difference between N.Y.S.E. readings
    again until not bull market
  elsif bear market then
    record beginning of bear market
    repeat
      record information for average daily decrease
      record another bear market day
      get next difference between N.Y.S.E. readings
    again until not bear market
  fi
again
calculate and print averages
```

One clear advantage of VAGUE_NYSE_2 over VAGUE_NYSE is that it is easy to see where to increase the counts of bull and bear market runs. This is because the form of the inner loops ensures that the beginnings of these market runs are clearly marked. In VAGUE_NYSE neither the beginnings nor the endings were clearly marked. Because VAGUE_NYSE_2 processes bull and bear markets separately, it is easy to determine their beginnings and endings: When it is already known that a bull or bear market is about to begin, then the question of which market depends solely on the sign of the difference in the N.Y.S.E. readings. When it is already known that a bull market is in progress, the question of continuance depends solely on whether the difference is negative. Similarly, continuance of a bear market is easy to identify by a positive difference.

Figure VAGUE_NYSE_2 seems to contain the better approach, a precise form is given in Figure NYSE.

Top-down design is an important tool for the computer scientist. It is an excellent approach for the vague-to-precise transition that is the backbone of problem solving. It results in abstract designs. And, as seen in the last example, it encourages a consideration of the alternatives. Such consideration is relatively

Figure NYSE   N.Y.S.E. Statistics Gatherer
This metacode depends on a *market change* data type that consists
of a partial sum of market differences and a count of the number of
differences that have been summed.

```
initialize increasing and decreasing market changes to 0
initialize bull and bear market day counts and run counts to 0
get the first nonzero difference between N.Y.S.E. readings
repeat while a difference was found
    {note that a bull or bear market run must always begin here}
    if difference > 0 then
        count another bull market run
        repeat
            update increasing market changes
            count another bull market day
            get next difference between N.Y.S.E. readings
        again until (no difference obtained) or (difference < 0)
    else
        count another bear market run
        repeat
            update decreasing market changes
            count another bear market day
            get next difference between N.Y.S.E. readings
        again until (no difference obtained) or (difference > 0)
    fi
again
calculate and print the average increasing market change,
    the average decreasing market change, the average bull
market run,
    and the average bear market run
```

painless before time is invested in any one alternative. But if a particular
vague-metacode plan is married before the alternatives have been considered,
then its problems will be hidden in the honeymoon of development and, if it
should require divorce, the severance will be painful.

EXERCISES

3.2.1 Write detailed metacode that matches the abstract metacode in Figure BINARY_
SEARCH.

3.2.2 The two comments in Figure BINARY_SEARCH seem to express the main
thought behind why the search technique works. Nothing in them states that the
interval must be halved each iteration. If the assignment to M is replaced with

$M \leftarrow 1 +$ (the lowest index of the search interval)

are the comments still true? How would you describe the action of this modified
binary search?

3.2.3 Write detailed metacode, matching the design in Figure NYSE.

3.2.4 Finish the design in Figure VAGUE_NYSE. Do you agree that it is worse than
the design in Figure NYSE_VAGUE_2? Explain.

3.2.5 Roman numerals depend on these letter-to-number conversions:

$$M = 1000$$
$$D = 500$$
$$C = 100$$
$$L = 50$$
$$X = 10$$
$$V = 5$$
$$I = 1$$

Evaluation is as simple as adding the corresponding values:

$$III = 3$$
$$MMI = 2001$$
$$MCLXVII = 1167$$
$$DCCCXI = 811$$

Letters appear in decreasing order of value. Letters V, L, and D may appear only once in an expression. The others may be repeated up to 4 times in sequence. This allows numbers up to 4999, or MMMMDCCCCLXXXXVIIII, to be written. Write both a metacode procedure which imports a character string Roman numeral and exports the integer form of the same number and a second metacode procedure which does the opposite. Implement those procedures, and test them on the numbers shown.

3.2.6 Write, implement, and test a metacode procedure to print all prime numbers less than 1000. Use the method of the Sieve of Eratosthenes: Your metacode should create a boolean vector whose Ith position is true if and only if I is prime for $1 < I < 1000$. Start with all positions true. Eliminate the multiples of 2, then the multiples of 3, etc. Don't bother to eliminate the multiples of a number that is already eliminated! Stop eliminating when all further multiples would be larger than 1000. When you test this program, note that the only primes between 875 and 885 are 877, 881, and 883.

3.2.7 Write, implement, and test metacode procedures to import two Roman numerals and export their sum and difference, also in Roman form. Do the arithmetic as the Roman would, without converting to integer form.

3.2.8 Sometimes a single I, X, or C will be written one place out of sequence in a kind of subtractive notation:

$$IV = 4$$
$$IX = 9$$
$$XL = 40$$
$$XC = 90$$
$$CD = 400$$
$$CM = 900$$
$$MCMXLIII = 1943$$
$$CMLXIV = 964$$
$$MMMCMXCIX = 3999$$

A letter being one place out of sequence means that there is exactly one letter to the right of it with a higher value. Modify your design and code of exercise

3.2.5 so that Roman numerals written in subtractive notation can be imported and will be exported. Implement and test the modification on these examples.

3.3 SIDE-TO-SIDE

Probably the richest source of ideas for solving problems is the store of similar problems known to the problem solver. A problem solver who has knowledge of similar problems has a clear advantage over one who does not. In this section we explore, with three examples, ways to capitalize on that advantage.

The first example concerns the sorting of data without actually rearranging it. Let V represent a vector of customer records. A customer record might be the kind of thing shown in Figure DATA_DICTIONARY of Section 2.3, or it might be something a little different. In any case, the Ith customer record contains a social security number, which we represent with $SSN(I)$.

Suppose, further, that the V's are stored in a form of alphabetical order and that order is convenient enough to preserve. But it is necessary to print these records for the tax people according to what they call "increasing social security numbers." Nobody else wants that order, and these records ought not be rearranged just for a government regulation. (Remember that this is a hypothetical situation!) The present problem is to find a way to print the records in order of nondecreasing social security numbers without actually rearranging them. (Since one customer may have more than one account, there is no assurance that social security numbers will not be duplicated. Hence, "nondecreasing" is correct.)

There are many ways to rearrange data into a sorted order. Most might be applied directly to the present problem. For example, an application of selection sort, Figure SELECT_SORT of Section 2.2, to order customer records by social security number is as follows:

```
repeat for I ← 1,2, ... , N−1
    find J such that SSN(J) is smallest of SSN(I), ... , SSN(N)
    interchange V(I) and V(J)
again
```

A small change would sort customer records by name. A conceivable solution to this problem would be to sort twice—once by social security number and once by name—and print the list for the tax people in between. Notice that if the customer records are large, the step "interchange $V(I)$ and $V(J)$" can involve a lot of interchanging! The amount of work a computer would have to do to accomplish this step, when multiplied by the necessary number of interchanges, is quite large. For that reason, the problem statement has forbidden the customer records to be rearranged.

A method is sought, therefore, to access these records one by one in order of nondecreasing social security numbers without actually rearranging them. Since this accessing is to be done only once a year, we will not keep any permanent files, indices, or whatever, to help.

There is one commonly used method of accessing records in a different order from that in which they are stored. It is to access the records through an indexing system rather than directly. Suppose *SSINDEX* is a vector which has the useful property that *SSINDEX*(1) is the index of a customer record with lowest social security number, *SSINDEX*(2) is the index of a customer record with next lowest social security number, and so on. This property can be stated more succinctly:

$$SSN(SSINDEX(1)) \leq SSN(SSINDEX(2)) \leq \ldots \leq SSN(SSINDEX(N)) \tag{3.1}$$

If such an *SSINDEX* existed, then the following algorithm could be used to print the customer records in order of increasing social security number:

repeat for each *I* from 1 to *N*
  print the record *V(SSINDEX(I))*
again

Our intention is, if possible, to use selection sort to aid in the creation of a vector *SSINDEX* which satisfies (3.1). It helps to think of the index in much more concrete terms first and, only later, to write an abstract version that is suitable for describing a computer algorithm. Suppose the index is on small cards in a file box. Each card contains the social security number *SSN(I)* and the index number *I* of some record *V(I)*. Because most of *V(I)* is not present on this card, the card is, in a sense, an abstraction of the record *V(I)*. When the file box is first set up, the cards are in the order of the corresponding *V*'s. Figure INDEX_CARDS shows this situation. Note that *SSN*(1) = 607 38 9914, *SSN*(2) = 506 12 4743, *SSN*(3) = 607 38 9914, and *SSN*(4) = 506 65 4872. The cards are then rearranged in nondecreasing order of the social security numbers. See Figure REARRANGED. By looking up the *V* indexed

Figure INDEX_CARDS

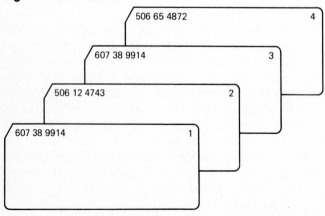

Figure REARRANGED

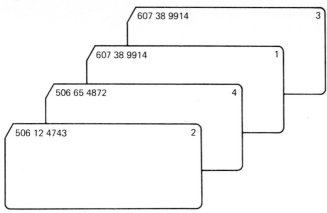

by the first card, then the V indexed by the second card, and so on, the V's can be accessed in order of nondecreasing social security number.

The file box analogy essentially requires that these "cards" or "lines" be rearranged into order of nondecreasing SSN's.

$SSN(1),1$
$SSN(2),2$

.

. (3.2)

.

$SSN(N),N$

(Here, the first card appears toward the top of the page whereas the first or top card in Figures INDEX_CARDS and REARRANGED appears toward the bottom.) To restate this requirement in abstract metacode is difficult. First, the integers 1, 2, . . . , N must be placed in some kind of vector before they can be manipulated with a computer program. Second, the SSN's may not really be rearranged because they are part of the V's. Third, it is not clear how to modify the sorting algorithm to fit this problem.

These difficulties might be enough reason to give up hope of applying the concepts of file box and selection sort to a solution of the problem, but they shouldn't be. By taking a little more time to describe the notion of file box in computer programming terms, the solution will fall into place.

The file box analogy indicates that a rearrangement of the integers 1, 2, . . . , N that is based on their "corresponding" social security numbers will provide the needed index system. To make this claim less vague, let's assume that the vector $SSINDEX$ contains N elements which are the integers 1, 2, . . . , N, in that order. Then list (3.2) can be rewritten as

$$SSN(SSINDEX(1)),SSINDEX(1)$$
$$SSN(SSINDEX(2)),SSINDEX(2)$$

.

.

.
                                                                                    (3.3)

$$SSN(SSINDEX(N)),SSINDEX(N)$$

In the analogy with the file box, $SSINDEX(I)$ corresponds to the index found in the Ith card. In the starting arrangement of cards, $SSINDEX(I) = I$ for each I and list (3.3) reduces to (3.2). In the final desired arrangement of the cards, $SSINDEX$ will satisfy (3.1). In understanding this analogy it is helpful to notice that interchanging the Jth and Kth cards is analogous to interchanging the values of $SSINDEX(J)$ and $SSINDEX(K)$.

The analogy suggests that the desired vector $SSINDEX$ can be obtained this way:

$SSINDEX(1), \ldots, SSINDEX(N) \leftarrow 1, \ldots, N$
sort $SSINDEX$ so that (3.1) holds

This expands into the metacode procedure found in Figure INDEX_SORT.

Figure INDEX_SORT Creating an Index to Access V in Order of Nondecreasing Social Security Number

$SSINDEX(1), \ldots, SSINDEX(N) \leftarrow 1, \ldots, N$
repeat for each I from 1 to $N-1$
    find J such that $SSN(SSINDEX(J))$ is smallest of
      $SSN(SSINDEX(I)), \ldots, SSN(SSINDEX(N))$
    interchange $SSINDEX(I)$ and $SSINDEX(J)$
again

This example has shown the side-to-side design technique at its slickest. The differences between the original SELECT_SORT and the new INDEX_SORT are not very large. Once the use of an index such as $SSINDEX$ is fully understood, all the work is essentially done.

The second example is different. The work will focus more on adapting known algorithms and less on adopting a correct point of view. It concerns the sorting of data which is too numerous to fit into computer memory. Specifically, we assume that a file IN_FILE of "objects" exists and that there are too many objects to fit into computer memory. It does not matter what an object is, but it must be possible to test two objects to see whether one is greater than the other. (To use mathematical jargon, the set of objects must be totally ordered.) A file $SORTED\_FILE$ is to be created which contains the same objects as IN_FILE but in nondecreasing order.

The two sorting algorithms in Section 2.2 are meant to be used when all the data to be sorted will fit into memory. Looking at SELECT_SORT, we can see that the method relies on the ability to find a lowest object from, in the first iteration, the entire set of objects. Looking at INSERT_SORT, we can see that this method relies on the ability to do an insertion which, in the last iteration, could involve all the data. It seems that an application of either algorithm to the present problem would require that the input file (or an analog of it) be reread many times. Such a solution would be slower than is desirable.

Since the two sorting techniques do not provide enough guidance, we search for another related problem. The FILE_MERGE algorithm of Section 2.3 is related. At first glance, it seems to be no help because its use would require not one, but two, input files—each of which is sorted. However, each input file could be half the length of the original. . .

Our present tools include a way of sorting data (as long as there isn't too much of it) and a way of combining files of sorted data into larger files of sorted data. Clearly, these tools are adequate if only we can put them together properly.

Using a combination of these tools, we could presumably sort a little at a time and merge the newly sorted data with a file of previously sorted data. Figure VAGUE_SORT expresses the thought:

Figure VAGUE_SORT   External Sort on a Data File

```
create an empty SORTED_FILE
input some of IN_FILE into V
repeat
    sort V
    lengthen SORTED_FILE by merging V into it
    input some of IN_FILE into V
again
```

The merge metastep is clearly different from FILE_MERGE because FILE_MERGE imports two files and exports a third whereas this metastep clearly requires an import of V and a single file, SORTED_FILE. The difference between an input and an import will be easy to accommodate, so we'll forget that problem for now. The single file is a greater problem. The only apparent

Figure SORT_MERGE   An External Sorting Routine

```
create two empty files SORTED_FILE and ALTERNATE_FILE
obtain first N objects from IN_FILE, determining N by doing the
    input until V can hold no more or IN_FILE is out of objects
repeat while N > 0
    sort V
    if SORTED_FILE's turn then
        merge V and SORTED_FILE, obtaining ALTERNATE_FILE
    else
        merge V and ALTERNATE_FILE, obtaining SORTED_FILE
    fi
    obtain next N objects from IN_FILE, determining N by doing the
        input until V can hold no more or IN_FILE is out of objects
again
if ALTERNATE_FILE's turn then
    copy ALTERNATE_FILE to SORTED_FILE
fi
```

way to adapt FILE_MERGE is to use *SORTED_FILE* as input and a scratch file as output. The scratch file can be copied into *SORTED_FILE* at the end of the metastep.

Recopying a file once each time through the loop isn't a practical solution. Perhaps the top level can be rewritten so as to alternate *SORTED_FILE* between input and output. This would require an alternate version of *SORTED_FILE* which is not impossible or unreasonable. Figure SORT_ MERGE shows the resulting top-level metacode.

An implementation of this metacode will require some sort of flag to keep track of whose "turn" it is, but that's not difficult. The metastep to merge *V* and one file to obtain another can be written as a subprogram. More detail is shown in Figure MERGE_V.

This example has shown that sometimes two known algorithms can be combined to obtain a new and different algorithm. Not only were algorithms combined, but the side-to-side method was combined with the top-down method as well.

Figure MERGE_V Merging a Sorted Vector and a Sorted File
A sorted vector *V* and a sorted file *F* are merged to obtain a sorted file *G*.

```
initialize input, getting first OBJ from F, if any
I ← 1
repeat while (I ≤ N) and (OBJ was obtained)
   if V(I) < N) then
      output V(I) onto G
      I ← I + 1
   else
      output OBJ onto G
      input another OBJ from F, if any
   fi
again
output remaining N + 1 − I objects in V onto G
copy rest of F onto G
```

The final example involves a situation in which the necessary building blocks are yet more difficult to find. A string *TEXT* is to be altered by replacing all occurrences of a substring *SUB* with an alternate substring *ALTSUB*. For example, *TEXT* might be as follows:

```
"
I ← 1
repeat while I ≤ N
   do something
   I ← I + 1
again
"
```

The substring *SUB* might be "I" and the alternate substring *ALTSUB* might be "LONG_VARIABLE_NAME." Input of these strings should cause the variable I in *TEXT* to be replaced with the variable "LONG_VARIABLE_ NAME". Staying in the spirit of this example and making the description of the problem as easy as possible, we assume that multiple occurrences of *SUB*, if any, are disjoint from one another. Our design is allowed to perform in any bizarre way if this condition is not met. For example, if *TEXT* is

"AAA"

SUB is "AA" and *ALTSUB* is "B", then the result can be "AB" or "BA" or anything.

It is also possible that *ALTSUB* has more characters than *SUB*. In this case, the string *TEXT* could grow in length to a size beyond its maximum capacity. In general, as many occurrences of *SUB* as possible are to be replaced with *ALTSUB;* and if there are any remaining, a message is to be printed that it was impossible to replace them all.

The only metacode procedure we have seen that is related to this problem is the PATTERN algorithm of Section 2.2. Its relevance stems from the need to find occurrences of the substring *SUB* in *TEXT*.

When we have a problem that is new and we lack sufficient guidance from previous work, we can choose to obtain that guidance by solving a related problem first. If this problem is related closely enough, its solution will add almost no extra time to what it will take to solve the original. If the original is difficult enough, the prior solution of a related problem may, in fact, be the only way to solve it.

An easy, but related, problem is that of replacing all occurrences of a letter L in *TEXT* with an alternate letter *ALTL*. Metacode to do this is shown in Figure LETTER_REPLACE.

Figure LETTER_REPLACE   Replacing a Single Letter

```
repeat for I ← 1,2, . . ., (length of TEXT)
   if TEXT (I) = L then
      TEXT (I) ← ALTL
   fi
again
```

Clearly this metacode won't work for string replacement. The metatest must test for equality of substrings. A substring, not a letter, must be replaced. Further, I cannot be advanced by 1 after a replacement is done without risking a replacement of newly replaced text. Correcting these problems leads to the vague metacode found in Figure VAGUE_REPLACE.

The major vague aspect of Figure VAGUE_REPLACE concerns the likelihood that *ALTSUB* and *SUB* are not the same length. The replacement step, if the lengths differ, is not going to be very easy. It will be particularly difficult if the length of *ALTSUB* is larger. In that case, it may be impossible to do the replacement because of a lack of room in *TEXT*.

Figure VAGUE_REPLACE   Vague Global Replacement Algorithm

$I \leftarrow 1$
repeat while $I <$ (length of *TEXT*) − (length of *SUB*) + 1
  if *TEXT* $(I), \ldots,$ *TEXT*$(I +$ (length of *SUB*) − 1) = *SUB* **then**
    replace *SUB* with *ALTSUB* in *TEXT*
    $I \leftarrow$ first position in *TEXT* after new *ALTSUB*
  else
    $I \leftarrow I + 1$
  fi
again

Once more, we avoid attempting to solve the entire problem in favor of gaining relevant experience with an easier problem. Two easier problems immediately come to mind. The first is to copy text to some "output" string, making the necessary changes along the way. The second is to assume that the length of *ALTSUB* is no longer than the length of *SUB*. Since most readers can easily solve the "output" string problems, it is omitted.

In the second easier problem we make the replacement within *TEXT*, but with the simplifying assumption that the length of *ALTSUB* is no longer than the length of *SUB*. In this case, *ALTSUB* can be copied into the place filled by *SUB*, but there may be a gap of unwanted characters after the copying is done.

This gap can be handled by using the knowledge we might have obtained from the "output" string version. We imagine that we are copying from an "input" *TEXT* to an "output" *TEXT*. Although they are the same string, we can distinguish between them by keeping an index *TO* which shows the next place where the "output" *TEXT* will receive a character and an index *FROM* which shows the next place of the "input" *TEXT* which has a character to copy. Of course, that character may not actually be copied because characters that are a part of substrings matching *SUB* are to be skipped rather than copied.

Figure SIMPLE_REPLACE shows metacode that handles the gap while copying. The metacode is an abstract solution of a problem which differs from the one we want to solve only in the assumption that *ALTSUB* is no longer than *SUB*.

A replacement algorithm must allow for the possibility that a substring is to be removed. In this algorithm, that means the possibility that *SUB* is to be replaced with the empty string. Notice that the metastep

TEXT $(TO), \ldots,$ *TEXT* $(TO +$ (length of *ALTSUB*) − 1) ← *ALTSUB*

has something to say about the case when *ALTSUB* is empty. This is because the left hand collapses to

TEXT $(TO), \ldots,$ *TEXT* $(TO - 1)$

which by convention is an empty subsequence of *TEXT*. The metastep, then, states that an empty substring of *TEXT* is to be have an empty string assigned to it, i.e., that no action is to take place. This convention dovetails nicely with the function of a loop that begins thus:

repeat for $K \leftarrow TO, \ldots, TO + $ (length of *ALTSUB*) $- 1$

Our final design must also work when the length of *ALTSUB* is larger than the length of *SUB*. In such case the string *TEXT* will get longer with each substitution. It is possible that it will grow beyond its maximum capacity, and this possibility should be checked by the procedure that does the replacing. The procedure should do as many replacements as is possible, and if that is not all of them, it should print a message. The metacode in Figure SIMPLE_REPLACE will need to be modified to accomplish this part of the task.

Figure SIMPLE_REPLACE   Simplified Global Replacement Algorithm

```
FROM ← 1
TO ← 1
repeat while
        FROM ≤ (original length of TEXT) − (length of SUB) + 1
    {note that TO ≤ FROM remains true}
    if TEXT(FROM), . . .,TEXT(FROM + (length of SUB − 1) = SUB then
        TEXT(TO), . . .,TEXT(TO + (length of ALTSUB) − 1) ← ALTSUB
        TO ← TO + (length of ALTSUB)
        FROM ← FROM + (length of SUB)
    else
        TEXT(TO) ← TEXT(FROM)
        TO ← TO + 1
        FROM ← FROM + 1
    fi
again
TEXT(TO),TEXT(TO + 1),. . ., TEXT(TO + (original length of TEXT) − FROM)
    ← TEXT(FROM),TEXT(FROM + 1),. . ., TEXT(original length of TEXT)
{note that the new length of TEXT is TO + (maximum length of TEXT) − FROM}
```

The main difficulty in making this alteration is that the relation $TO < FROM$ may fail, and so characters will be overwritten before they are used. A simple way to solve this problem is to copy the characters in *TEXT* from the left side of the entire string to the right side. After this has been done, the relation $TO \leq FROM$ can fail only when a replacement of *SUB* by *ALTSUB* causes *TEXT* to grow too large. Figure REPLACE_STRING shows this design and solves the original problem.

The three examples in this section have shown a range of situations in which the side-to-side technique is useful. In the first example, the difficulty lay in understanding the applicability to a new problem of a small change in a known algorithm. In the second, the difficulty lay in combining two known algorithms to solve a new problem. And in this last example, the difficulty

Figure REPLACE_STRING   Global Replacement Algorithm

shift the text in *TEXT* so that it is right justified and
  let *FROM* be the index of the first textual character
TO ← 1
repeat while
      FROM ≤ (maximum length of *TEXT*) − (length of *SUB*) + 1
      and *TO* + (length of *ALTSUB*) ≤ *FROM*
    TEXT(TO), . . .,*TEXT(TO* + (length of *ALTSUB*) − 1) ← *ALTSUB*
    TEXT(TO), . . .,*TEXT(TO* + (length of *ALTSUB*) − 1) ← *ALTSUB*
    TO ← *TO* + (length of *ALTSUB*)
    FROM ← *FROM* + (length of *SUB*)
  else
    TEXT(TO) ← *TEXT(FROM)*
    TO ← *TO* + 1
    FROM ← *FROM* + 1
  fi
again
if   (*FROM* ≤ (maximum length of *TEXT*) − (length of *SUB*) + 1)
    and *TEXT(FROM)*, . . ., *TEXT(FROM* + (length of *SUB*) − 1) = *SUB* **then**
  print a message that not all occurrences of *SUB*
    have been replaced
fi
TEXT(TO), *TEXT(TO* + 1), . . .,*TEXT(TO* + (maximum length of *TEXT*) − *FROM*)
    ← *TEXT(FROM)*,*TEXT(FROM* + 1), . . .,*TEXT*(maximum length of *TEXT*)
{note that the new length of *TEXT* is *TO* + (maximum length of *TEXT*) − *FROM*}

involved first creating a relevant, but simpler, ''known'' algorithm where there was none.

A warning about possible misinterpretations of the material in this chapter is necessary. Problem solving has been presented as the act of moving from the vague to the precise. In making the presentation, several algorithms have been given first a vague form and then a precise form. In spite of appearances, that vague form was not a representation of the algorithm. In all cases, it was a vague generality of dubious value. It would not have appeared on the pages of this book but for the problem-solving emphasis. Proper designs are related to their implementations along the principles begun in Chapter 2 and continued in Chapter 4. This relationship is very different from that between vague metacode and precise metacode, found in Chapters 3 and 5.

If the vague forms are of dubious value, why present them? The value is dubious only in a special sense. Vague metacode makes poor designs. Its value lies in its aid to problem solving. I have tried to write vague metacode for you that will seem to be a natural part of the thinking process. Perhaps through the magic granted by an audience to a storyteller, I succeeded. Be that as it may, once a development story is told, all that remains is a design and a vicarious experience of a development process. The vague metacode of this chapter is a part of the experience, not of the design.

EXERCISES

3.3.1 Write detailed metacode matching Figure INDEX_SORT.

3.3.2 Design another index sort that is based on quicksort, if you know it, or on insertion sort, otherwise.

3.3.3 Write Pascal or FORTRAN code, implementing the design in Figures SORT_ MERGE and MERGE_V. The objects to be sorted can be integers. Test your program.

3.3.4 Alter the design in Figures SORT_MERGE and MERG_V so that it runs faster if the file is already sorted. Try to do this in a way that doesn't add much complexity to the algorithm or much processing time to the sorting of files.

3.3.5 Write Pascal or FORTRAN code, implementing the design in Figure PATTERN_REPLACE. Test your implementation with three cases; the first involves an empty *ALTSUB*, the second involves a nonempty *ALTSUB* that is shorter than *SUB*, and the third involves a nonempty *ALTSUB* that is longer than *SUB* and will cause the length of *TEXT* to be exceeded. All these cases should involve multiple substitutions.

3.3.6 Figure REPLACE_EXERCISE shows another vague plan for solving the pattern-replacing problem of this section. It is the kind of plan one might concoct while under the influence of Figure PATTERN of Section 2.2. What is the major difference between REPLACE_EXERCISE and VAGUE_REPLACE? Write a design based on REPLACE_EXERCISE that shows the same difference when compared with PATTERN_REPLACE.

Figure REPLACE_EXERCISE   Replacing a String by Using PATTERN Search Algorithm

$I \leftarrow$ first column of *TEXT* that begins a copy of *SUB*
    (if there is any—0 otherwise)
repeat while $I = 0$
  do the replacement
  $I \leftarrow$ next column of *TEXT* that begins a copy of *SUB*
    (if there is any—0 otherwise)
again

3.3.7 In using the N.Y.S.E. statistics-gathering program of the last section, it is found that the input data often contains errors. This method is chosen to correct for the errors: A data item D is validated when it lies close enough to the previous data item P and the next data item N. In particular, D is validated if it is less than the largest of

$$N + 4 \times N - P , N - 4 \times N - P , P + 4 \times N - P , P - 4 \times N - P$$

and greater than the smallest of them. When an invalid data item is found, it is replaced with the average $(N+P)/2$.

Another problem is that the definition of bull and bear market is too simple. A small improvement would be to replace the concept of an increasing or decreasing difference with the concept of two consecutive increasing or decreasing differences. Of course, the length of the resulting bull or bear market would be counted from the first of these consecutive differences and would include any singleton difference of the wrong sign that occurred during the run.

Revise the metacode in Figure NYSE to accommodate these changes.

3.3.8 Rewrite the sort in Figure INDEX_SORT so that it is possible not only to print the customer records in order of nondecreasing social security number but to print them in their original order with a number appended to each that gives its position in the nondecreasing social security sequence. That is, the alphabetically first customer will have the number 27 appended if that customer appears 27th in order of nondecreasing social security numbers.

3.3.9 Another way of combining a vector sort with a file merge to sort objects in a file has this somewhat vague description: Begin with one pass through *IN_FILE* that reads N records at a time, sorts, them, and outputs them to files *F1* and *F2*. The first N records go to *F1*; all the rest go to *F2*. Then the first N records of *F2* are merged with *F1* onto *F3*. More merging takes place until *F1* or *F3* contains the desired result. Convert this to a design.

REFERENCES

[SUZ]: Suzuki, D. T.: "Lectures on Zen Buddhism" from *Zen Buddhism and Psychoanalysis* by D. T. Suzuki, Erich Fromm, and Richard DeMartino, Grove Press, 1960.

CHAPTER 4

DATA ABSTRACTION

Programmers typically deal with integers, real numbers, characters, strings, boolean values, and organizations of these things into arrays, records, and files. The reason is that these are the concepts of the programming languages in which they must write. However, these concepts are not natural to almost any given programming problem.

Examples abound. A simple instance is a problem requiring that student grades be recorded, averaged, and analyzed. The problem statement will be in terms of grades, average grades, students, etc. A program performing the specified task, however, will deal with real numbers and character strings.

Traditionally programmers have used two methods to bridge the gap between the data natural to the problem and the data of the programming language. The first is the insertion of comments which say something like "When I say *X*, I mean student." The second is the choice of mnemonic variable names, such as *STUDENT*.

In more recent times, a third method of bridging this gap has become popular. Data is defined in the two-step process of Section 2.3. With this method, the programmer-designer first describes what a *Student* is and second declares variables, say *STUD* and *COED*, to be of type *Student*.

All these methods describe data by its form, not its function. Form, however, is seldom as significant as function. This point becomes quite clear when we consider that the form in which programmers view integers and the form in which computers view integers are quite different. A compiler can replace one form by the other because it is the addition, subtraction, and multiplication of integers which is important. Within the range of integers available to the computer, these functions are the same for the programmer and for the computer. (Division is a little trickier. It functions the same way in both forms, but that function must be explained to the novice programmer who, more often than not, would prefer to see ½ equal 0.5, which is not an integer, rather than 0, which is.)

A fourth method of bridging the gap is to describe what data is for—not how it is named or how it looks. Under this method a student record might, in part, be something which has a grade that can be looked up or altered. Exactly how that grade is recorded is not described.

This *functional* description of data is a central theme of this book. The concept is tied up with such buzzwords as "data abstraction," "Parnas module," "information hiding," and "object-oriented design". Although it is not a new concept, the approach taken here is new. As seen in Chapter 5, many problems can be solved and designs written by using this approach. Chapter 7 links this approach to others which use mathematics to achieve a greater degree of abstraction.

A functional description of data may be accomplished by listing and explaining a set of basic actions that can be taken with the data. Each action can be implemented later as a subprogram, although another implementation method is sometimes used in the appendixes. These action implementations and nothing else may be used to create, look up, alter, or destroy the data. All actions which a program unit takes with the abstracted data must make direct use of one of the listed basic actions. The data may not be handled directly. The basic actions are the tools by which data is manipulated.

Data which cannot be used is, of course, without value. Further, the value of data increases with its ease of use, and the ease of use increases with the appropriateness of the basic manipulations that are available. A design process that views data from a functional point of view tends to be concerned with the finding of appropriate basic actions.

For example, a computer which will add and subtract integers, but not multiply and divide them, does not have an integer data type that is as valuable as a computer which will add, substract, multiply, and divide integers. For general use, the four arithmetic operations are a more appropriate basic set of actions than just addition and subtraction. The reason lies in the convenience of one-step operations for multiplication and division, in spite of the fact that everything that can be done with the four operations can also be done with the two. Multiplication of integers can, after all, be obtained from repeated additions, and division of integers can be obtained from repeated subtractions. It is the convenience of the four arithmetic operations, not their necessity, which makes them a good basic set.

Likewise, when a program designer decides to establish a new kind of data, the value of that data is enhanced if some basic operations are developed early in the design process. Further, the basic operations should be designed before the form of the underlying data is determined, because when form comes first, it affects function in ways that are unrelated to convenience of use.

Often there will be more than one way to write the subprograms that implement a functional data definition. If some of these implementations do not satisfy the intent of the person who wrote the functional data description but do faithfully represent the description itself, then the description is a vague generality. The description writer's goal, of course, is to write an abstractions. Such abstractions are called *data abstractions*.

This chapter provides two main frameworks for defining data abstractions: *object* modules and *object-type* modules. (These terms should not be confused with the usage of "object code" to mean executable machine code.) Object modules can be viewed in two ways: as *containing* object modules and as *interfacing* object modules.

From the containment perspective, we visualize an object such as a gas tank or a recipe box and design a "container" that controls access to the object while suppressing, or *hiding,* information about the form of the data "inside" the container. Object modules are described in Section 4.1; the cleanest examples of containing object modules arise from objects known as data structures and are discussed in Section 4.2

From the interface perspective, we define object modules that form an interface between our software and external data objects such as input-output (I/O) devices. This perspective, which is discussed in Section 4.4, seems to be less abstract than the containment perspective, for it often seems to require more detailed metacode descriptions of the basic actions.

In the object-type module framework, we create a data type by defining the actions which will combine and otherwise manipulate objects of that data type. For example, the data type *Matrix* can use operations of addition, multiplication, inversion, etc. The concept of an object-type module is introduced in Section 4.5.

There is reason to believe that programs which have been implemented from functional data descriptions tend to exhibit a cleaner and easier-to-debug structure than those which have not. This is discussed in Section 4.3.

Although they are discussed in separate sections, containing object modules, interfacing object modules, and object-type modules are not mutually exclusive concepts. One design can involve all three. And as some examples of this chapter show, sometimes the same basic data organization can be described from more than one of these points of view. Then the designer can choose the point of view which seems most appropriate. The choice can even be left to the implementor by writing the design at the level of abstraction shown in Chapter 7.

Remark: All the subprograms that are used to implement the actions of a module may make the computer work a little harder at run time, but the computer is supposed to work for us, not the other way around. We shouldn't mind sacrificing some computer time if we can thereby decrease development time.

At first it may seem that the use of functional data descriptions will increase rather than decrease the development time. After all, it takes time to list and describe actions in a precise way. Subprograms don't write themselves either.

Clearly, there is work involved in defining functional data abstractions. And if our point of view is so narrow that we never look beyond that work, we will see no productivity improvements.

A wider point of view includes the time taken to debug the program as part of the development time. It also includes the time spent coordinating the efforts of a team of programmers. Finally, it may include the time spent in updating the program to meet new demands. Even though functional data descriptions may increase the time taken to create a design and write the original version of the code, the overall development time is decreased because the use of functional descriptions of data can make the interactions of the pieces of a program much more apparent. This is very valuable to programmers who are looking for bugs, who are reusing code written by others, and who are rewriting code written by others.

Further, it is not uncommon to find that a single designer-programmer working on a program many pages in length will save enough time in the coding and debugging stage to make up for the lost time in writing careful functional descriptions at design time. This fact is not obvious. Most people have to try it both ways before being convinced.

Sometimes even the design time is decreased by the use of functional data descriptions. This is true when the designer needs help in organizing thoughts about a difficult new problem. Chapter 5 discusses the use of functional data descriptions in problem solving.

Of course, there are applications in which machine efficiency is so important that the use of extra subprograms is unacceptable. In such situations, however, there are two problems: getting it right and getting it fast. It is best to solve these two problems in four steps:

1 Create a good design.

2 Make algorithmic changes at the design level, if there are any, that will make it faster.

3 Code this design, and make sure the code is correct.

4 Using this code as a detailed design, write "optimized" code that does it fast.

A book has been written which is devoted to the fourth step, see [BEN].

4.1 OBJECT MODULES: PROBING AND OPERATING ON A STATE

To set the stage, consider a simulated container:

> The content of a car's gas tank is modeled by keeping information about the amount of each brand in the tank and providing answers to questions about whether a single brand makes up 90% of the mixture.

A limited model of this type could be useful in any program which must calculate mileage by brand. Such a calculation requires that running totals be kept, for each brand, of the miles traveled and the amount of gas used. These totals cannot be updated without knowing whether the tank can be considered to be purely one brand.

An object module is a set of actions pertaining to some data object. We can say the data object is *contained* by the module because the only permitted ways to manipulate or investigate the object are the actions described in the object module.

Finding language in which to describe an object module's action can be difficult. The description should avoid considerations of the overall problem on one side and of the particular data implementation on the other. Of course, such considerations will often be on the designer's mind, but she doesn't write them when describing the object module. Instead she writes a careful description of the basic actions that manipulate and investigate the contained object.

One descriptive technique, explained in Chapter 7, uses the mathematical concept of axiom. Another less formal approach is described here. It involves the concept of a container which holds an abstract object and enables its use. The object can be used with any of a list of acceptable actions which are described in terms of what they do to, or discover about, a *state*. States are described by using any precise terminology that is familiar to all. They represent the essential features of the contained data object.

For example, the state of our simulated gas tank can be defined with the familiar words "set" and "amount" as a set of brands together with the amount of each. This description can be used to define actions taken with the gas tank:

initialize: The tank is initialized with a specified amount of an unknown brand.

refill: A brand and an amount are specified; the tank is drained by that amount, with each brand decremented by the same proportion, and then filled with that amount of the imported brand.

An object module that satisfies our limited needs for keeping track of a gas tank's contents need not have its state modified in any other fashion, but some other actions are necesssary to provide information about the state. Possible descriptions of those are as follows:

pure: Exports true or false; true iff the tank contains one brand that makes up at least 90% of its present contents.

pure_brand: Exports the brand, if any, that makes up at least 90% of the tank's present contents.

An *object module* is a set (called the *state space*) of states, a set of actions (called *operations*), and a set of actions (called *probes*). The primitive concepts of "state" and "action" are undefined, but a state can be thought of as any composition of data that can be described, and an action can be thought of as a subprogram.

A state of the gas-tank module is a set of brands and associated amounts.

The *initialization* operation causes an initial state to exist. The *refill* operation is used to change the state. The actions *pure* and *pure_brand* are probes. They are used to report information about the state to a program unit that uses the module.

Each execution of a module operation establishes an element of the state space. The element established by the most recently executed operation is called simply *the state*. Execution of a probe exports to the invoking program unit some information about the state.

All object modules have an *initialize* operation, and their states are undefined until it has executed.[1] The imports of the *initialize* operation are called *parameters*. They are part of the state, but they remain unchanged by all other operations.

The sole purpose of an operation is to establish a new state, so there is a rule that no operation may export or update data.

The state and the state space are known to, and shared by, the probes and operations of the module. Thus in any implementation of the module, the state represents data that is global to each probe and operation. However, access to the state by a probe or operation of the module is not considered to be an import, export, or update. These terms are used in the sense of data that flows to or from the module as a whole.

The sole purpose of a probe is to report about some aspect of the module's state. So a probe must have exactly one export and may neither update data nor change the state of the module.

An object module can be implemented as a set of subprograms, one for each operation and probe. These subprograms must share the "global" data that represents the state. Program units which are not a part of the module are not permitted to access this data. It is to be contained by the module. Secret data sharing between a set of subprograms is supported in FORTRAN with use of a COMMON statement (Appendixes F2 and F4). It is supported in some versions of Pascal through the mechanism of external compilation. It is supported in ANSI COBOL through multiple-entry subprograms [LEV]. It is well supported in Ada[2] through the package concept [BAR]. It is possible to implement object modules when there is no language support, but in such implementations the programmer is responsible for seeing that all the rules are followed. Programmers in assembly language, BASIC, or even ANSI Pascal have no language support for enforcing the rules—only self-imposed discipline can produce correct implementations. (A discipline for enforcing the proper data sharing in ANSI Pascal appears in Appendixes P2 and P4.)

Modules in this book are described in a standardized format, called a *module chart,* which presents both what the module will do and what it will not do. As an example, Figure TANK is a module chart for the gas-tank module. Of

---

[1] The *initialize* operation may be implemented as part of the instantiation process that is available to languages which support abstract data types.

[2] Ada is a trademark of the U. S. government, Joint Ada Program Office.

course, it has sections for the state space, the probes, and the operations. At the beginning there are sections discussing the module's purpose and describing its data coupling. The coupling section mentions any nonstandard data types that will be involved in an import or export of a probe or an operation. The data types *Integer, Real, Character,* and *Boolean* are considered to be standard and are not described. In Figure TANK, for example, the coupling section mentions that there must be a *Brand* data type which is shared by the module and any invoking unit. The nature of this data type is left to the implementor.

Figure TANK   Tank Module

Discussion   The contents of a tank are recorded in such a way as to permit questions about whether a single brand makes up 90 percent of the mixture to be answered.

Coupling   *Brand* (unspecified)

State Space   A *Real* parameter *SIZE* and a set of brands together with the amount of gas attributable to each. The available brands are those in the *Brand* data type and an extra unknown brand which is different from any in *Brand*.

Probes
pure
   export: *Boolean*
   description: export true iff one *Brand* comprises 90 percent of the contents
                 of the tank.
pure_brand
   export: *Brand*
   preconditions: *pure* is true.
   description: export the *Brand* that comprises 90 percent of the contents of
                 the tank.

Operations
initialize
   imports: *Real, SIZE*
   preconditions: $SIZE > 0$
   description: initialize the tank with quantity *SIZE* of an unknown
                 brand and 0 for all known *Brands*
refill
   imports: *Real, Q; Brand, B*
   preconditions: $0 < Q \leq SIZE$
   description: multiply the amount of each brand in the tank
                 by $(SIZE-Q)/SIZE$
                 increase the amount of *B* by *Q*

The concept of *precondition* is used to explain what a module will not do. A probe or operation will not perform its function unless its precondition is met. Preconditions allow designers to define the limitations of their modules. For the TANK module, there are preconditions to ensure that the tank size is positive and that the tank is never refilled with more liquid than it contains.

By merely stating a precondition, the designer is giving the implementor a blank check. The implementor can cause the module to do anything, including creating misleading values or aborting, if the precondition is violated. The designer allows this freedom because it is expected that the module will be used in such a way that the precondition is never violated. For modules that will be used in many different situations by many different programmer-designers, each probe and operation should check that its precondition is satisfied and a modulewide standard should be adopted to establish what happens when a violation is detected. These things are discussed in Section 6.3.

The descriptions of the various probes and operations are written in matacode. Often, but by no means always, the metacode will consist of exactly one fairly abstract metastep. For the TANK module, only the *refill* operation requires more than one metastep.

Code written to Figure TANK's specification would provide the defined services for any program unit which uses it. The nature of this usage can be exemplified by looking at a simple program to test the tank module. Implementations of both appear in Appendixes F4 and P4.

Input for this test program is a text file whose lines represent gas stops. Each line contains first the *Brand* used and then the amount refilled. The first line is different. It contains only an amount; this will become the *SIZE* parameter.

The test program simply reads the gas-stop information and for each gas stop prints the *Brand*, if any, that comprises 90 percent of the gas tank. It is given in Figure TANK_TEST. Implementations of the program described in Figures TANK_TEST and TANK are shown in Appendixes P4 and F4.

Figure TANK_TEST   Top-Level Metacode to Test the Gas-Tank Module

```
initialize input, obtaining T and both Brand B and amount A of
    first refill, if they exist, and echoing the input
initialize, using T
repeat while there A and B were input
    refill using amount A of Brand B
    if pure then
        output that pure_brand makes up
            at least 90 percent of the tank
    fi
    advance input, obtaining new Brand B and amount A, if they exist,
        and echoing the input
again
```

Notice that although probes and operations can be viewed as subprograms, their imports are shown more casually than would be the case if we were writing in a programming language. This is consistent with previous metacode examples and is done because metacode is often more readable if parameter lists are presented with words rather than in the common coding language format of "$(P_1, P_2, \ldots, P_k)$". Probes are always written as if they were function subprograms—even when the export cannot be made throught a function in the intended coding language.

Figures TANK and TANK_TEST comprise a design for a small program that does nothing more than provide information about when a gas tank is 90% pure.

In situations where several modules are being used, there is another notation which can make metacode more readable. It is the prefixing of each probe and operation with the name of the module to which it belongs. Thus in TANK_TEST the prefix "*tank.*" would appear with each operation or probe, as in "*tank.pure*" or "*tank.refill*". Another way to prevent confusion between modules in hardcopy of code and metacode is to highlight the probes and operations of each module with a different color. Of course, the implementation may require another convention.

In a multiprogrammer environment, the implementors of modules and the users of modules must agree on the kind of subprogram or variable that is to be used in implementing each probe and operation. Also, the naming convention used in the code must be documented so different programmers will use the same names for the same subprograms. Such information is included in the module chart with the addition of another line or lines, called the *interface description*, to each probe and operation. When probes are to be implemented as variables, this line must state "variable" and give the name of the variable. When the probes and operations are to be implemented as subprograms, this extra line need only contain the first line of that subprogram. For example, FORTRAN interface descriptions for the *refill* operation might be as follows:

```
      SUBROUTINE TANKFILL (A,B)
C     A IS THE AMOUNT OF REFILL AND B THE BRAND; BOTH ARE IMPORTS
```

and a Pascal interface description might be like this:

```
procedure TankFill (A : Amount; B : Brand);
```

The interface descriptions are not placed into the design until everything else has been finished and checked. This makes the design as flexible as possible until the last minute, and it helps keep the designer's mind away from implementation details.

Figure TANK could be viewed as nothing more than a presentation of the metacode expansions of two metatests, labeled *pure* and *pure_brand*, and two metasteps, labeled *initialize* and *refill*. The level of abstraction is not much greater than would have been the case if the metatests and metasteps had been described without reference to the concept of object module. Clearly, the achievement of a high level of abstraction is not the reason for defining such an object module. Rather, the reason is to achieve the kind of organization provided by the module concept. Reasons for desiring this can be found piecemeal throughout the book, beginning in Section 4.3 and continuing in Chapters 5 and 6. Finally, in Section 7.2 a mathematical descriptive technique is given which fits well with the object-module concept and which, in its fully axiomatic form, raises the level of abstraction a great deal.

A somewhat higher level of abstraction can be achieved without the mathematics by leaving out details which the designer is sure that the implementor can and should fill in for herself. If the implementor understands the problem statement, then the designer's main task is to organize the form of the solution, not to restate the problem. The design's organization, of course, should not be loose enough to encourage the implementor to create an unsatisfactory implementation. But unless the program being designed contains many thousands of lines and requires a team of implementors, the designer can often assume the implementor will obtain some details from the problem statement. In Chapter 1 we said that the difference between an abstraction and a vague generality is partially dependent on the amount of understanding which the communicator-designer and the communicatee-implementor share. This common understanding can include the problem statement and a shared knowledge of techniques to solve certain subproblems.

Two concepts for increasing the level of abstraction in a module chart are *conditions* and an **either** construct. They are probably more useful in describing input modules (compare Section 4.4) than in describing gas tanks. But the gas-tank example gives a good opportunity to demonstrate the effect of their use because we have seen in Figure TANK what a design is like without them.

A *condition* is a data type which assumes one of a list of values and which is used to replace detail in a state space. For example, a percentage grade might be replaced with one of

excellent/good/ok/fair/poor

In the TANK module, a state contained a list of brands and their quantities. The whole purpose of this list was to inform the invoking program unit about whether one *Brand* could be considered to be the only *Brand* in the tank. A more abstract state could have a two-way condition: pure/impure and a *Brand*, say *P_BRAND*, which is defined only when the condition is pure.[3] The definition of a pure tank and the way a brand is chosen to represent the entire contents of the tank are abstracted from this description.

The **either** construct may appear with any positive number of **or**'s. It shows that an action is to be selected but provides no criteria by which the reader can know which action. It is used to abstract such criteria from the design. For example,

```
either
    set pure
    set P_BRAND
or
    set impure
end
```

[3] *"Brand"* refers to one of the brands in the coupling and is defined in some data dictionary while "brand" refers to any brand. The use of "brand" is necessary when we speak of the state because an unknown brand that is different from those in *Brand* is included.

could be used to describe the *refill* operation of the abstracted tank module. It assumes the state given above and says that *refill* either will cause the condition to be pure and a *P_BRAND* to be defined or will cause the condition to be impure.

Conditions and **either**'s introduce a new dimension to our understanding of what it means for code to match metacode. Since Chapter 2, we have followed the rule that all variables that appear in metacode must appear in the same way in the code. All **if** and **repeat** constructs that appear in metacode must appear in the same way in the code. (Extra variables and control constructs beyond those appearing in the metacode were allowed.)

For conditions and **either**'s there is no requirement of exact matching in the implemented code. A condition may be replaced by sets of variables or even by a probe to another module. Any code variables that implement conditions must be altered in a way that corresponds to the alteration of the condition in the metacode. An **either** may be replaced with any sequence of statements. The metacode that appears within the **either** is not matched in the code either. Only the effect of the construct must be matched. This means the implementation must alter variables in the same way as the corresponding **either** statement does.

Figure TANK_ABS shows a module chart for an object module which is an abstraction of the TANK module. Note the difference between "*pure*" and "pure". The first is a probe; the second is a condition.

Many more implementations would satisfy TANK_ABS than would satisfy TANK. Not all designs having Figure TANK as part of them could accept Figure TANK_ABS in its place. The abstraction in Figure TANK_ABS places a greater burden of understanding on the implementor. But in either design the implementor is told what is to be achieved with the tank module and how that module is to interface with an invoking program unit.

Figure TANK_ABS   Abstract Tank Module

Discussion   The contents of a tank are recorded in such a way as to permit questions about whether a single brand makes up 90 percent of the mixture to be answered.

Coupling   *Brand* (unspecified)

State Space   A *Real* parameter *SIZE*, a two-way condition:
    pure/impure
and a *Brand P_BRAND*.
    Note: *P_BRAND* is defined iff pure is set.

Probes
pure
    export: *Boolean*
    description: export true iff pure is set
pure_brand
    export: *Brand*
    preconditions: *pure*
    description: export *P_BRAND*

Figure TANK_ABS   **(continued)**

Operations
initialize
   imports: *Real SIZE*
   preconditions: *SIZE* > 0
   description: set impure
refill
   imports: *Real Q*; *Brand B*
   preconditions: 0 < *Q* ≤ *SIZE*;
   description: **either**
               set pure
               set *P_BRAND*
            or
               set impure
            end

The two versions of the tank module show a wide range in the level of abstraction that can be applied to a given problem. A designer wants to write as abstractly as possible without causing the intended reader to encounter vagueness. A reason for this is the problem of overspecification. *Overspecification* happens when a design forces the implementor to do things which are not necessary.

Overspecification can happen when the notation used for the state space implies something more than the designer wishes. For example, suppose that

Figure LAST_THREE   **Saving Last Three Items**

Discussion   Reports on the last three *Items* which have been received.

Coupling   *Item* (unspecified)

State Space   A sequence
   $i_1, \ldots, i_K$
of *Items* where K is a nonnegative integer.

Probes
recent
   export: *Item*
   preconditions: $K > 0$
   description: export i_K
second_recent
   export: *Item*
   preconditions: $K > 1$
   description: export i_{K-1}
third_recent
   export: *Item*
   preconditions: $K > 2$
   description: export i_{K-2}

Operations
initialize
   description: $K \leftarrow 0$
accept
   imports: *Item I*
   description: $K \leftarrow K + 1$
             $i_K \leftarrow I$

we wish to define an object module which accepts values, called *Items*, from its invoking program unit and which can be probed for the three most recent values. Figure LAST_THREE shows a possible design. It is based on the mathematical concept of a sequence.

What is this module chart saying to the implementor? That a sequence should be implemented? That a vector should be used? That anything which provides the last three accepted *Items* is permissible?

If the implementor perceives that a vector is required, then overspecification has certainly taken place. But the implementor should not perceive that because although the mathematical concept of sequence can be implemented in a vector, there are also other techniques for implementing sequences. Nothing in the design suggests one implementation of sequence over another.

Whether the design of the LAST_THREE module implies the use of the entire sequence of all those *Items* which have been accepted is questionable. Any implementation which saved only the last three accepted *Items* could certainly provide the described service to any invoking program unit. Moreover, an implementation which kept a whole sequence might not provide the described service because of difficulty with memory limitations. The abstract state, however, contains the entire sequence of accepted *Items*, and there is a possibility that the designer wanted the entire sequence implemented. Perhaps she expected the design to be modified at a later date in such a way that the entire sequence would be needed. However, were that the case, the designer ought have said so in a way that was clearer. The discussion section of the module chart can be used to make such points.

In this book, a module such as LAST_THREE will not require that an implementation match those parts of the abstract state which never appear in the descriptions of the probes and operations. Also an abstract state which contains extra parts will not be considered an overspecification. It will be considered "almost" an overspecification.

An object module is a concept for giving a functional data description to a data object. It can be written so that it explains more about how to use the object than about how to implement it.

An object module doesn't just contain an object; it contains a messy, low-level object and makes it appear to be a clean, abstract object.

An object module adds to the computer's repertoire instructions relevant to the purpose of the object. These instructions make the job at hand easier and allow the object being contained to be dealt with in a cleaner, more abstract way. They form a virtual machine for dealing with the object. Roughly speaking, a *virtual machine* is the machine you wish you had, but don't. It is a set of routines coded to run on the machine you do have. Using this set of routines, in place of the set of commands available on your machine, can give you the impression that you are using a machine which has the kind of commands you want. A virtual machine thus makes the machine which you do have appear to behave as the machine which you wish you had.

A good definition of a particular virtual machine describes not how the machine works, but what it does. From the virtual-machine point of view, an object module ought to be a description of a "machine" which is to be "built" in some unspecified way to facilitate specified manipulations of data.

The concept of object module as a virtual machine helps problem solving by enabling the definition of tools tailored to make a solution easier to write. Examples appear in Chapter 5. In multiprogrammer projects, it helps by dividing the work between tool builders and tool users. It has other benefits, as discussed in Chapter 6.

Implementation Notes

Before you write code for an object module, there are some decisions to make:

1 Add interface descriptions, as discussed above, to all probes and operations.

2 Determine the data structures that will implement the state space.

3 Determine any support units that will make the implementation of the probes and operations easier.

Support units are subprograms that access the state variables but are not probes or operations. They are invoked by two or more operations or probes (those probes that are subprograms), and by nothing else. They are created to make the implementation of the module easier. They are considered to be part of the module, but programmers using the module need not know of their existence.

Since the data coupling of a module is limited to the listed imports, exports, and updates of the probes and operations, support units may not share data with any program unit outside the module. Since probes may not alter a module's state, support units which alter the module's state may not be invoked by probes.

EXERCISES

4.4.1 Look for and restate rules about the following:
    a Permitted exports and updates for probes
    b Permitted exports and updates for operations
    c The *initialize* operation
    d Use of the state space by probes and operations
    e Program units that use module probes and operations

4.1.2 Cite the object-module rule violations in Figure BAD_TANK.

4.1.3 It is sometimes desirable to have a module check whether the preconditions to probes and operations have been satisfied and report back to the invoking program unit whether everything is OK. Explain how this could be done without violating any module rules.

4.1.4 Make a module chart for a module that imitates a light switch. A probe should be included to tell whether the switch is on or off.

4.1.5 Figure TANK has been implemented in Appendixes P4 and F4 with functions

Figure BAD_TANK   Incorrectly Defined Tank Module

Discussion   The contents of a tank are recorded in such a way as to permit questions about whether a single brand makes up 90 percent of the mixture to be answered.

Coupling   Brand (unspecified)

State Space   *Real* parameters *SIZE* and *PERCENT* and a set of brands together with the amount of gas attributable to each. The available brands are those in the *Brand* data type and an extra unknown brand which is different from any in *Brand*.

Probes
pure
   export: *Brand, B,* and *Boolean, P*
   description: set *P* to be true if the percentage of some *Brand* is at least *PERCENT*
            and false otherwise
          if *P* **then**
              B ← that *Brand*
          fi

Operations
initialize
   imports: *Real, SIZE, PERCENT,* and *Q; Brand, B*
   preconditions: *SIZE* > 0, 0 < *Q* ≤ *SIZE*, and 0 < *PERCENT* < 100
   description: initialize the tank with quantity *SIZE* of an unknown
            brand and 0 for all known *Brand*s
         multiply the amount of each brand in the tank
            by (*SIZE-Q*)/*SIZE*
         increase the amount of *B* by *Q*

refill
   imports: *Real, Q; Brand, B*
   precondition: 0 < *Q* ≤ *SIZE*
   export: *Boolean, OK*
   description: **if** 0 < *Q* ≤ *SIZE* **then**
         OK ← true
         multiply the amount of each brand in the tank
            by (*SIZE-Q*)/*SIZE*
         increase the amount of *B* by *Q*
      else
         OK ← false
      fi

for the probes *pure* and *pure_brand*. It is possible to write an implementation with variables for *pure* and *pure_brand*. What implementation decisions should be made first? Write an implementation of this type, and test it with a tank test program as in Figure TANK_TEST. (The implementation technique to use when probes are variables is shown in Appendixes P2 and F2 for input modules.) Also explain how it is easier to misuse an implemented object module whose probes are variables than one whose probes are functions.

4.1.6a Does the implementation in Appendix P4 or F4 match the design in Figure TANK_ ABS? Explain.

b Is the phrase "Note *P_BRAND* is defined if and only if pure is set." in the state-space section of Figure TANK_ABS redundant? That is, if this restriction were removed, could it be violated during execution of an implementation that matched the rest of Figure TANK_ABS?

4.1.7 Design and implement a program which calculates miles-per-gallon and cost-per-mile statistics about a car's fuel usage. The statistics are to be kept by brand. Information about a sequence of fuel stops is provided on a sequence of input lines. Each line contains a brand code, a decimal number representing price per gallon, an integer number representing the odometer reading, and a decimal number representing the number of gallons purchased. It is assumed that each purchase refills a 20-gallon tank. The input data is assumed to be correct.

The statistics printed are overall and by brand, miles per gallon, and cost per mile. The overall cost is calculated by adding all the purchase prices except the first. The by-brand statistics are included only for those miles driven when the tank is 90 percent pure. The by-brand cost is calculated from the price for the brand which was most recently paid when the miles were driven. The output shows the total miles counted for each brand.

Your design should, of course, use the TANK module of this section, and the code should use an implementation from the appendixes.

This test data will help you in making sure your program works correctly. It assumes brands A, B, and C:

A	1.14	0001	19.5
B	1.02	0400	11.0
B	1.12	0800	18.0
A	1.50	1200	19.0
C	1.50	1600	10.0
C	1.50	2000	10.0

This is the output which would be produced by that test data:

Overall statistics:

mileage accounted for:	1999
miles per gallon:	29.4
cost per mile:	0.045

By-brand statistics:

brand	mileage	m.p.g.	c.p.m.
A	799	38	0.034
B	400	21.1	0.053

4.1.8 Write a module chart for a module that represents a checkerboard (substitute another board game if you like). Define whatever probes and operations you think are appropriate. Remember that a program which uses your board module will have no access to the board other than what you provide in probes and modules!

4.1.9 Rewrite LAST_THREE so that it shows the same kind of abstraction found in TANK_ABS.

4.2 DATA STRUCTURES

The study of data structures is concerned with the development of efficient data organizations that can be applied in multiple situations. It has become a central part of computer science, and it provides for one of the more clear-cut applications of the concept of a object module.

One very common data structure can be thought of as a "recipe box." What one does with a recipe box is to place recipes into it and to look up recipes that are already there. With the particular kind of recipe box being described here, looking up a recipe does not cause it to be removed from the box. (Perhaps the recipe box should be visualized as a "recipe wheel" which is rotated to find a particular recipe.)

In defining a recipe-box object module, more precise descriptions of what it means to add or find recipes are needed, and these descriptions must utilize the language presented in a definition of some state space. One possible state space is a set of strings called recipes. Then the action of adding a recipe R is easy to describe: Simply augment the state set of recipes with R. Finding R is trickier. How, precisely, is the look-up to be accomplished?

There are at least two bad answers. One is: Provide, inside the module, a mechanism to look at the recipes one by one, and have a program unit which uses the module look at the recipes one by one until the correct one is found. The overall effect of this method is to remove the problem of how to find the recipe from the recipe-box module and give it to whatever program unit uses the module. That doesn't make the recipe-box module very useful.

A second bad answer is to say: Let each recipe begin with a name to aid in locating it, and let the state of the recipe box be a vector of recipes which is alphabetized by name. To look up a recipe, give the recipe box the desired name and let it perform a binary search to find a matching name in its state. This answer certainly does prescribe a way for the module itself to look up a recipe, namely to use an alphabetized vector and a binary search. Therein lies the problem. This answer is an overspecification. A functional data definition ought not commit the implementor to a particular way of accomplishing the functions of the module.

A better answer also incorporates the use of names to identify recipes but does not specify either how the recipes are to be stored or how they are to be looked up: Let the state consist of a set of recipe strings, each of which has an associated name string that is different from the name string of any other recipe. As above, the look-up probe imports a name and exports the recipe which has that name. Since there will be at most one recipe with that name, we know the look-up is possible without being told how to accomplish it. The operation of placing a recipe in the box imports the recipe and its associated name. Again, the method of accomplishing this is left to the implementor.

Of course, a recipe-box module can be used to save and retrieve all kinds of data, not just recipes. To store and retrieve other kinds of data is essentially the same as storing and retrieving recipes. The usual name for this kind of module is a *symbol table*. Symbols are objects of an unspecified type having associated names, just as recipes are strings and have associated names. The reason for the symbol table nomenclature is that the first uses such modules involved computer language translators and not recipe boxes. A computer language translator must be able to store the symbols which a programmer has chosen for variable names. It must be able to look up a variable by name to identify the what the programmer means with that name.

A module chart for a symbol table is found in Figure SYMBOL_TABLE.

Figure SYMBOL_TABLE   A Symbol Table Module

Discussion   This module is used to store and retrieve values by name.

Coupling   *Name* (a fixed-length character string)
Value (unspecified)

State Space   A state is a two-way condition: full/not_full and a set of *Values* which may be empty; each *Value* has a unique *Name* associated with it.

Probes
full
   export: *Boolean*
   description: export true iff full is set
value
   imports: *Name, N*
   preconditions: the state must contain a *Value* whose associated name
               is *N*
   export: *Value*
   description: export the unique *Value* having the name *N*
exists
   imports: *Name, N*
   export: *Boolean*
   description: true iff the state contains a *Value* whose *Name* is *N*

Operations
initialize
   description: set an empty state;
             set not_full
put
   imports: *Name, N,* and *Value, R*
   preconditions: not_full is set and the state must not already contain a
               Value whose *Name* is *N*
   description: places *R* in the state under the name *N*;
           either
             set full
           or
             set not_full
           end
delete
   imports: *Name, N*
   description: **if** the state contains a *Value* whose associated
             Name is *N*
           then
             delete that *Value*;
             set no_full
         fi

With the use of a vector in the implementation, clearly the full condition depends on whether the vector has been filled with data. With other implementation methods it is less clear what the full condition depends on. Even so, it is possible to imagine situations in which it can be determined that no more memory is available for storing symbols. By including the abstract condition full/not_full in the state, the probe *full* can be described without reference to any of this. The way in which the condition full/not_full is implemented is left to the implementor. The condition may even stay not_full throughout execution.

The use of a symbol table module can be illustrated with an example. Suppose that a survey of population changes is to be made. A file *F1980* exists in which each line contains a town name and that town's 1980 population. Another file *F1990* exists which has the same format but for 1990. A report of all those names in *F1990* which represent new towns or old towns with a population increase of at least 50 percent is wanted. Figure POP_SURVEY contains metacode for the program.

Figure POP_SURVEY   Obtaining a Population Survey

This algorithm uses module SYMBOL_TABLE as if it were a
TOWN_TABLE module. The values of this town module are
integers, not strings.
> *town.initialize*
> input first *TOWN_NAME* and *TOWN_POPULATION* from *F1980*, if any
> **repeat while** there is input data and not *town.full*
> > *town.put* the *TOWN_POPULATION* of *TOWN_NAME*
> > input next *TOWN_NAME* and *TOWN_POPULATION* from *F1980*, if any
>
> **again**
> **if** *town.full* and there is input data **then**
> > output that the table is full and some data has been lost
>
> **fi**
> input first *TOWN_NAME* and *TOWN_POPULATION* from *F1990*, if any
> **repeat while** data is available
> > **if** not *Town.exists TOWN_NAME* **then**
> > > output that *TOWN_NAME* is a new town
> >
> > **else if** *town.value* of *TOWN_NAME* > 1.5 × *TOWN_POPULATION* **then**
> > > output that *TOWN_NAME* has grown by more than 50 percent
> >
> > **fi**
> > input next *TOWN_NAME* and *TOWN_POPULATION* from *F1990*, if any
>
> **again**

To recap, object modules which describe data structures provide probes and operations for storing and retrieving data. Although data structures are always implemented with some particular data representation, this particular representation is not part of the module chart of a data structure.

As another example, consider the *stack*. A stack is an organization of data that is analogous to a stack of trays in a cafeteria — except it is data that is being stacked. Data is placed on the "top," and data is removed from the "top." If two data items *X* and *Y* are placed into a stack in that order, then *Y* must be removed before *X*. Thus a stack is said to be a last-in first-out type of data organization. We assume that a data type *Item* has been defined elsewhere and that the stack contains data of type *Item*.

An object module which contains a stack must have operations to initialize the stack, to place (*push*) *Items* on the stack, and to remove (*pop*) *Items* from the stack. Probes are necessary to find out whether the stack is empty or full and what is on the top of the stack, i.e., to find out what would be popped next.

A module chart is given in Figure STACK. One notable convention is introduced in this chart. The description for *empty* says "exports $K = 0$" rather than "exports true iff $K = 0$". The convention is to omit the "true iff" whenever the *Boolean* value being exported is a simple result of a boolean expression. The omitted words are redundant anyway.

Figure STACK   Stack Module

Discussion   Contains a last-in first-out data structure

Coupling   *Item* (unspecified)

State Space   A state is a two-way condition, full/not_full, and a sequence:

$$i_1, i_2, \cdots, i_K$$

of *Items*; where K is a nonnegative integer.

Probes
top
  preconditions: $K \neq 0$
  export: *Item*
  description: export i_K
full
  export: *Boolean*
  description: export true iff full is set
empty
  export: *Boolean*
  description: export $K = 0$

Operations
initialize
  description: create an empty sequence;
                 set not_full
push
  preconditions: not_full is set
  imports: *Item*, *I*
  description: $K \leftarrow K + 1$
                $i_K \leftarrow I$;
                either
                   set full
                or
                   set not_full
                end
pop
  preconditions: not *empty*
  description: $K \leftarrow K - 1$;
              set not_full

To implement a stack requires that a sequence be implemented. Readers who have not studied data structures will probably implement stacks in vectors. Others will be able to choose an implementation that fits the needs of the day.

A use for the stack module is given in the exercises.

A final very common data structure is the *queue*. A queue is organized as a line of people waiting for tickets at a movie theater. Data is placed at the "rear" and removed from the "front." If two data items X and Y are placed into a queue in that order, then X must be removed before Y. Thus a queue is said to be a first-in first-out type of data organization.

A module which contains a queue must have operations to initialize the queue, to place (*enter*) *Items* in the queue, and to remove *Items* from the

Figure QUEUE   Queue Module

Discussion   Contains a first-in first-out data structure

Coupling   *Item* (unspecified)

State Space   A state is a two way-condition, full/not_full, and a sequence

$$i_1, \cdots, i_K$$

of *Items*; where K is a nonnegative integer.

Probes
front
  preconditions: $K \neq 0$
  export: *Item*
  description: export i_1
full
  export: *Boolean*
  description: export true iff full is set
empty
  export: *Boolean*
  description: export $K = 0$

Operations
initialize
  description: create an empty sequence
           set not_full
enter
  preconditions: not_full is set
  imports: *Items, I*
  description: $K \leftarrow K + 1$;
          $i_K \leftarrow I$
          either
            set full
          or
            set not_full
          end
remove
  preconditions: not *empty*
  description: remove first element from sequence and relabel
           set not_full

queue. Probes are necessary to find out both whether the queue is empty or full and what is at the front of the queue, i.e., to find out what would be removed from the queue the next time *leave* is executed. A module chart is given in Figure QUEUE.

A use for a data object similar to the queue module is given in the exercises.

In this section three of the more common data structures have been introduced with functional data descriptions. Readers are referred to any data-structures text for a discussion of implementation methods.

EXERCISES

Exercises 4.2.1 through 4.2.4 are for readers who have not studied data structures. Exercises 4.2.5 through 4.2.8 are for readers who have studied data structures. Exercises 4.2.9 through 4.2.11 are for all readers.

4.2.1 Write an implementation of Figure STACK, assuming that real numbers will be stacked. Implement the stack in a vector of five real numbers.

Test this stack with a program that inputs and stacks real numbers until the stack is full, then pops and prints the number until the stack is empty. This filling and emptying is repeated a second time. It is controlled by the probes *full* and *empty* and not by counting. An input file of ten real numbers should be used.

4.2.2 Write an implementation of Figure QUEUE, assuming that pairs of *Integers* will be queued. Implement the queue in a vector which can hold at most five pairs. Figure QUEUE gives no guidance about how to implement the *remove* operation. Figure CIRCULAR_QUEUE provides some implementation guidance. The first element of the vector C is viewed as following the last. You will need to keep track of the indices F and L of the first and last *Item*s in the queue and to keep a boolean variable that indicates whether or not the queue is full.

Figure CIRCULAR_QUEUE   A Method for Implementing a Queue in a Vector

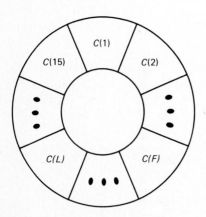

Then i_1 will be the element $C(F)$, and i_K will be $C(L)$. The *remove* operation causes the queue to become empty if F moves clockwise past L. The *enter* operation causes the queue to become full if L moves to the position just one place counterclockwise of F.

Test your implementation with a program in the same way as the stack of exercise 4.2.1 is tested.

4.2.3 Implement a symbol table as described in Figure SYMBOL_TABLE. Implement the table in a vector of *TableRecords* where a *TableRecord* consists of a *String* (the name of the record) and an *Integer* (the value of the record). *TableRecords* should be kept in increasing order of name and should be looked up with a binary search.

To this end, *Boolean* functions *equal* and *less* should be written which return true iff the first *String* parameter is equal to or less than the second, respectively. "String A is less than string B" means that there exists an index I such that

(the numeric code for A (I)) $<$ (the numeric code for B(I))
and $A(J) = B(K)$ for any J with $1 \leq J < I$.

Test your implementation.

FORTRAN programmers should implement the vector of *TableRecords* as two one-dimensional arrays, NAME and VALUE. The Ith *TableRecord* would thus be (NAME(I),VALUE(I)).

4.2.4 An arithmetic expression is said to be in *postfix* notation when the operators appear to the right of their operands. Thus, in postfix notation, the famous expression "2 + 2" appears this way: "2 2 +". The subtraction "5 − 7" appears "5 7 −". The expression "5 + 7 + 2" would be written "5 7 + 2 +" or "5 7 2 + +" depending, respectively, on whether the leftmost or rightmost numbers were to be added first. This last example hints at one of the nice properties of the notation: Parentheses are never needed to explain the order in which the operations should be evaluated. Another nice property is that there is such an easy rule to follow in evaluating an expression. You simply start reading the expression at the left and stack up operands. Whenever an operator *OP* is found, you pop an operand (call it *RIGHT*), pop another (call it *LEFT*), perform the operation "*RIGHT OP LEFT*", and push the result back on the stack. Then you start reading the expression again. When there is no more expression, the stack will contain one number, the result of the evaluation.

Write metacode using the STACK module which evaluates the expressions on an input file with one postfix expression per line that is composed of nonnegative real numbers and these binary operations: +, −, *, and /. There are blanks between operands and operators. If a division by zero is attempted or if there is a mismatch of operands with operators, your metacode should print an error message and skip to the next expression. Implement and test your design. Make up your own test data, but include these expressions:

8.0 5.0 5.0 − / 4.0 +	{division by 0}
8.0 7.0 / 6.0 3.0 2.0 + *	{mismatch of operands}
8.0 / 4.0 +	{mismatch of operands}
8.0 7.0 2.0 / 6.0 3.0 2.0 + * + −	{−25.5}

4.2.5   Figure FREE_NODE shows an incomplete module chart for a free node list. Complete it. Then implement and test your design.

Figure FREE_NODE   Free Node List

Discussion   Allocates and deallocates *Node*s for the invoking program unit

Coupling *Node* (unspecified)

Probes
node_available

Operations
initialize
free
get

4.2.6   Implement Figure STACK, using a linked list and a free node list as in exercise 4.2.5. Set your free node list so that it contains only five nodes, and test your stack as described in exercise 4.2.1.

4.2.7   Implement a symbol table as described in Figure SYMBOL_TABLE. Implement the symbol table in a 3-2 tree or in a height-balanced tree. The nodes of your tree should contain *TableRecord*s where a *TableRecord* consists of a *String* (the name of the record) and an *Integer* (the value of the record). Use *Boolean* functions *equal* and *less* as described in exercise 4.2.3 to determine the ordering of the *Name*s. Test your implementation.

4.2.8   Design an object module that acts as a matrix. Implement it with a technique suitable for storing sparse matrices. Test your implementation.

4.2.9   Design the function *less* of exercises 4.2.3 and 4.2.7 so that it returns true iff the first string parameter comes before the second in alphabetical order.

4.2.10   It is not necessary to insist on the precondition *full* for the add operation of a queue. Instead it is possible to have the *enter* operation make room for the new element, if necessary, by invoking the *leave* operation. Another change that can be made to the queue concept is to allow an invoking program unit to see all the *Item*s in the queue—not just the front. What results is not quite a queue; let's call it a "matching queue." Write a design for a matching queue. Using a matching queue that holds at most two *Item*s, design and implement a program which reads a text file and prints another, replacing "(*" with "{" and "*)" with "}". Implement and test your design.

4.2.11   Redo your implementation of Figure SYMBOL_TABLE (exercise 4.2.3 or 4.2.7) as follows:

a All searching of the table is done by a *look_up* support unit that imports a *Name* and exports an *Integer* (a pointer to a tree node if you are working from exercise 4.2.7). This integer references the *TableRecord* that is sought, if it exists, or is zero (nil) otherwise. The only other data coupling allowed for *look_up* consists of the state space.

b An *Integer* (a pointer) *CACHE* is kept in the state so that *look_up* can avoid searching the tree twice in a row for the same thing. At the end of its execution *look_up* always resets *CACHE* to the value it is exporting.

4.3   ESTABLISHING CLEAN DATA ENVIRONMENTS

These days it seems that everybody is aware of the value of clean environments. Unfortunately, many programmers do not understand that the environment of a computer program can suffer from data litter. This section discusses the data environment(s) of a program and the avoidance of extraneous variables in the code as well as in the design. Once again, the presentation is backwards—we proceed from detailed metacode to abstract design.

An example is given in detailed metacode which suffers from data litter. An object module design is created from the detailed metacode. Then the implementation techniques of Appendixes F2, F4, P2, and P4 can be used to create code which, in theory, has no data litter.

A *data environment* is defined in terms of variables. All the variables which a statement is permitted to use by the language, or by the more restrictive and rigidly enforced set of rules concerning object modules, comprise its data environment. Statements have data environments, variables have scopes; there is a difference. Ideally, a variable is in the data environment of a statement if the statement is in the scope of the variable. Unfortunately, the lack of proper support for object modules in many programming languages makes this statement false. For example, in the ANSI Pascal code of Appendix P4, the scope of the variables that implement the state space of an object module is very large—it includes everything. In defining data environments, we pretend that this isn't so, that the data environment of a statement outside the module does *not* include the variables which implement the module's state space.

Another situation in which the ideal differs from the actual occurs when variables are used to implement probes. These variables belong to the data environment of all statements within the module. However, they do not belong to the data environment of a statement in an invoking program unit even though their scope must include such statements—probe variables may not be changed in invoking program units, so they are not considered to be variables there.

A single data environment for a large program means that all statements can access all variables. This is bad. It causes population problems which manifest themselves in the form of bugs. Consider a program which consists of these statements:

$$S_1$$
$$S_2$$
.
.
.
$$S_K$$

A common way in which bugs are spontaneously generated seems to be the inadvertent alteration of data in statement S_I in a way that was not expected when statement S_J was written. The number of possibilities for such spontaneous generation increases with the number of ordered pairs (S_I, S_J) of statements which can be found in the program. For a program with K statements this is $K(K - 1)$. Comparing a program with 1000 statements to a program with 100 statements, we find a ratio of about 100:1 in the number of ordered pairs of statements.

This tends to imply that with a constant data environment, the 1000-statement program will be 100 times harder to debug than the 100-statement program even though it is only 10 times longer. In general, the analysis says that the difficulty of debugging a program should increase with the square of its size. Even though the analysis is rather simple-minded, it does give us a feel for why longer programs are much harder to debug than shorter ones—unless they have been effectively broken into relatively independent pieces. I refer to this fact as the *N-squared* rule.

One obvious way to combat the *N*-squared rule is to divide the program so that each subset of statements has a small data environment. A useful concept in deciding how to spread variables around the subsets is the *need-to-know* principle. If variable A isn't necessary for accomplishing the task of statements $S_1, \ldots, S_J$, then arrange for variable A to be unavailable to those statements. The use of subprograms with few imports, exports, and updates is one way to accomplish this.

To justify the need-to-know principle, consider a program with a bug involving variable A. Imagine you are looking for that bug and you have looked at all the statements which might reasonably alter A but have not found it. Have you missed something? Or is A altered in some unreasonable place? If you have not looked at every statement that could alter A, then you cannot know which possibility is true. By following a need-to-know principle, you will not need to look at so much code to find that bug.

The need-to-know principle can be enforced by eliminating extraneous variables from design and code. In Chapter 2, we eliminated extraneous variables with an appropriately defined metastep. A subprogram which implements the metastep can enforce the need-to-know principle by defining those extraneous variables locally.

Often, however, an extraneous variable cannot be buried in a single metastep. Even so, it can probably be buried within a set of appropriately defined metasteps. For example, the variables needed to implement "save A" and "get A" may not be local to either metastep, but they may be local to the two of them together. The concept of object module provides a good framework for defining a related set of metasteps to hide extraneous variables. The rules of object module usage remove those variables from any kind of consideration in program units external to the module.

Rules for using object modules can be enforced by the underlying programming language, by a preprocessor, or by the programmer. However it is done, there should be no need—when you are chasing bugs—to consider whether a variable has been altered in a forbidden place. At bug-chasing time, such checking has already been done.

A program that shows extraneous variables can be likened to a program which shows a convoluted flow of control. The extra variables cause convoluted data references. Both kinds of convolutions make a program harder to understand, debug, and modify.

To present an example of such a program, consider a real-life problem statement:

A certain college has a problem with its registration procedures. Students are standing in long lines and grumbling. Since no other college has a similar problem, some of the professors are beginning to worry that students will begin to go elsewhere. One professor decides to take action. She will do a study and write a paper. This study will take the form of an interview with the last twelve students who register for each class. Luckily (for her programmer) the registrar keeps class lists on the administration's computer in chronological order of enrollment so that it is a simple matter to read these lists and extract the names of the last twelve students. She has a program written which will extract the last twelve students that have registered in a class and print their names in the order in which they registered.

Fairly detailed metacode to solve the programmer's problem is shown in Figure EXTRACT_DETAIL. A vector *LAST_TWELVE* is used to contain up to twelve student names. The student names, of course, are character strings of some fixed length.

Figure EXTRACT_DETAIL   Obtaining the Last Twelve Student Names in a File

```
{input up to 12 students}
   I ← 1
   get first input name
   repeat while I ≤ 12 and input name is available
      LAST_TWELVE(I) ← the input name
      I ← I + 1
      get next input name
   again
      if input name is available then
         {input rest of students}
            I ← 1
            repeat
               LAST_TWELVE(I) ← the input name
               I ← (I mod 12) + 1
               get next input name
            again until no input name is available
         {output last twelve students}
            JLARGE ← ( (I + 10) mod 12) + 1
               repeat for twelve times
                  output LAST_TWELVE(JLARGE)
                  JLARGE ← (JLARGE mod 12) + 1
               again
   else
      {output all students}
         repeat for J ← 1, . . . , I − 1
           output LAST_TWELVE(J)
         again
   fi
```

Variables *I* and *JLARGE* are extraneous. They aid in storing names in, and retrieving names from, *LAST_TWELVE*. To understand how they perform this aid requires a little thought. The vector *LAST_TWELVE* must be filled in this order:

LAST_TWELVE(1),*LAST_TWELVE*(2), . . . , *LAST_TWELVE*(12),   *LAST_TWELVE*(1), *LAST_TWELVE*(2), . . . , *LAST_TWELVE*(12),*LAST_TWELVE*(1), . . .

which is obtained from this set of indices:

1,2, . . . , 12, 1,2, . . . , 12, 1, . . .

which is obtained through this pattern:

1,(1 mod 12) + 1, . . . , (11 mod 12) + 1, (12 mod 12) + 1,
    (1 mod 12) + 1, . . . , (11 mod 12) + 1, (12 mod 12) + 1, . . .

Variable *I* relies on this pattern to sequence through the correct values. The expression $(I + 10) \bmod 12 + 1$ obtains the value that occurs in this sequence just before *I*. Thus *JLARGE* sequences through this pattern from the position just before the *I*th.

A first attempt at creating an object module should try to remove *I* and *JLARGE*. Prior to defining the module we can obtain a better idea of what is involved by defining reasonable metasteps to which these variables are local. Figure PLAN_MODULE lists all the statements of Figure EXTRACT_DETAIL which contain these variables. The list is organized into functional groups. For example, statements $I \leftarrow I + 1$ and $I \leftarrow (I \bmod 12) + 1$ perform the function of "advance for next addition"; the first is used for the first twelve names, and the second for all subsequent names.

Figure PLAN_MODULE   Statements of EXTRACT_DETAIL Organized by Function

Statement	*Function*
$I \leftarrow 1$	initialize for storage
$JLARGE \leftarrow ((I + 10) \bmod 12) + 1$	initialize for inspection
repeat for $J \leftarrow 1, \ldots, I - 1$	
LAST_TWELVE(*I*) $\leftarrow$ the input name	add a name
$I \leftarrow I + 1$	advance for next addition
$I \leftarrow (I \bmod 12) + 1$	
output *LAST_TWELVE*(*JLARGE*)	inspect a name
output *LAST_TWELVE*(*J*)	
$JLARGE \leftarrow (JLARGE \bmod 12) + 1$	advance for next inspection
repeat for $J \leftarrow 1, \ldots, I - 1$	
repeat while $I \leq 12$	first twelve names added?

Now we try to define an object module whose probes and operations correspond roughly to the metasteps identified in Figure PLAN_MODULE.

The actual probes and operations which we define may look rather different from the first functions which we identified. The reason is that we bring our experience with object modules into play when writing the module definition. In the present context, our experience tells us that the usage of *LAST_TWELVE* looks rather like a queue because names are retrieved in the order in which they are stored.

We must then decide whether the module is to be a queue as in Figure QUEUE of Section 4.2 or something different. This calls for an identification of the differences between the usage here and the definition there. Each difference must be questioned: Does it serve a useful purpose? If not, then we should not incorporate it into our new design.

The add-a-name operation of Figure PLAN_MODULE arranges that the oldest name be replaced with the new addition when the storage area is full. This, of course, is different from a queue; but it is also what the problem requires, so this difference is justified.

The inspect-a-name operation also represents a difference from the standard queue. To inspect a queue, one has to remove the contents one by one. Of course, when the contents are removed, they no longer sit in the queue. The advantage of the kind of inspection shown in Figure PLAN_MODULE is that the inspection could be done more than once. However, this problem does not require multiple inspections of the stored names, so the deviation from the standard queue is not justified.

The module implied by Figure PLAN_MODULE actually seems to have two different add-a-name operations. This isn't necessary. The first twelve names can be added in the same way as subsequent ones. The same is true of the inspect-a-name operation—the distinction between the different versions is not necessary.

A queue does not have separate steps for adding a name and advancing for next addition. The present problem doesn't require separate steps either.

Enough preliminaries. Let's define the "almost-queue." We could describe it with the same kind of state space shown in Section 4.2, but it seems worthwhile to illustrate another approach. A state of this module must include a set of names organized in such a way that the order in which names were placed in the set is known. Simply put, a state is a set of ordered pairs of names and arrival times. An arrival time can be an *Integer T* which expresses that the associated name was the Tth to enter following initialization. As was the case when we described a queue using the sequence $I_1, \ldots, I_K$ in Section 4.2, this description isn't a prescription for an implementation method. Rather, it is a way of using everyday mathematics to describe a model of what is going on. An implementation, in other words, need not really keep track of the *Integer, T*.

Following the plan of allowing the almost-queue to be inspected only as it is disassembled, the probe which returns an inspection name will simply return the oldest element in the state, and the operation which advances the inspection name will remove the oldest element in the state.

Figure STORED_NAMES   Stored-Names Module

Discussion   Keeps track of a "small" number of names and the order in which they appear. Addition of a new name will cause the oldest name to be removed, if necessary, to keep the total number within bounds. The oldest name can be examined and removed by command of the invoking program unit.

Coupling   *Name* (fixed-length character string)

State Space   A positive *Integer* parameter *SIZE* and set *SP* of ordered pairs of *Names* and positive *Integers*.

Note that no two ordered pairs of *SP* may contain the same *Integer* and *SP* never has more than *SIZE* ordered pairs in it.

Probes
empty
　Export: *Boolean*
　description: export $SP = 0$
oldest
　preconditions: not *empty*
　export: *Name*
　description: export the *Name* associated with the lowest integer

Operations
initialize
　imports: *Integer SIZE*
　preconditions: $SIZE > 0$
　description: $SP \leftarrow 0$
cull
　description: removes the pair of *SP,* if any, with the lowest integer
name
　imports: *Name, N*
　description: **if** cardinality of $SP = SIZE$ **then**
　　　　　　　　cull
　　　　　　fi
　　　　　　add pair *N,M* to *SP* where *M* is any integer
　　　　　　larger than those presently associated with names

Will the STORED_NAMES module allow the code in EXTRACT_DETAIL to be replicated? As it happens, it will. Figure EXTRACT_LONG shows a translation of EXTRACT_DETAIL which uses STORED_NAMES to avoid the extraneous variables. The translation is almost one for one the same as the original.

Notice that the input loops and the output loops in EXTRACT_LONG have become more similar to each other than those in EXTRACT_DETAIL. The difference between the two input loops is that the first one stops before the business is finished. The difference between the two output loops is that one repeats twelve times instead of as many times as there are names. Since twelve times is just the number of names when the output loop is executed, it is possible to replace the two output loops with one that continues as long as there are names left.

Figure EXTRACT shows the result of eliminating the excess loops.

Figure EXTRACT_LONG   Version of EXTRACT_DETAIL Using STORED_NAMES

```
{input up to 12 students}
    store.initialize
    get first input name
    repeat while number of interations ≤ 12
                and input name is available
        store.name the input name
        get next input name
    again
if input name is available then
    {input rest of students}
        repeat
            store.name the input name
            get next input name
        again until input name is not available
    {output last twelve students}
        repeat for twelve times
            output store.oldest
            store.cull
        again
else
    {output all students}
        repeat while not store.empty
            output store.oldest
            store.cull
        again
fi
```

Figure EXTRACT   Extracting Metacode with Nonconvoluted Data Manipulations

```
store.initialize
get first input name
repeat while there is another name
    store.name the input name
    get next input name
again
repeat while not store.empty
    output store.oldest
    store.cull
again
```

In this section we have eliminated extraneous variables from existing metacode with a three-step process: (1) Identify sets of related extraneous variables. (2) Group the statements which reference those variables by function. (3) Define an object module whose probes and operations can carry out the indicated functions. This process can be applied in many situations to existing designs and can result in new designs whose data environments are cleaner. Cleaner data environment is our way of combating the N-squared rule.

Removal of extraneous variables was discussed first in Section 2.3. The tenchique shown here can be used to remove extraneous variables that are scattered throughout existing metacode. The concept of a clean data environment given here provides a better understanding of why extraneous variables ought be eliminated. With that understanding, we will sometimes see that not all variables of temporary significance are bad for a design. The use of a temporary variable to replace several repetitions of a complicated arithmetic expression can even increase clarity. The key to a good design is not so much the removal of all temporary variables as the insistence on clean data environments.

EXERCISES

4.3.1 Give an example that shows an extraneous variable which cannot be removed with a single metastep but can be removed with an object module.

4.3.2 Look at the example in Appendix P4 or F4, and identify all the places where a statement lies within the scope of a variable but the variable is not considered to be in the data environment of the statement.

4.3.3 In light of the discussion about clean data environments and the difference between data environments and variable scopes, why is it important that all designers and implementors of object modules agree on the rules for their usage?

4.3.4 This exercise requires a random-number generator. One is described in Figure RANDOM. With RANDOM it is possible to cause a statement S to execute with probability 0.1, that is, to execute in "a random fashion" approximately 10 percent of the time. This is done as follows:

> **if** *random.value* < 0.1 **then**
>   *S*
> **fi**
> *random.get*

RANDOM may be implemented with the help of your system's random-number generator. Or if your system doesn't have one, it may be implemented so that it state varies through this pattern:

$$0.5, 0.5, \ldots, 0.5, 0.09, 0.5, 0.5, \ldots, 0.5, 0.09, 0.5, \ldots$$

Here each repetition of 0.5 is done 9 times. This will not produce random or even pseudorandom numbers, but it will be good enough for our purposes. (In fact, it is even better for testing a program that uses RANDOM. Why?)

The problem is to redesign EXTRACT so that the students are chosen randomly. Each student is to have a 0.1 probability of being chosen. The total number of students chosen is not fixed by this method, but when you implement your design, you may assume that it is never more that twenty-five.

4.3.5 Design an estimates module for use with a program such as that described in Figure ROOT of Section 2.3 for finding a root of a function f. Make your design so that the metacode using it need have no variables corresponding to X and Y. Write that metacode as well. Make the whole design such that any change in

Figure RANDOM   A Random-Number Generating Module

DISCUSSION   Successive *get* operations produce a sequence of real numbers between 0 and 1 inclusive. The idea is that each time a new number is generated, the choice of it is to be random, and every number between 0 and 1 is to have an equal chance of being chosen. Actually, pseudorandom numbers are acceptable, so any technique of generating the numbers that is statistically indistinguishable from a "purely random" method is fine.

State Space   A *Real, R.*
   Note that $0 \le R \le 1$.

Probes
value
   export: *Real*
   description: export *R*

Operations
initialize
   description: causes *R* to be given a random value from a uniform
                [0,1] distribution
get
   description: cause *R* to be given a random value from a uniform
                [0,1] distribution

what is meant by "significantly large" can be made at the top level rather than inside the object module.

When your design is complete, implement it, using the "method of bisection." That is, improve the two estimates X, Y by finding the midpoint M of the interval $[X, Y]$ and assigning $Y \leftarrow M$ if $f(Y)$ and $f(M)$ have the same sign and $X \leftarrow M$, otherwise. Test it by finding a root of $sin(X)$ between $\pi/4$ and $-\pi/4$.

4.3.6 Consider your implementation of exercise 3.3.7. Are there convoluted data manipulations, or did you manage to design an appropriate input module without the benefit of this chapter to explain what to do? Revise your design and implementation as necessary to meet the standards of this section.

4.4   DATA FILES

Any software system needs to interact with things external to it. External objects are defined outside the system being designed, and a designer doesn't want to recreate that definition in the design. Thus there is a need for a way to incorporate an external object into a design as is and with minimal comment.

Further, many design problems are easier to solve if the existing external objects are altered or abstracted to fit the problem. These problems require a way to incorporate an external object into a design that simplifies its use. The inclusion in a design of simplified external objects, particularly data files, is an approach to problem solving which is discussed in Chapter 5.

In this section the "containment" of external objects by object modules is discussed. "Containment" appears in quotes because the concept begins to break down when the thing being contained is an external object. For example, a container that holds an input file is "filled" from outside the system. A container that holds an output file is "emptied" to the outside. Object modules which abstract external objects are better considered as *interfaces* between the software system and the external object.

An object module might interface a master file of customer records whose data requires formatting or type conversions. Actions such as "get a delinquent customer," "get another delinquent customer," "send polite dunning letter to this customer," and "send customer's name to collection agency" might be available in this module.

An object module might interface an input file so that it presents to invoking units something that is easier to use. Actions such as "get the next valid data item" might be available. Similarly, an object module might interface an output file. Actions such as "plot this point," "change the graph's scale," and "print the graph" might be available to an object module which makes graph plotting easier.

Although the examples in this book are mostly limited to those external objects which are data files, the techniques explained here can be applied to many other kinds, including some that require a technique known as *real-time programming*. *Real-time* systems control external devices whose timing is critical and must, therefore, operate within the time limits imposed on those devices.

A robot's arm, a robot's eyes, the injectors in a car's fuel injection system, or the sensors that provide data to a fuel injection system are examples of devices which must be operated in real time. These devices appear to the controlling software as data that is input or output. The relevant input/output actions can be abstracted by an object module.

Some actions which might be suitable for an object module that contains a robot's arm are "move the hand X centimeters to the right" and "return the arm to resting position."

Some actions which would be suitable for an object module that contains the sensors on a fuel injection system are "get the ambient temperature" and "get the intake manifold pressure."

The difference between the module chart of an external interface module and that of a containment module is the inclusion of two new sections, a *external data objects* section and a *drivers* section in the interface module chart.

Drivers are like operations, but drivers do not change the state of the module. Instead they merely manipulate the external object. Drivers cannot be classified as probes because they have no exports, and they cannot be classified as operations because they do not change the state of the module. To an invoking program unit, drivers appear to be the same thing as operations. An action which both changes the state of a module and manipulates an external object is considered to be an operation.

In this section, we consider object modules that interface textual input and output devices. In such modules, the external data objects section contains a list of the actions which are possible on that external object. The actions are not defined; their description belongs elsewhere. In the descriptions of the interface module's probes and operations, these actions often appear with the notation "[ ]", as in "$X \leftarrow$ [ ]" or "[ ] $\leftarrow X$", indicating, respectively, input from or output to the external object.

As a simple example of an external interface module, consider the module shown in Figure OUTPUT which interfaces an output file of characters. As stated in the External Data Object section, it is assumed that there are actions that output characters, create new output lines, and eject pages. No mention is made of how those actions are accomplished. They may not actually be separate commands to begin output lines and eject pages; these things may be accomplished by sending special characters. The implementor and the designer must know from some place other than the design what the output mechanism is.

Figure OUTPUT   Character-Output External Interface Module

Discussion   Enables character-by-character output on a default printing device.

Coupling

External Data Object   Any output device which accepts actions to output single characters, start new output lines, and eject pages.

State Space

Probes

Operations

Drivers
initialize
   description: establishes the ability to output on the default printer
out_char
   imports: *Character, C*
   description: [ ] $\leftarrow C$
new_line
   description: [ ] $\leftarrow$ new-line command
new_page
   description: [ ] $\leftarrow$ page ejection command

Since this is a very simple module that makes no alterations in the characteristics of the external device, it has no state space. Thus there are no operations to change the state. An output module often has no use for probes. This one has only drivers, and their sole purpose is to the make three output actions available to an invoking program unit. The drivers are to be used by the invoking program unit as if they were operations.

Many interface modules will have no state. When a state is present, the reason is to provide an invoking program unit with an object having characteristics different from those of the existing external object. In these cases we say the interface module *adds value*. Examples of external interface modules that add value are given below.

Notice that the *initialize* "operation" is permitted to be a driver. However, it may not be omitted. An implementation of this module may need to open a connection to a default printer or print file. On the other hand, it may not. This is an implementation decision. To make sure the implementor can decide, the *initialize* operation must be there and must be used by invoking program units.

The output module in Figure OUTPUT is rather primitive compared to the built-in writing capacity available to most programming languages. It could, however, be expanded. For example, drivers for the output of integers and real numbers could be added. Further, the capacity to handle multiple files could be added by placing file identifiers in the coupling and importing them to the various drivers. Other extensions are limited only by the designer's imagination.

One possible extension is given in Figure DUAL_OUTPUT. In this extension, the character output can be sent either to a data file or to a video screen.

Figure DUAL_OUTPUT   Printer/Screen Output Module

Discussion   Enables output of characters and integers on a default printer and/or video screen.

Coupling   *Device* which may be "printer" or "screen".

External Data Object   Any two devices, printer and screen, which accept actions to output single characters, output integers within a given field length, start new output lines, and eject pages.

State Space   A *Device*, OUT_DEVICE

Probes

Operations
initialize
   imports: *Device, D*
   description: *OUT_DEVICE ← D*

Driver
out_char
   imports: *Character, C*
   description: [*OUT_DEVICE*] ← *C*
out_integer
   imports: *Integers, FIELD_LENGTH,* and *OUTPUT_VALUE*
   description: [*OUT_DEVICE*] ← *OUTPUT_VALUE, FIELD_LENGTH*
new_line
   description: [*OUT_DEVICE*] ← new-line command
new_page
   description: [*OUT_DEVICE*] ← page-ejection command

Note that when there are multiple external objects, say a printer and a screen, the "[ ]" notation is extended to "[printer]" and "[screen]" to allow for a distinction between output devices. In Figure DUAL_OUTPUT the state variable *OUT_DEVICE* is used, as in "[*OUT_DEVICE*]", to indicate that the actual output device being manipulated depends on the state.

Of course, the meaning of the three output actions would be different for these two output objects. The ejection of a page on a line printer, for example, would mean to advance to the next perforation whereas on a video screen it would probably mean to clear the screen and place the cursor in the upper left-hand corner. The effect of these actions is not controlled by the design. The point of the "[ ]" notation is to emphasize that something is happening which involves communication with the unknown.

When the external interface module adds value to the external interface, the use of drivers is much less pronounced. As a simple example, consider a character output module which automatically ejects a page when a certain number of lines has been output. To do this, it is necessary to keep track of the page size and the present line number, or "row," in the state space. Other than alterations involving this count, the module, which is shown in Figure PAGE_OUTPUT, is essentially the same as that in Figure OUTPUT. An exercise suggests that this example be extended to include line length.

Often our input and output modules will have a different set of actions from those of our programming language. Even so, we are influenced by those programming languages familiar to us. Indeed, one purpose of designing input and output modules is to add an input-output feature to one language which we have grown to appreciate in a different language.

The object module concept was introduced on the sly in Appendixes F2 and P2 as a pair of subprograms that enables the style of the input to be altered. These subprograms were necessary because of the differences in how FORTRAN and Pascal perform input. The problem arises from the use of the same metacode for both kinds of input and the requirement, stated in Section 2.1, that the structure of repetitions and selections of the design be faithfully reproduced in the code. This faithful implementation of the same design in both languages requires that the input mechanism of one of these languages be modified. To understand the problem, consider a typical input-until-end-of-file loop in both languages. In Pascal, the way to use the *read* procedure is to check for end of file first and read only if there is more data, so the loop looks something like this:

```
repeat while there is a current input item
   read
   do something, using value that was read in
again
```

Figure PAGE_OUTPUT   Character Output with Automatic Pagination

Discussion: Enables character-by-character output on a default printing device that is organized into lines and pages. Upon initialization the maximum number of text lines per page is imported. Pages are automatically ejected when the line count reaches this maximum number. No concept of line length is known to the module.

State Space   An *Integer* parameter *MAX_ROW* and an *Integer ROW*. Note that $0 \leq ROW \leq MAX\_ROW$.

External Data Objects   Any output device which has actions to output single characters, start new output lines, and eject pages.

Probes
room_for
  imports: *Integer, I*
  export: *Boolean*
  description: exports $ROW + I \leq MAX\_ROW$

Operations
initialize
  imports: *Integer, I*
  precondition: $I > 0$
  description: $MAX\_ROW \leftarrow I$; $ROW \leftarrow 0$;
            [ ] ← page ejection command

new_page
  description: [ ] ← page ejection command
             $ROW \leftarrow 0$

new_line
  description: **if** $ROW < MAX\_ROW$ **then**
            [ ] ← new-line command
            $ROW \leftarrow ROW + 1$
      else
        new_page
      fi

Drivers
out_char
  imports: *Character, C*
  description: [ ] ← *C*

In FORTRAN, the reading principle is to READ first and ask questions later, so the loop looks something like this:

```
repeat
  READ
exit when the READ operation encountered the end of file
  do something, using value that was read in
again
```

Neither style has been used in the appendixes. The pair of subprograms introduced in Appendixes F2 and P2 supports input that looks like this:

> *initialize* input
> **repeat while** item was input
>   do something, using current input item
>   *advance* input
> **again**

This style of input was modeled after the basic *reset* and *get* mechanism of Pascal. Essentially it depends on an object module with two operations—one to initialize the input and obtain the first input item, and another to advance the input to obtain the next input item. Probes are used to find out both what the input items are and whether there are any more input items.

The analogy with Pascal's basic input mechanism is apparent when the *eof* function and the file buffer[1] are considered to be probes and the *reset* and *get* procedures are considered to be operations. The analogy is close, but the object module approach can be applied in more situations.

The object module style of input is different from almost any other programming language. Although it fits with the basic input mechanism of Pascal, it does not fit Pascal's *read* or *readln* procedure. As with most computer languages, these procedures combine the actions of obtaining an input item and of advancing to the next item. This combination is forbidden to us by the rules of object modules. An input integer can be obtained only with a probe, whereas advancement to the next input integer requires an operation or a driver. This rule is enforced because it encourages designers to define actions which are very basic and because very basic actions make the resulting designs more flexible.

Consider the input of integers from a text file which contains a sequence of integers. This can be described at a level of abstraction that omits discussion of an external interface. Figure INPUT_INTEGER shows such a description. Of course, the description in INPUT_INTEGER makes it impossible to distinguish between input from a text file and input from a file containing integers in arthmetic form. However, it covers enough detail for an invoking program unit to be written which inputs integers.

This module's two operations look the same, but they are not. Their difference lies in the rules of module usage. Nothing is defined until *initialize* has been executed.

When it is necessary to provide a design that shows some detail about how this sequence of integers is obtained, the external interface concept can be incorporated into the module chart. Figures INPUT_F and INPUT_P show two different module charts which could provide the same sequence of integers that is described in Figure INPUT_INTEGER. The difference between INPUT_F and INPUT_P lies in the natures of the underlying input actions. INPUT_F assumes FORTRAN-like input, and INPUT_P assumes Pascal-like input.

Figure INPUT_F tells what the FORTRAN-based integer input module does and how FORTRAN is utilized to obtain the results. But there is no

---

[1] The file buffer was known as the *file window* in the early descriptions of Pascal.

Figure INPUT_INTEGER   Abstract Integer Input

Discussion   Provides a sequence of integers.

State Space   An *Integer, CURRENT_INTEGER*, and a two-way condition: has_data/end_of_file.

Note *CURRENT_INTEGER* is defined iff condition is has_data.

Probes
has_integer
  export: *Boolean*
  description: exports true iff has_data is set
current_integer
  preconditions: *has_integer*
  export: *Integer*
  description: exports *CURRENT_INTEGER*

Operations
initialize
  description: **either**
          set end_of_file
      or
        set has_data
        CURRENT_INTEGER ← ?
      end
advance_integer
  description: **either**
          set end_of_file
          CURRENT_INTEGER← **undef**
      or
        set has_data
        CURRENT_INTEGER ← ?
      end

explanation of why the results are obtained in that particular way. The next two paragraphs explain some of the reasons.

The integer input module is intended to advance the integers of the input file one by one—regardless of how they have been arranged into lines. FORTRAN provides a way of reading integers without regard to their positions on the input lines; it is called *list-directed input*. List-directed input does not meet the requirement that integers be read one by one when the number of integers per line is not known because list-directed input will not begin searching for an integer in the middle of a line. The only way to overcome this problem is to read the underlying file line by line into the *LINE* string of the state space and then search for integers within *LINE*. Thus the form of input described in the external interface section is line by line.

The probe *has_integer* reports whether another integer is available. An integer is unavailable if it is not on the present *LINE* and if all subsequent lines are blank. The only way to find this out is to read ahead. The variable *CURRENT_INTEGER* appears in the state to contain the integer that has been found by looking ahead, and the *Boolean END_FILE* simply tells whether there is a *CURRENT_INTEGER*.

Figure INPUT_P also omits an explanation of why the input module is

Figure INPUT_F   FORTRAN-Based Integer Input

Discussion   Interfaces a formatted FORTRAN input file so that it appears to be a sequence of integers. The integers in the file must be separated by blanks or line boundaries.

Coupling

External Data Objects   A default input file and one input action are assumed. This action inputs a character string representing a whole line of input and a *Boolean* which is true iff the end of the file was encountered while attempting to input the character string.

State Space   A character string *LINE; Integers I* and *CURRENT_INTEGER;* and a *Boolean END_FILE*
Note that *END_FILE* is false iff *CURRENT_INTEGER* is defined.

Probes
has_integer
   export: *Boolean*
   description: exports not *END_FILE*
current_integer
   preconditions: *has_integer*
   export: *Integer*
   description: exports *CURRENT_INTEGER*

Operations
initialize
   description: arrange for input from the default file
                perform *LINE,END_FILE* ← [ ] until a nonblank character
                   is found within *LINE* or *END_FILE* becomes true
                if not *END_FILE* **then**
                   CURRENT_INTEGER ← integer that begins with the
                      nonblank character
                   I ← position of the next character in *LINE*
                      after that integer, if any, and 0 otherwise
                fi
advance_integer
   description: advance *I* (modulo length of LINE) until it points to a
                nonblank character or *END_FILE* becomes true—
                   whenever *I* = 0 perform *LINE,END_FILE* ← [ ]
                if not *END_FILE* **then**
                   CURRENT_INTEGER ← integer that begins with the
                      nonblank character
                   I ← position of the next character in *LINE*
                      after that integer, if any, and 0 otherwise
                fi

designed as it is. Pascal allows for reading of integers to happen one by one without regard to line boundaries, so there is less difficulty in describing a Pascal version of this module. However, the end-of-file test provided by Pascal tests for end of file—not for the existence of another integer. Thus to answer the question posed by the *has_integer* probe, it is necessary to look ahead to see whether the remainder of the file contains another integer or merely some trailing blanks. To search for these trailing blanks without causing an error condition, it is necessary to use the Pascal operations for peeking at the next character (the file buffer of text file) and for advancing over the next character

Figure INPUT_P   Pascal-Based Integer Input

Discussion   Interfaces a Pascal text file so that it appears to be a sequence of integers. The integers in the file must be separated by blanks or line boundaries.

External Data Object   A default input file and four input actions are assumed: One obtains the next integer in the file advancing over it, one peeks at the next character, one advances over the next character, and the last obtains a *Boolean* that is true iff the end of the file has been reached.

State Space   An *Integer CURRENT_INTEGER;* and a *Boolean END_FILE.*
Note that *END_FILE* is false iff *CURRENT_INTEGER* is defined.

Probes
has_integer
   export: *Boolean*
   description: exports not *END_FILE*
current_integer
   preconditions: *has_integer*
   export: *Integer*
   description: exports *CURRENT_INTEGER*

Operations
initialize
   description: using *END_FILE* ← [ ], *NEXT_CHARACTER* ← [ ] and
                  [ ] ← advance character, get either *END_FILE* = true or
                  NEXT_CHARACTER = the next nonblank character
              if not *END_FILE* **then**
                  CURRENT_INTEGER ← [ ]
              fi
advance_integer
   description: using *END_FILE* ← [ ], *NEST_CHARACTER* ← [ ], and
                  [ ] ← advance character, get either *END_FILE* = true
                  or *NEXT_CHARACTER* = next nonblank character
              if not *END_FILE* **then**
                  CURRENT_INTEGER ← [ ]
              fi

(the *get* procedure of a text file). It is not necessary, however, to input the integers in character form. The *read* procedure of Pascal can be used when the file is positioned on the first character of an integer.

   Neither Figure INPUT_F nor Figure INPUT_P describes what may happen if the input file contains something other than a sequence of integers. Until such things have been defined, the modules are not very practical. However, a discussion of the handling of error situations is left to Section 6.3.

   The modules of this section have a dual nature. On one side, they describe alterations to a state and are concerned with the services provided to invoking program units. On the other side, they describe interface actions and are concerned with services provided to the module by already built software or an external device. From a theoretical point of view, this duality is unclean.

But from the point of view of somebody who is trying to implement a design or understand why all aspects of it are correct, this duality can be helpful.

Whatever point of view is taken, an object module is primarily a set of actions, called probes and operations, which are described in terms of a state. (The difference between drivers and operations will disappear at the level of abstraction discussed in Chapter 7.) If an object is contained within the module, then the state is an abstraction of that object and the "real" object lurks inside, hidden from invoking program units. If an object is interfaced by the module, then the state, if any, is an abstraction of some aspect of that idealized object. The real object appears inside the module as interface actions. It is difficult to sustain the same level of abstraction when we speak in terms of interface actions and drivers that is possible when we speak in terms of a state. For this reason, the use of such descriptions should be considered a secondary aspect of object module definitions and should be limited to situations in which it cannot reasonably be avoided.

EXERCISES

For exercise 4.4.12 you must be able to do output of individual pixels. For exercises 4.4.13 to 4.4.15, you must have a working version of the module requested in exercise 4.4.12.

4.4.1 Extend the module in Figure DUAL_OUTPUT so that it is possible to write real numbers and to skip both rightward and downward.

4.4.2 Make up your own extension to the module in Figure DUAL_OUTPUT. Anything goes, as long as it follows the rules and adds value to the external interface.

4.4.3 Implement and test the module in Figure PAGE_OUTPUT.

4.4.4 Extend the module chart in Figure PAGE_OUTPUT so that it handles lines in a way similar to the way it now handles pages. Also make an extension that allows the output of integers and real numbers with imported formats. Then implement your design. Test your implementation with a suitable test program and data.

4.4.5 Pascal programmers: Write a code segment demonstrating Pascal-style input of integers from a text file. Will your code segment work properly if there is a blank character between the last integer and the end of file?

4.4.6 FORTRAN programmers: Write a code segment demonstrating FORTRAN-style input of integers from a text file. Will your code segment work properly if the number of integers per line varies?

4.4.7 Implement and test either Figure INPUT_P or INPUT_F.

4.4.8 Define a module which makes the plotting of a graph on a line printer easier. It should be possible to plot points on a "scratch pad" and output them all when the graph is complete. Points should automatically transformed thus:

$$(X, Y) \rightarrow (A \times X + B, C \times Y + D)$$

And the coefficients should be determined during initialization of the module. A count should be kept of the points that cannot be plotted because they lie out of range. (Make your own decisions as to what "out of range" means.) Implement and test the module with a suitable test program.

4.4.9 Define an input module suitable for use in implementing the design in Figure FILE_MERGE of Section 2.4. Is the implementation of Figure FILE_MERGE given in Appendix P3 or F3 also an implementation of your module? Explain why or why not.

4.4.10 Define and implement a module which inputs a text file word by word. A *word* is defined to be a string of consecutive nonblank characters which is bounded by blanks or line boundaries. Test this with a program that inputs text and prints it, one word per line.

4.4.11 Using the input module of exercise 4.4.10 and the output module of exercise 4.4.4, design a program to read a single paragraph and reformat it to another line length. Each line of the output, including the first, is to begin in column 1. No word is to be split between lines. Words are to be separated with single spaces in the output, regardless of the separation in the input. (This will leave the right margin ragged.) Implement and test your module.

4.4.12 Design, implement, and test a module which allows output of individual pixels on paper or a screen.

4.4.13 Using the pixel module of exercise 4.4.12, design, implement, and test a graphics package with drivers that allow line segments to be drawn between two given endpoints and circles to be drawn with a given center point and radius.

4.4.14 Extend exercise 4.4.13 so that it is possible to change the scale of the drawings in a way similar to exercise 4.4.8.

4.4.15 Extend exercise 4.4.13 with a driver or an operation that draws a third-degree polynomial between (X_1, Y_1) and (X_4, Y_4) that fits the points $(X_1, Y_1), (X_2, Y_2), (X_3, Y_3), (X_4, Y_4)$.

4.5   OBJECT-TYPE MODULES

In Section 2.3 the concept of data type was described. Data types identify kinds of data, not particular data items. When we say, "let D be the distance traveled . . . ," we are both describing a kind of data and naming a variable, D, to represent that data. When we say, "one kind of distance, called *Distance*, is the distance traveled . . . ," we are describing and naming a type of data. We can later say, "let D be a variable of type *Distance*" when we want to deal with particular data items of that type.

Object modules are analogous to variables; they describe particular data objects. The difference, of course, is that object modules describe those data objects from a functional point of view.

The *object-type* modules of this section are analogous to data types; they describe a kind of data from a functional point of view. A program unit which uses an object-type module will declare and use the variables whose functions are described by the module. The module's actions import, export, or update those variables.

An example can make the concept clear. Consider the stack-data-type module of Figure STACK_TYPE, and compare it with the stack object module in Figure STACK of Section 4.2. Figure STACK_TYPE shows these differences from Figure STACK:

1 In the Discussion section, the object module "contains" a stack, and the data-type module "supports" stacks.

2 The State Space section is replaced by a Supported Data Type section which describes a state for each stack in an unspecified set of stacks.

3 Stacks are imported by probes and exported or updated by operations.

These differences reflect the fact that the object module appears to its invoking unit as an actual stack whereas the type module appears to its invoking unit as a set of actions that are possible with stacks.

An implementation of the stack module implements a particular stack. Variables to implement the state space of that stack are contained within the implementation. No variables implementing the stack are accessed by the invoking program unit. Probes may be variables, but must not have their values changed outside of the module.

Figure STACK_TYPE   Stack-Data-Type Module

Discussion   Supports a last-in-first-out data structure.

Coupling   *Item* (an unspecified data type)

Supported Data Type   *Stack*; for each *Stack S* a typical state is a sequence

$$i_{S,1}, \ldots, i_{S,K(S)}$$

of *K(S) Items*; *K(S)* may be 0, in which case the sequence is said to be empty.

Probes

top
   imports: *Stack S*
   preconditions: $K(S) \neq 0$
   export: *Item*
   description: export $i_{S,K(S)}$

full
   imports: *Stack S*
   export: *Boolean*
   description: export true iff it would be impossible to push another
                  Item on *S*

empty
   emports: *Stack S*
   export: *Boolean*
   description: export $K(S) = 0$

Operations

initialize
   export: *Stack S*
   description: $K(S) \leftarrow 0$

push
   updates: *Stack S*
   imports: *Item I*
   preconditions: not *full(S)*
   description: $K(S) \leftarrow K(S) + 1; i_{S,K(S)} \leftarrow I$

pop
   updates: *Stack S*
   preconditions: not *empty(S)*
   description: $K(S) \leftarrow K(S) - 1$

An implementation of the stack-type module implements no particular stack. Instead, it provides probes and operations that may be used on any stack which an invoking program unit might declare. Stacks declared by invoking program units are not manipulated except by means of the probes and operations of the module. Probes and operations of the module use variables that reference stacks, but these variables reference no particular stack unless the probe or operation is executing. When a probe or operation begins execution, these variables are bound to stacks of the invoking program unit.

Object modules and type modules are essentially two sides of the same coin, and rules that apply to one have a counterpart in the rules that apply to the other. In one case, the object being described is abstracted with a state that is a special preserve of the module. In the other, a kind of object, called a *supported data type*, is being described. This association between states and supported data types forms the basis of comparison between the rules of the two kinds of modules:

All probes and operations of an object module must have something to do with the state—all probes and operations of a type module must import, export, or update a supported data type.

A probe of an object module must not alter the state and must export exactly one data type—a probe of a type module must export exactly one data type, and that data type may not be supported by the module.

An operation of an object module must alter the state and must export or update nothing—an operation of a type module must export or update a supported data type and must export or update no unsupported data type.

The state of an object module is not directly accessible by an invoking program unit—variables of a supported data type are not directly accessible by the program unit using them; i.e., the only actions permitted on those variables are those defined in the type module that does the supporting. The data-type module should provide all basic actions necessary to utilize the supported data, and the programmer of the invoking program unit should resist the temptation to use supported data with any of the primitive actions directly available in the programming language. This is called the data-type *encapsulation* rule.

Although they represent two sides of the same coin, the implementations of these two kinds of modules are different. Languages such as FORTRAN and Pascal provide even less enforcement of the type module rules than they do for the object module rules. Data-type modules are difficult to use properly in these languages and should be avoided when object modules are possible.

The rules concerning the *initialize* operation are the same. The *initialize* operation must be invoked for each variable of the supported data type before any other probe or operation. The imports of the *initialize* operation are called *parameters* and may not be changed by any other operation.

It might be thought that any situation which requires multiple data objects of the same type is a situation requiring a type module rather than a object module. This isn't true. The combination of a printer and a screen in Figure DUAL_OUTPUT in Section 4.4 shows that it is possible for object modules to deal with multiple objects. It is also possible to make multiple implementations of an object module. (This would be done, for example, if the program needed one stack of integers and another of real numbers.) Thus object modules are not limited to single objects.

In some situations, however, the concept of object module seems too constraining. After all, a concept which ties data together into a usable package is not likely to be good for explanations of how pieces of data can be combined to get other pieces of data.

A situation requiring such an explanation is the use of real numbers on a computer that only supports integers. Addition, multiplication, subtraction, and division are operations that combine pieces of data (namely, two real numbers) to make another piece of data (the result of the arithmetic operation). Another such situation is the development of "infinite" precision real numbers on almost any computer. Development of a fractions data type represents a third situation.

Anybody who has needed to add two fractions knows the value of having a single-step addition operation to support a *Fraction* data type. Such an operation would import two fractions, add them, and export the result.

Object type modules are used in defining programs by defining relevant actions as soon as it is known that a particuar data type will be needed. These actions are packaged as a set of actions that support the data type. A designer who needs a fraction, for example, would create a data-type module which contains the primitive arithmetic operations that apply to fractions. This module would be designed and perhaps even coded before the program which uses it were designed. Then the portions of that program which utilize fractions would be easier to design because the fractions would be easier to use.

A *Fraction* object-type module is described in Figure FRACTIONS. Its description relies on our common knowledge of fractions and not on a mathematical model. No mathematical representation of a *Fraction* appears in the Supported Data Type section. Such a state-free description is possible with an object-type module but not with an object module.[2]

There are a lot of probes in the fractions module. This is due to the encapsulation rule which makes it impossible to obtain information about any of the parts of a *Fraction* without using a probe. Thus, for example, there must be some probes to help an invoking program unit discover what the numerator and the demoninator of a particular *Fraction* actually are.

---

[2] This observation is false at a high level of abstraction where the distinction between the two types of modules is blurred. Such a level is reached in Chapter 7 where even a queue module is defined without reliance on the concept of a state.

Figure FRACTIONS *Fraction* **Data-Type Module**

Discussion   Supports arithmetic operations on fractions.

Supported Data Types   *Fraction*

Probes

equal
  imports: two *Fractions F1* and *F2*
  export: *Boolean*
  description: export *F1* = *F2*

greater
  imports: two *Fractions F1* and *F2*
  export: *Boolean*
  description: export *F1* > *F2*

is_zero
  imports: *Fraction F1*
  export: *Boolean*
  description: export *F1* = 0

is_positive
  imports: *Fraction F1*
  export: *Boolean*
  description: export *F1* > 0

integer_part
  imports: *Fraction F1*
  export: *Integer*
  description: export 0 if *F1* is proper, otherwise export
                     integer part of that mixed number equivalent to *F1*

numerator
  imports: *Fraction F1*
  export: *Integer*
  description: export the numerator of *F1*

denominator
  imports: *Fraction F1*
  export: *Integer*
  description: export the denominator of *F1*

Operations

define
  imports: *Integers N* and *D*
  preconditions: $D \neq 0$
  export: *Fraction*
  description: export reduced *Fraction* that equals *N/D*

add
  imports: two *Fractions F1* and *F2*
  export: *Fraction*
  description: export *F1* + *F2* in fully reduced form

subtract
  imports: two *Fractions F1* and *F2*
  export: *Fraction*
  description: export *F1* + *F2* in fully reduced form

multiply
  imports: two *Fractions F1* and *F2*
  export: *Fraction*
  description: export *F1* × *F2* in fully reduced form

divide
   imports: two *Fractions* F1 and F2
   preconditions: not *is_zero*(F2)
   export: *Fraction*
   description: export F1/F2 in fully reduced form
fractional_part
   imports: *Fraction* F1
   export: *Fraction*
   description: export F1 if F1 is proper, otherwise export the
                         fractional part of that mixed number equivalent to F1

The concept of data type truely comes into its own when it is possible to build definitions of data types upon other definitions of data types. A customer record as described in Section 2.3 is nice. A customer record that can be a part of an array, a file, or a symbol table is much nicer. A stack as in Figure STACK_TYPE is nice. A stack which can stack up symbol tables as well as real numbers or *Fractions* is much nicer.

Although we can imagine such things, without a programming language that provides substantial support for abstract data types, we risk inadvertent misuse when we fill our designs with type modules. Several languages which give some of the necessary support are Ada,[3] Alphard, CLU, Concurrent Pascal, Euclid, Gypsy, Modula, Russell and Simula [SHA]. None of these is on a list of best sellers. Ada may get there, but for now the best approach seems to be to emphasize object modules over type modules whenever appropriate.

EXERCISES

4.5.1 Redo exercise 4.2.1 or 4.2.6, using Figure STACK_TYPE rather than Figure STACK as a guide.

4.5.2 Define a queue-type module.

4.5.3 Define a symbol table type module.

4.5.4 Convert your symbol table object module of exercise 4.2.3 or 4.2.7 to a symbol table type module. Convert the test program as well. (*Hint*: FORTRAN programmers who are converting exercise 4.2.3 should make VALUE and NAME into two-dimensional arrays whose *I*th row represents the VALUE and NAME of a single symbol table. Then the *SymbolTable* data type will be simply INTEGER.)

4.5.5 Implement and test a stack of symbol tables. Use Figure STACK of Section 4.2 to guide the implementation of the stack, and utilize the symbol table of exercise 4.5.4 for the symbol tables being stacked.

4.5.6 One of the more useful type modules for FORTRAN and especially Pascal programmers is a *String*-type module. No example of one has been given. Make up your own. In addition to operations for cutting and pasting, do not forget that the data type must be encapsulated, and so methods of putting characters into strings and removing them from strings are needed as well. Do not implement.

---

[3] Ada is a registered trademark of the U.S. government, Ada Joint Program Office.

4.5.7   Have a friend, who is also reading this book, read your *String* module chart when you are absent. Then have her comment on your choice of probes and operations and explain the implementation decisions she would make for the module. Don't argue with your friend—your goal is to see your module chart through her eyes. Module charts are for communicating as well as for planning. Without the kind of practice this exercise provides you won't learn to write them properly. Rewrite your module chart, taking advantage of any inspirations you had while listening to your friend.

4.5.8   Implement and test your string module.

4.5.9   Implement and test a stack of strings, using your string module.

4.5.10 Implement Figure SYMBOL_TABLE of Section 4.2 so that it makes full use of your *String*-type module. The *Value* data type should also be a *String* data type. Test your implementation.

4.5.11 Redo the word input module of exercise 4.4.10, making full use of your *String* type module.

4.5.12 Using the symbol table of exercise 4.5.10 and the word input module of exercise 4.5.11, design, implement, and test a program which reads a dictionary of words and their synonyms, then reads a text, and prints the text with the words replaced by their synonyms.

REFERENCES

[BAR]: Barnes, J. G. P. *Programming in Ada*, Addison-Wesley, Reading, Mass., 1982.

[BEN]: Bentley, J. L. *Writing Efficient Programs*, Prentice-Hall, Englewood Cliffs, N.J., 1982.

[LEV]: Levy, M. R. "Modularity and the Sequential File Update Problem," *Communications of the Association for Computing Machinery*, June 1982, pp. 362–367.

[SHA]: Shaw, M. "The Impact of Abstraction Concerns on Modern Programming Languages," in Peter Hibbard, Andy Hisgen, Jonathan Rosenberg, Mary Shaw, and Mark Sherman; *Studies in Ada Style*, Springer-Verlag, New York, 1981, pp. 5–29.

5

PROBLEM SOLVING WITH DATA ABSTRACTION

Problem solving, as discussed so far, involves the creation of vague metacode and the work of making it precise. Object modules can ease the burden of that work, and they can allow the designer to begin with something other than vague metacode.

Object modules can be viewed as virtual machines that provide the designer and programmer with the illusion of one set of actions whereas, in reality, a very different set is doing the job. When an existing algorithm that requires one set of actions must be adapted to a situation where another set of actions is available, this aspect of object modules can be very handy. Problem solving by defining object modules that adapt known algorithms to new problems is discussed in Section 5.1.

One good way to show the interactions between the metasteps of top-level metacode is to define object modules whose operations correspond to the metasteps. The definition of metacode first and a refinement of the metasteps second comprise top-down design. The use of object modules in creating that refinement is discussed in Section 5.2.

In the bottom-up approach, metasteps tend to be designed before a use for them has been determined. Not surprisingly, such metasteps don't always fit together very well. However, object modules which are designed before their exact use is known, are much easier to fit together. Since object modules are little more than cooperating sets of metatests (probes) and metasteps (operations), a designer who begins with a couple of object modules is practicing bottom-up in a form that works. The idea behind this form is to begin the design process with the creation of a *false bottom* for the metacode, i.e., a virtual machine that makes input, output, and temporary data storage easier to do. This approach is exemplified with the longest and most complex example of the book in Section 5.3. Not all readers will wish to wade through that section, but those who do will see how the action and data abstractions of the book can be applied to larger, more realistic problems.

We are coming to the point where our techniques can be used to create nontrivial designs. As the complexity of a design increases, so does the number of places where bugs can hide. Our emphasis on clarity of exposition is a protection against bugs. Like cockroaches, bugs in designs can't stand the light of day. They need a place to hide, and a well-written design provides little of that. However, bugs will appear. Some will be discovered during coding. Others will be discovered during testing. Still others will be discovered by irate users. When bugs are discovered, the design must shine.

Implemented code which does not match its design in exactly the manner discussed in Chapter 2 in terrain where the sun never shines. A design can shed no light on the reason why such code is malfunctioning. Here is what you must do to prevent the waste of a good design. The same steps can also help to transform a bad design into a good one.

When a bug appears, first check the code against the design. Ask questions later.

Don't chase bugs in a code which does not match its design. Instead, change the code to match the design; or if you have a very good reason, change the design to match the code.

When a bug is traced to the design, fix both the design and the code so that the correspondence between them is as strong as ever and so that both are improved. Remember that a decrease in clarity is not an improvement!

When you feel that this process involves too much busy work, think of the parable of the tortoise and the hare. The hare is fast because it is capable of skipping the busy work and guessing what needs to be done. The tortoise cannot, or will not, skip the busy work. On easy problems (those that can be completed with two or three bursts of speed) the hare wins. On larger problems, the hare gets lost from time to time. "Why was this decision made?" and "Why, this bug could be anyplace!" are a hare's comments. The tortoise, who patiently writes and updates a design, is never confused by past decisions. When bug hunting, the tortoise has a map of the terrain that clearly shows possible hiding places. The tortoise often finishes while the hare is searching for that "last" bug!

5.1 SIDE-TO-SIDE

Side-to-side problem solving is the adaptation of known algorithms to new problems. Examples were introduced in Section 3.3. but without the use of object modules. With the object module concept, known algorithms can sometimes be applied to new problems with little or no change. The idea is to create a virtual machine that revamps those aspects of the problem which do not fit the algorithm.

In a sense, an example of this design technique has already been shown. The algorithms of this book rely on a certain kind of input mechanism. This input mechanism is not directly available in FORTRAN, and in Pascal it is available only through the *reset* and *get* mechanism, a mechanism which has limited applicability. In this book, the problem of implementing the same repetitious metacode input in both FORTRAN and Pascal is solved (compare Section 4.4 and Appendixes F2 and P2) by defining object modules that change the input mechanism to fit the metacode.

As a more direct illustration of the technique, let's reconsider the global replacement algorithm of Section 3.3. The purpose of that algorithm is to replace all copies in a string *TEXT* of a substring *SUB* with another substring *ALT*. (It is assumed that all such copies are disjoint from each other.) Our approach in Section 3.3 began with two similar problems. One was the replacement of letters in text with other letters. Figure LETTER_REPLACE of that section, which is reproduced here for easy reference, shows a simple letter-replacement algorithm.

Figure LETTER_REPLACE   Replacing a Single Letter

```
repeat for I ← 1,2, . . . , (length of TEXT)
  if TEXT(I) = L then
    TEXT(I) ← ALTL
  fi
again
```

For the present approach, we begin with a restatement of LETTER_ REPLACE which replaces the string *TEXT* with an object module that contains a sequence of characters. This module is not defined—the top level is merely organized as if it had been defined. Figure LETTER_REPLACE_2 shows this top level. The index *I* is missing because its purpose is to help step through the characters in the string, and the string is being contained by the imagined module. In place of *I* are operations for stepping through the string. Since the algorithm must update a string *TEXT*, provision must be made at the beginning to transfer *TEXT* to the module and at the end to obtain *TEXT* from the module.

Figure LETTER_REPLACE_2   Replacing a Single Letter in Text that Is Contained by a Module

```
set up for consideration of first letter in TEXT
repeat while there is another character to look at
  if that character = L then
    replace that character with ALTL
  fi
  advance to next character
again
obtain TEXT from module
```

Next we make minimal modifications to LETTER_REPLACE_2 to allow for the fact that substrings, not letters, are going to be replaced. Substrings have a length associated with them. Before doing a replacement, the algorithm must check to see whether there is room for the new substring, and it must not advance just one character each time through the loop. Figure STRING_REPLACE shows the results of these modifications.

Figure STRING_REPLACE

> set up for considering substrings of *TEXT* that begin with
>   the first character of *TEXT*
> **repeat while** there are another length of *SUB* characters
>   **if** a copy of *SUB* begins at this position and
>   there is room for a switch of *SUB* with a string of size of *ALT*
>
>   **then**
>   replace *SUB* with *ALT*
>   set up for considering substrings of *TEXT* that begin immediately
>
>   after the inserted *ALT*
>   **else**
>   set up for considering substrings of *TEXT* which begin with
>   the next character of *TEXT*
>   **fi**
> **again**

In Section 3.3, vague metacode was written and made precise to furnish the details about how the steps of LETTER_REPLACE could be altered to accommodate strings. This time, we define probes and operations inspired from the metatests and metasteps of STRING_REPLACE; i.e., we create a virtual machine for dealing with strings whose actions include many of the metatests and metasteps of STRING_REPLACE. A difficulty we have in Section 3.3 was the description of how the cutting of *SUB* and the pasting of *ALT* were to be done. This is an implementation problem, and it is avoided in the object module through the magic of mathematics. The state is a sequence of characters—not a character string. Figure TEXT_OPERATIONS shows a definition of a module for recognizing substrings and inserting new substrings.

The description of *adv_replace* shows an assignment of the sequence

$$c_1, \ldots, c_{P-1}, A(1), \ldots, A(\text{length of } A), c_{P+I}, \ldots, c_K$$

to *C*. Because of its complicated use of sequence notation, this assignment bears some explanation. If the length of *A* is 0, this sequence reduces to

$$c, \ldots, c_{P-1}, c_{P+I}, \ldots, c_K$$

and the effect is to remove a copy of *SUB* from *C*. Otherwise, if $P = 1$, the sequence reduces to $A(1), \ldots, A(\text{length of } A), c_{I+1}, \ldots, c_K$, in which case

Figure TEXT_OPERATIONS   A Substring Manipulation Module

Discussion   Contains a character string which can examined character by character for purposes of identifying and replacing substrings.

Coupling   *String*
   Note that the *I*th element of a *String S* is indicated by $S(I)$

State Space   A state consists of a positive integer parameter *MAX_K*, an *Integer P*, and a sequence of *Characters*
   $C = c_1, c_2, \ldots, c_K$
   Note $0 \le K \le MAX\_K, 1 \le P \le K + 1$.

Probes
remaining
   imports: *Integer, I*
   export: *Boolean*
   description: export $P + I - 1 \le K$
points_to
   imports: *String S*
   precondition: $P + (\text{length of } S) - 1 \le K$
   export: *Boolean*
   description: export
      $c_P, \ldots, c_{P + (\text{length of } S) - 1} = S(1), \ldots, S(\text{length of } S)$
roomfor
   imports: *Integer, I*
   export: *Boolean*
   description: export $K + I \le MAX\_K$
string
   export: *String*
   description: export the string represented by C

Operations
initialize:
   description: $MAX\_K \leftarrow$ maximum string length
set_string
   imports: *String S*
   precondition: length of $S \le MAX\_K$
   description: $C \leftarrow S(1), S(2), \ldots, S(\text{length of } S)$
               $P \leftarrow 1$
adv_char
   preconditions: $P < K$
   description: $P \leftarrow P + 1$
adv_replace
   imports: *Integer I* and *String A*
   preconditions: $K + (\text{length of } A) - I \le MAX\_K$
   description:
      $C \leftarrow c_1, \ldots, c_{P-1}, A(1), \ldots, A(\text{length of } A), c_{P+I}, \ldots, c_K$
      $P \leftarrow P + \text{length of } A$

the replacement is to the first part of C. If K is also 0, the sequence would reduce to

   $A(1), \ldots, A(\text{length of } A)$

in which case the assignment is merely $C \leftarrow A$. (This last case would not occur in the design, but the notation allows it.) If, instead, $P > 1$ and $K < P + I$, the sequence reduces to

$$c_1, \ldots, c_{p-1}, A(1), \ldots, A(\text{length of } A)$$

in which case the replacement is to the last part of C.

Whatever the sequence on the right is, the expression

$$c_1 \ldots, c_K$$

will refer to the new C after the assignment has been completed.

Top-level metacode that is based on module TEXT_OPERATIONS appears in Figure TEX_REPLACE; it is essentially the same thing as Figure STRING_REPLACE, having been changed to accommodate the names of the probes and operations. Figures TEXT_REPLACE and TEXT_OPER-ATIONS comprise a design for a global replacement algorithm. The design is written at a higher level of abstraction than appears in Section 3.3. That level is concerned with the details of how to represent the string being altered. At the present level, such details are avoided.

Figure TEXT_REPLACE   Global Replacement Algorithm

```
initialize
set_string TEXT
repeat while remaining is length of SUB
  if points_to SUB
      and roomfor is (length of ALT) − (length of SUB)
    then
      adv_replace next (length of SUB) characters with ALT
  else
      adv_char
  fi
again
TEXT ← string
```

It may seem to some readers that the present design punts the real problem. But, as is well known, to punt with precision can often get you out of trouble.

Figures TEXT_OPERATIONS and TEXT_REPLACE punt over the question of how to store the characters of *TEXT* while the replacements are being made. This is accomplished by using the matematical entity, sequence, to keep track of *TEXT* while the replacements are occurring. Some readers would implement that state in a string and cause the right side to be recopied each time *adv_replace* were invoked, others would utilize a linked list, and still others would utilize the trick described in Section 3.3. Be that as it may, implementation of the text operations module is a more straightforward programming exercise than implementation of the entire global replacement program.

This is precision punting because the global replacement problem is replaced with an easier problem whose solution can be changed as implementation requirements change. A implementation which is easy to program might work at first. Later an implementation that runs faster or saves memory might be necessary. The overall design is impervious to such changes.

If the designer felt it necessary to control the particular method of implementation, then a little more detail would be necessary. This detail could be given in some implementation guidelines.

For example, a designer wanting to guide the implementor toward the kind of solution found in Section 3.3 might provide an implementation guideline stating that the sequence of c_I's is to be implemented as a character string STR with $STR(I) = c_I$ for $I = 1, 2, \ldots, P-1$ and

$STR((\text{length of } STR) - (\text{length of original } TEXT) + I) = c_I$

for $I = P, P+1, \ldots,$ (length of original $TEXT$).

Such guidance will ensure an implementation that has much of the flavor of the detailed metacode in Section 3.3, but that metacode specifies replacement within $TEXT$—not within a second string STR. To match REPLACE_STRING's use of $TEXT$, the module TEXT_OPERATIONS must be redefined. Exercise 5.1.4 asks for such a change.

All that has been accomplished so far in this section is to rework a problem that was solved earlier. The usefulness of object modules in helping to adapt a known algorithm to a new problem really has not been documented. Now let's adapt the design of Figures TEXT_REPLACE and TEXT_OPERATIONS to work while copying data from one textual file to another.

Since the original problem statement involved working with a given string $TEXT$ and the new problem statement involves copying from input to output, clearly references to $TEXT$ must be removed from the top-level metacode. The first reference is easy to remove—just drop the *set_string* operation. Removal of the second reference requires that the *string* probe be replaced with an operation, say *epilogue*, which ensures that the altered text is completely copied over to output. Figure COPY_REPLACE shows the revised top level. No further changes are needed at the top.

Figure COPY_REPLACE   External Global Replacement Algorithm

```
initialize
repeat while remaining is length of SUB
   if points_to SUB then
      adv_replace next (length of SUB) characters with ALT
   else
      adv_char
   fi
again
epilogue
```

The text operations module must be altered to contain external interfaces for input and output. These can consist of simple actions to read and write one character at a time. The *points_to* operation seems to require a comparison of its import with a sequence of characters in the state, and this, in turn,

Figure COPY_OPERATIONS

Discussion   Interfaces textual input and output files so as to facilitate copying from input to output while identifying certain substrings and cutting and pasting other substrings. There is an implementation-dependent maximum length on the substrings.

Coupling   *String* (varying length with fixed maximum length)
Note that the *I*th element of a *String S* is denoted $S(I)$.

External Data Objects   An input file with two actions: reading a single character and detecting end of file. An output file with one action: writing a single character.

State Space   A state consists of a positive integer parameter *MAX_K* and a sequence *C* of characters
  $c_1, c_2, \ldots, c_K$
where $0 \leq K \leq MAX\_K$

Probes
points_to
  imports: *String, S*
  precondition: length of $S \leq K$
  export: *Boolean*
  description: export
    $c_1, c_2, \ldots, c_{\min (K, \text{length of } S)} = S(1), S(2), \ldots, S(\text{length of } S)$
remaining
  imports: *Integer, I*
  export: *Boolean*
  description: export $I \leq K$

Operations
initialize:
  description: *MAX_K* ← maximum string length
            input as many characters as possible into *C*
adv_char
  preconditions: *remaining* 1
  description: remove and output the leftmost character from *C*
            if not end of input data **then**
                input single character into *C* on right
            fi
adv_replace
  imports: *Integer, J*; *String, A*
  preconditions: *remaining J*
  description: output *A*
            remove first *J* characters of *C*
            input as many characters as possible into *C* on the right

Drivers
epilogue
  description: output remaining characters in *C*

requires that the state contain a sequence of characters. Since the text being altered is stored in a file, we cannot hope to keep the entire text internal to the module. Luckily, there is no need because the sequence of characters in the state can be handled in a queuelike fashion. The queue will be filled (as much as possible) by *initialize* and refilled by *adv_char* and *adv_replace* as characters are copied from the front to output. A revision of Figure TEXT_OPERATIONS that arises from these considerations is shown in Figure COPY_OPERATIONS.

One of the goals of the software designer is to produce modules that can be reused in other algorithms with no change. Section 6.2 gives some pointers for designing modules that have a better chance of being reused.

Often, however, modules must be altered before they can be reused. In these cases, the process of alteration is one of side-to-side problem solving. The development of COPY_REPLACE and COPY_OPERATIONS from TEXT_REPLACE and TEXT_OPERATIONS is an example of this kind of alteration.

The more modules you have designed, the greater is your opportunity to apply the side-to-side problem solving of this section.

EXERCISES

5.1.1 Let

$$C = c_1, c_2, \ldots, c_K$$
$$D = d_1, d_2, \ldots, d_L$$
$$E = f_1, f_2, \ldots, f_M$$

be empty sequences. Assume that the following metacode has been executed, and answer the questions below.

$$C \leftarrow 2,4,6,8,16,32,64,128,256,512$$
$$D \leftarrow 1,3,5,7,9,11,13,15$$
$$E \leftarrow c_1, \ldots, c_L, d_2, \ldots, d_{L-1}, c_{K-1}, \ldots, c_1$$
$$D \leftarrow d_1, c_1, d_2, c_2, \ldots, d_L, c_L$$

  a What values are K, L, and M?
  b List the values of D.
  c List the values of E.
  d Is $D = d_1, c_1, d_2, c_2, \ldots, d_L, c_L$?
  e Is $C = d_2, d_4, \ldots, d_L$?

5.1.2 Rewrite the design in Figure TEXT_REPLACE and TEXT_OPERATIONS so that the rightmost occurrence of *SUB* is replaced first, the second-to-rightmost; occurrence is replaced next, etc.

5.1.3 Implement and test the design in Figures COPY_REPLACE and COPY_OPERATIONS.

5.1.4 Redesign the string replacement algorithm of Figures TEXT_REPLACE and TEXT_OPERATIONS so that it can be implemented in a way that matches Figure PATTERN_REPLACE of Section 3.3. The "match" will not be exact because of the subprogram invocations required by a modular design. But you can make the match close enough that given the same data, the metacode of your design and the metacode in PATTERN_REPLACE would cause the same sequence of changes to be made to the string TEXT. Since your design is for a segment of code which imports and exports TEXT, it will be necessary to use a type module rather than an object module to describe the alterations which TEXT can undergo.

5.1.5 Design, implement, and test a new version of the synonym-replacing program of exercise 4.5.12 so that it replaces variables in the source code of a program rather than words in a text.

5.1.6 Design, implement, and test a new version of the N.Y.S.E. statistics-gathering program of Figure NYSE in Section 3.3. This version can be defined by denoting the sequence of N.Y.S.E. composite index readings with

$$N_1, N_2, \ldots, N_K$$

and then defining the beginning of a *bull* market as a the Ith day iff

$$N_I > \text{all of } N_{I-5}, N_{I-4}, \ldots, N_{I-1}$$
$$N_I \leq \text{all of } N_{I+1}, N_{I+2}, \ldots, N_{I+5}$$

and each of $N_I, N_{I+1}, \ldots, N_{I+5}$ is greater than the average of the five preceding values.

A bull market continues through all J that satisfy the property that N_J is greater than the average of the five preceding values. A *bear* market is defined similarly but with the inequities reversed.

5.2   TOP-DOWN

One nice thing about top-down design is that the top level can be written in a language which is natural to the problem rather than to a particular computer system. One disadvantage is that the top-level language is likely to be ambiguous or pedantic. If the top-level language is ambiguous, then the design usually achieves its precision from the inclusion of lower-level metacode expanding some of the top-level metatests and metasteps. If the top level is pedantic, it probably reads so poorly that it is hard to see the forest for the trees.

Another way to give precise meaning to the top-level metacode is to define object modules whose probes and operations are the top-level metatests and metasteps.

There are two advantages to this use of object modules as opposed to merely expanding the ambiguous metatests and metasteps:

1 First, the exercise of writing a module chart forces the designer to consider a state space and the use which each metatest or metastep makes of that state space, which encourages the discovery of unworkable metatests or metasteps.

2 The use of module probes and operations in the top-level metacode enables code to be written which is as abstract as the metacode design. The reason is that probes and operations don't require an expansion into several statements as ordinary metatests and metasteps do. The details required to carry out their actions are buried within an object module.

To illustrate this approach, let's consider a program which keeps track of bowling scores. A game of bowling is divided into ten *frames*. In each frame, the player tries to knock down a set of ten pins by rolling a ball at them. Two rolls are permitted toward this end. Each roll contributes to the player's frame score by the number of pins knocked down.

If not all the pins are knocked down, then the frame score is the sum of the scores for the two rolls. This situation is called a *break*. If all ten pins are knocked down, a bonus is added to the frame score. There are two situations: (1) All ten pins are knocked down by the first roll. This is called a *strike*. Then there is no second roll for a strike frame. The next two balls to be rolled count for the strike frame as well as for whatever frame(s) they belong to. (2) The last of the ten pins are knocked down by the second roll. This is called a *spare*. The next ball to be rolled counts for the spare frame as well as for the frame to which it belongs. The frame is said to be *open* until the scores for bonus rolls are known.

A game score is, of course, the sum of the frame scores. A strike or spare in the last, or tenth, frame allows the player to take one or two extra rolls that count for the bonus in the tenth frame and, possibly, the ninth frame as well. Figure PERFECT_BOWL shows the final part of a score sheet for a perfect game in which all ten pins are knocked down on every roll.

Figure PERFECT_BOWL   Last Three Frames of a Perfect Game

Frame	1st Ball	2d Ball	Status	Bonus	Frame Score	Score
9	10	—	strike	20	30	270
10	10	—	strike	20	30	300
*	10	10	*	*	*	*

Figure SCREEN_BOWL   A Screen Display for a Game in Progress

Player	Frame	1st Ball	2d Ball	Status	Bonus	Frame Score	Score
A	4	6	0	break	—	6	32
A	5	7	3	spare	1	11	43
A	6	1	6	break	—	7	50
B	3	10	—	strike	8	18	24
B	4	8	0	break	—	8	42
B	5	3	7	spare	0+	10+	52+

Please enter player B's pin counts for frame 6.

Figure SCREEN_BOWL shows a game between two players as it might appear on a video screen before the second player begins the sixth frame. We shall design a program that operates a display of this type. An exact description of the CRT display would add unnecessary detail to the example, so we assume an external interface for the output of the CRT display which accepts the commands given in Figure SCREEN_OUTPUT. The results of these commands can be given substance by the reader from Figures PERFECT_BOWL and SCREEN_BOWL. Of course, no real terminal driver accepts commands such as these. By postulating an interface of this kind, we are, for purposes of simplifying the example, merely removing many output details from the design.

Figure SCREEN_OUTPUT   External Interface for Screen Displays

A screen output device is assumed which accepts output by line. Lines are identified by counting from the top of the screen. There are five actions:

   1 initialize and clear screen
   2 output *String* in line *L*
   3 output open-frame entries for *X* in line *L*
imports *Player X, Pin_counts, Status*, and integers:
frame number, bonus, frame score, score, and line number *L*
   4 output closed-frame entries for *X* in line *L*
imports *Player X, Pin_counts, Status*, and integers:
frame number, bonus, frame score, score, and line number *L*
   5 output extra roll line for *X* in line *L*
imports player id *X, Pin_counts*, and line number *L*

   The environment for this driver includes a *Player* data type that includes representations of A and B; a *Pin_counts* data type that consists of two integers, one for each pin count—the first is nonnegative; and a *Status* data type that contains a representation for each of these conditions: strike, spare, break.
   When a negative second pin count is imported, it is output as a " − ."

   Metacode to display the three most recent frames of each player might follow this vague plan:

   repeat
      get *Pin_counts* for next frame
      display entries for three most recent frames, updating them
         using these *Pin_counts* and remembering previous actions
   again

   There are two metasteps. The first acquires some *Pin_counts*, and the second uses them. Both are rather vague. We can be somewhat systematic in identifying their vagueness by considering what data is left unmentioned.

One way to look for what is unsaid is to look for data objects mentioned in the problem which are missing in the metacode. The concepts of player and frame are missing. Data involving these concepts will be needed by both metasteps. (The "display . . ." step clearly needs player and frame information. The "get . . ." step also needs both because prompting for interactive input belongs to the input step.)

The vague metacode seems to make no provision for any extra rolls. Data about extra rolls is required by both metasteps. It could be represented as the *Pin_counts* for an imaginary eleventh frame.

Data that is needed by both metasteps can be visible at the top level or hidden in some module that is available to both metasteps.

There are two different ways to hide data in a module that is available to both metasteps:

1 Both metasteps are placed in same module which hides the data.
2 Both metasteps make use of some object module that hides the data.

There seems to be no possibility of a coherent module that contains both metasteps. A module containing both metasteps could be defined, but its unifying theme would seem to be "metasteps needed by the bowling metacode," and that isn't enough. Therefore, we remove possibility 1 from consideration.

Because frame, *Player*, and *Pin_counts* information is interrelated—nothing is extraneous—it can be made visible in a coherent top level. Thus there is no need for further effort to find a way to hide some of it as in possibility 2.

Once we know what information is going to be at the top level, we should require that the information be used in an enlightened manner. In particular, if the eleventh frame is different from the others, then the difference should be apparent at the top level. The top level ought not to say, "update and output using *Pin_counts*, *Player*, and frame". It ought to say, "update output table entries, knowing X's Fth frame is *Pin_counts*", and it ought to say, "update output table entries, knowing X's extra rolls are . . .".

Using information in "an enlightened manner" calls for judgments that are not always easy to make. For example, the first and second frames are different from the others because they must be displayed differently. We might decide that there should be separate metasteps for these frames as well. However, we don't because their difference seems to be closely related to output and to have nothing to do with input.

The difference between the eleventh frame and the others is more fundamental than the difference between the first two and the others. For one thing, the eleventh frame is imaginary. For another, its differences with the others involve input as well as output.

Judgments about which differences are more fundamental and should be visible at the top level often seem obvious after they have been made. This does not mean they can be made without both common sense and skill. On the contrary, these judgments are not obvious before they have been correctly made. Unfortunately, the only real guidance that can be given here is that of examples.

Enough decisions have now been made to write top-level metacode for the bowling program whose metasteps will make good operations or drivers. An output module which contains an as yet undefined way to remember past frames is assumed. Figure PLAN_BOWL shows the metacode.

Figure PLAN_BOWL   Top-Level Metacode for Keeping Track of Bowling Scores

```
initialize module(s)
repeat for F ← 1,2, . . . , 10
  repeat for X ← A,B
    obtain Pin_counts for X's Fth frame
    update output entries, knowing X's Fth frame is Pin_counts
    if F = 10
          and Pin_counts shows a strike or a spare
        then
      obtain Pin_counts for X's extra rolls
      update output entries, knowing X's extra rolls are Pin_counts
    fi
  again
again
```

What about the two "obtain . . . " metasteps—do they represent an input module? No data need be shared between them; the only data sharing required is the sharing with the top-level environment. They can be designed as a part of an input module or not, as we please. Largely for reasons given in Section 6.2, the choice made here is to define an input module.

Let's consider this input module first.

The two "obtain . . . " metasteps require different prompts and different error checking. They should be two different actions. Obtaining *Pin_counts* information requires a prompt. When this prompt requests pin counts for X's *F*th frame, the action must import X and F. When it requests pin counts for extra rolls, no import is needed.

It is clear from Figure SCREEN_BOWL that a keyboard input device of some kind is assumed. As in Section 4.4, we can define an external data object to model this keyboard, or we can describe our input module without reference to the origin of the data. The latter is simpler and sufficient for present needs.

Figure INPUT_BOWL shows an input module that arises from these considerations. A *Frame* data type is assumed which includes representations of eleven frames.

Now to consider the output module. There are two kinds of "update . . ." steps in Figure PLAN_BOWL. Each will require a different screen output. A look through the example output in Figure SCREEN_BOWL establishes that there are only two other kinds of screen output: prompting (which is already planned for) and titles (which can be handled in the *initialize* operation).

Figure INPUT_BOWL   Input for Keeping Track of Bowling Scores

Discussion   Obtains keyboard input for one or two counts of pins knocked over by a single roll. Negative counts or counts that are too large are rejected, and new values are requested.

Coupling   Player, Frame, and *Pin_counts*

External Data Object   An output device as described in Figure SCREEN_OUTPUT.

State Space   A *Pin_counts COUNTS*

Probes
pincounts
   export: *Pin_counts*
   description: export *COUNTS*

Operations
get_counts
   imports: *Player, X; Frame, F*
   precondition: $1 \leq F \leq 10$
   description:
      {using the *String* output action of SCREEN_OUTPUT to prompt for
         X's *F*th frame in the 14th line (and to reprompt as necessary)}
      either
         $COUNTS \leftarrow (10, -1)$
      or
         $COUNTS \leftarrow (I,J)$ with $0 \leq I,J < 10$ and $I + J \leq 10$
      end

get_extra
   description:
      {using the *String* output action of SCREEN_OUTPUT to prompt in
         the 14th line (and to reprompt as necessary)}
      $COUNTS \leftarrow (I,J)$ with $0 \leq I,J \leq 10$

Drivers
initialize
   description: no visible effect

No other kind of output is required, but the "update . . . ." steps themselves require some provision for a shortened table when frames 1 and 2 are first shown, and some provision must be made to ensure that open frames are notated with the " + " symbol.

The "update . . ." steps, however, must do more than output—they must remember information about previous frames; they must determine whether a frame is a break, a spare, or a strike; and they must calculate the bonus, frame, and total scores. The output module description should give some aid in understanding how these things will be accomplished.

The level of abstraction we will adopt is that which permits metasteps, such as "display entries for the $(F-1)$st frame using . . .", to be made in a context where enough information has been predetermined to make the work easy. The following information would be enough: pin counts for the frame, the bonus (as much of it as can be known) for the frame, the total accumulated score, the screen line number on which the display is to be put, and whether the frame is still open.

Making this information available is an auxiliary problem that introduces

Figure OUTPUT_BOWL   Calculating and Displaying a Bowling Score Card

Discussion   Converts *Pin_counts* for a given player and frame into output about the three previous frames. The *update* operation must be invoked for frames 1, 2, . . ., 10 in sequence

Coupling   *Frame, Pin_counts*

External Data Object   A screen output object as shown in Figure SCREEN_OUTPUT.

Modules Used   Output table module.

State space   A vector parameter *FIRST_LINE* of two integers which is indexed by *Player.*

Probes

Operations
initialize
   description: *FIRST_LINE*(A) ← 4
                    FIRST_LINE(B) ← 8
                    [ ] ← initialize and clear
                    [ ] ← table header in line 2
                    initialize the output table module
update
   imports: *Player, X; Frame, F; Pin_counts, P*
   preconditions: $1 \leq F \leq 10$
   description:
     LINE ← *FIRST_LINE*(X)
     record *Pin_counts* for *X*'s *F*th frame
     if $F > 2$ **then**
        display entries for $(F - 2)$d frame on line *LINE*
           using recorded information and screen display device
        LINE ← *LINE* + 1
     fi
     if $F > 1$ **then**
        display entries for $(F - 1)$st frame on line *LINE*
           using recorded information and screen display device
        LINE ← *LINE* + 1
     fi
     calculate and display frame *F* in line *LINE*
        using recorded information and screen display device
update_extra
   imports: *Player, X; Pin_counts, P*
   description:
     LINE ← *FIRST_LINE* (X)
     record *P* as extra rolls in dummy 11th frame
     display frames 9 and 10 on lines *LINE* and *LINE* + 1
        using recorded information and screen display module
     display extra rolls in line *LINE* + 2 using *P*

Figure RECORD_BOWL   Store Information about Previous Frames

Discussion   Saves information about *Pin_counts* and reports this information together with the corresponding bonus values and the total accumlated scores (as far as they are known).

Coupling   *Player, Frame, Pin_counts*

State Space   A state consists of two sequences:

$A = a_1, \ldots, a_{11}$ and $B = b_1, \ldots, b_{11}$

whose elements may be *Pin_counts* or **undef** and whose indices represent the 11 *Frames*; two *Integers*, BONUS and TOTAL.

Note that in this module chart when X is a variable of type *Player*, the notations X and x_i will refer, respectively, to the sequence that is obtained when X is replaced with its value and the lth element of that sequence.

Probes

pin_counts
 imports: *Player, X; Frame, F*
 preconditions: $x_F \neq$ **undef**
 exports: *Pin_counts*
 description: export x_F

bonus
 imports: *Player, X; Frame, F*
 preconditions: $1 \leq F \leq 10$
 export: *Integer*
 description:
  export the sum of the first two nonnegative integers associated with this
   sequence
   x_{F+1}, x_{F+2}
   {or as many nonnegative integers as there are}

total
 imports: *Player, X; Frame, F*
 preconditions: $1 \leq F \leq 10$
 export: *Integer*
 description:
  export the sum of the all nonnegative integers in X and of all the
  values that *bonus* would export if invoked for frames
   $1, 2, \ldots, F$

Operations

initialize
 description: fill A and B with **undef**
record
 imports: *Player, X; Frame, F; Pin_counts, P*
 preconditions: $1 \leq F \leq 11$
 description: $x_F \leftarrow P$

greater complication at this level of abstraction than is useful, so we postulate another object module representing a recorded output table. This additional module contains all known pin counts and will provide information about bonuses (insofar as such information is known) and total accumulated scores.

By postulating this module we can push a major nonoutput activity out of the output module to a lower level of abstraction.

Another activity of the output module is the calculation of the screen line numbers for the various players and frames. This activity is accomplished entirely within the output module.

A possible module chart is shown in Figure OUTPUT_BOWL.

The output module requires that a recorded output table module be defined. Little needs to be said about this module because its characteristics are well determined by decisions already made. Figure RECORD_BOWL shows a possible module chart.

The bowling example is now essentially finished. Top-level metacode in Figure PLAN_BOWL has been explained with input and output modules in Figures INPUT_BOWL and OUTPUT_BOWL. Although the metasteps in the output module are fairly detailed, they do not explain the origins of the bonus and total accumulated total scores. This information appears in Figure RECORD_BOWL.

A goal in defining the modules of Figures INPUT_BOWL, OUTPUT_BOWL, and RECORD_BOWL was to make the metacode in Figure PLAN_BOWL precise. This has been achieved. This top-level metacode need not be revised to make it precise. The only reason that a revision might be wanted would be to make the references to the probes and operations of the modules clearer. Figure BOWL shows such a revision. It differs from Figure PLAN_BOWL only in the way the metasteps are phrased.

**Figure BOWL   Top-Level Metacode for Keeping Track of
Bowling Scores**

```
initialize the input and output modules
repeat for F ← 1, 2, . . ., 10
  repeat for X ← A, B
    input_bowl.get Pin_counts for X's Fth frame
    output_bowl.update for X's Fth frame using Pin_counts
    if   (F = 10) and (Pin_counts show a strike or a spare) then
      input_bowl.get_extra Pin_counts for X
      output_bowl.update_extra for X using Pin_counts
    fi
  again
```

Our final version of the bowling scorekeeper is found in Figures BOWL, INPUT_BOWL, OUTPUT_BOWL, RECORD_BOWL, and SCREEN_OUT-PUT. (A revision of the output module in Figure OUTPUT_BOWL that utilizes the names of the probes and operations of the output table module could have been made. Again, the only purpose would be to ensure that the references to the probes and operations of the recorded output table module were crystal-clear.)

This example has shown how top-down design and the use of object modules can be combined. Unlike the examples in Chapter 3, there was no need to rewrite the first fairly complete top-level metacode—the finessing of details was taken care of with the definition of object modules whose probes and operations matched the metatests and metasteps. Another difference with the top-down approach of Section 3.2 is that with the use of object modules even the top level of the implemented code will be close to the early metacode.

Of course, a designer will not always be so lucky as to avoid a major rewrite of the first serious top-level metacode. However, even when such a rewrite is necessary, the object module discipline is useful because it will probably cause the designer to realize that necessity earlier than with a traditional metastep-by-metastep expansion of the metacode.

EXERCISES

5.2.1 Why were player, frame, and *Pin_counts* information made available to the top level rather than being buried within some module or modules?

5.2.2 Frames 1, 2, and 10 require different actions from the others. In the top-level metacode, it is apparent that frame 10 is handled differently from the others but not that frames 1 and 2 are. Why?

5.2.3 In a game of bowling, the players may get extra rolls beyond the ordinary tenth frame. These rolls might be allowed during an extended tenth frame or after both players have rolled their one or two tenth-frame balls. The game description given in this section doesn't say which way it is done. Which will players using a program based on Figure BOWL need to play? Rewrite the design so that the alternative timing of the extra rolls is enforced.

5.2.4 Rewrite Figure OUTPUT_BOWL so that its metasteps clearly show the usage of the RECORD_BOWL module.

5.2.5 Write detailed metacode for the *update* operation of OUTPUT_BOWL which utilizes the probes of RECORD_BOWL and the external action of SCREEN_OUTPUT.

5.2.6 If your system can be used interactively, design, implement, and test the external interface SCREEN_OUTPUT. When that is done, implement and test the bowling program of this section.

5.2.7 A somewhat simpler problem is to calculate and output a complete table of frame scores and accumulate total scores for a single player whose pin counts have been placed in a text file, one set of pin counts per line. Design, implement, and test a solution to this problem. Your solution should dispense with a records module in favor of an input module with a look-ahead feature.

5.3   FALSE-BOTTOM

Bottom-up design has gotten a bad press without having been given a good definition. What is a bottom, and how does one begin one's design there? Well. . .

Whatever a bottom is, it includes input and output. For many programming problems, input and output have distinctive characteristics that are ignored with difficulty. Beginning with the details of how these characteristics will be implemented is an example of bottom-up design. It can be contrasted with a top-down approach which seems to encourage the designer to pretend that the distinctive input and output details don't exist.

The false-bottom approach combines good features of both bottom-up and top-down design. Messy aspects of the specified input and demanding aspects of the required output are identified and hidden with a false bottom made from object modules. By defining these modules, the designer determines the I/O abstractions that will be used in the upper-level metacode.

Although the previous section demonstrated a top-down approach, a false bottom was used without having been described as such. The telltale sentence was: "An exact description of the CRT display would add unnecessary detail to the example, so we assume an external interface for the output of CRT display. . . ." This external interface was a false bottom. It was written before the top-down design process was begun, and it abstracted the details of output to a CRT.

Another aspect of programming which can be considered bottom level is the implementation of data structures. A false-bottom approach applies here as well. The need for a data structure is identified, and a stack, queue, symbol table, or other data structure is described in an object module. Then design work procedes from the top in an environment that has predefined actions on appropriate data structures. This approach and the concomitant implementations are the subject matter of data structures books. Here we limit ourselves to input and output related false bottoms.

Once a false bottom has been defined, the designer again has her choice of design methods. If she chooses a false-bottom approach, she is moving in a bottom-up direction, but without many of the problems of the usual haphazard and ill-defined technique we call bottom-up design.

In this section a text formatter is designed. A *text formatter* is a program which copies textual input to textual output, altering line lengths and dividing into pages along the way. There may be provision for special effects such as handling display text or controlling different fonts. A fancier version of the formatter discussed in this section was used in formatting the manuscript of this book.

Although too simple to be of much practical use, the example of this section is the most complicated of the book, and some readers will wish to skip it upon first reading. Others may wish to enhance it with the suggestions made in the exercises.

This text formatter packs words found in input lines into output lines. It does not justify the right margin, so different output lines will tend to have different lengths. When text such as you are now reading is being formatted, the mechanism of adjusting line lengths ought not be applied to embedded figures and program segments. These things should be kept as they are typed and should, if possible, appear on one page. This formatter has a rudimentary mechanism for identifying such *display-mode* text and keeping it all together on one page.

A careful description of this text formatter is given in Figure SPECIFI-CATION. It is not particularly pleasant reading, but it does explain exactly what the formatter will do.

Figure SPECIFICATION Description of a Text Formatter

This program copies textual input to textual output, altering line lengths and dividing into pages along the way. This specification assumes an input file which consists of printable characters and line boundaries.

Parameters and General Format

Lines beginning with a ">" are called *command lines*. They are used to control the copy process. Nothing on a control line is copied to the output file. The first command line has four integer arguments separated by blanks. The first is the amount of margin to be placed at the left of each output line. The second is the maximum number of characters per output line. The third is the number of lines in the top margin. The fourth is the maximum number of text lines per page on the output file. All numbers have implementation-dependent ranges. If the first line is not a command line or is a command line of the wrong format or if the numbers are out of range, then an error message is output and the formatter stops.

The way in which the output file shows that it is divided into pages is implementation-dependent. It may involve format control characters or the placing of an exact number of lines (including top and bottom margins) on each page.

Control Lines

All subsequent command lines consist of two optional parts: a command (a single lowercase letter in column 2) and a comment (anything beyond column 2). If both parts are present, then the comment must appear to the right of the command. If a command line (other than the first) is found to be incorrect, it is treated as if there were no command present on the command line—see the table below.

The formatter functions in pack mode or display mode. It begins in pack mode. The meaning of the modes is discussed below. The following commands can alter the modes:

Command	Meaning
p	pack mode
d	display mode

and the following commands affect the vertical spacing:

Command	Meaning
e	eject page
{no command present}	finish the line

Figure SPECIFICATION *(continued)*

When the formatter is in a particular mode, a command to enter that mode has no effect. All correct command lines cause the present output line to be "finished," i.e., no more output is placed on that line. A command line with no command does nothing more. Comments are possible on all command lines.

Pack Mode

A *word* is defined to be a sequence of consecutive characters that is bounded by blanks or line boundaries but contains neither. A word is said to *begin a paragraph* when it is the first word on an input line which follows a command line and is indented. A word is said to *begin a follow-up sentence* when it begins with an uppercase letter, a quotation mark, or a "(" and the preceding word ends with ".", "?", "!", ")" or a quotation mark, is separated from this word by at least one blank or one line boundary, and is not separated from this word by a command line.

In pack mode, words which do not begin paragraphs and do not immediately follow command lines are packed into the lines of the output file—regardless of input line boundaries. The right margin of an output line is not justified; i.e., it is left ragged. Words that begin paragraphs are indented over exactly five blanks of an output line. (Other parts of this specification imply that the indentation will be at the beginning of an output line.) An extra blank line is inserted between each two consecutive paragraphs on the same page.

Regardless of the spacing in the input file, only one or two blanks are placed between words that lie on the same line of the output file. The general rule is that there is one blank between consecutive words, but there are two blanks if the second word begins a follow-up sentence.

Display Mode

In display mode, lines are copied into the output file exactly as they appear in input. A line longer than the designated text length is simply truncated, and any excess on the right is lost. Blank lines and empty lines are copied just as any other lines.

Pagination

The eject-page command causes the present page to be finished. However, spacing for the top margin on the next page is not to be begun until after it is known that there is text to go on that page.

Pages are ejected automatically when and only when (1) the formatting process starts; (2) the end of the input file has been reached; (3) a line of output is about to be copied which would be one line too many for the present page; (4) a line of output is about to be copied which is the first text line after display mode is begun, which is not already the first line of an output page, and after which the succeeding display mode text — or as much of it as there is before a page ejection command — will not fit on the present page.

The heart of the specification is the explanation of how word packing is done. The input text is divided into blanks and/or line boundaries, which are pretty much ignored, and nonblank characters called words, which are stuffed into output lines as tightly as possible with one space in between and a ragged right margin. Words that begin sentences are preceded with an extra space. Words that begin paragraphs are indented and follow a blank line. When the formatter is not packing, it is displaying. In display mode it copies the input lines, including empty ones, without change.

This problem is complex enough to warrant two false bottoms. The higher of these will establish a language similar to that used in the problem specification: it deals with concepts of line, word, sentence, and paragraph. The lower will establish primitive actions which are closer to the programming environment. The top-level metacode will make use of both bottoms, but mostly it will use the upper bottom.

The function of the top-level metacode will be to copy text or to initiate the performance of commands. Some of these commands reset the mode from pack to display or from display to pack. The text copying done at the top level will be word by word or line by line according to whether the mode is pack or display. Knowledge of the mode can be limited to the top level.

The lower bottom should be designed with a good knowledge of the requirements placed on input and output by the specification. One effective way to obtain this knowledge is to read the specification twice: once to be sure of the input requirements and once to be sure of the output requirements. It can be helpful to highlight the I/O references in two colors: one for input and one for output.

Sometimes some part of the specification seems to have a close relationship to both input and output. In Figure SPECIFICATION, for example, the section on pagination describes a nasty complication. A page is to be ejected at the beginning of display mode — maybe. The decision to eject or not to eject is explained in point 4, and it depends on the succeeding display mode text as well as the lines already on the present output page. To make such a decision, it is necessary either to read ahead or to delay printing. If reading ahead is chosen, the decision is based on look-ahead information provided by the basic input module and page usage information that belongs in the output module. If delaying printing is chosen, the decision is based on information that can be contained in the output module. A more cohesive design will probably arise from delaying printing.

Consider now the needs of input. From the definition of a command line it is apparent that the first character of each input line must be checked to see whether it is a ">". This means that the input mechanism of the lower bottom should not ignore line position.

There are two ways to describe line position within an input module: Define an external data object which makes line position apparent, or define an abstract state which makes line position apparent. The second method is chosen here, and the first is left as an exercise so that the reader can compare them.

Line position can be made apparent by placing a four-way condition in the state:

first_of_line/farther_down_line/end_of_line/end_of_file

Lacking an external data object, we depend on the implementor's good sense to make the proper connections between the actual input file and changes to the state of the module.

The specification defines input in terms of characters, for example, ">", strings, e.g., "sequence of characters", and unsigned integers. When strings are input, there is always the question of how many characters are enough. For this application we will need to deal with commands, comments, words, and lines, all of which can be input by reading either to the end of the current line or to the next blank (if there is one on the current line). Our lower-level input module should incorporate both kinds of string input.

A *String* data type is required by all the parts of our program. We assume a data-type dictionary that defines it. Since the specification permits lines and words that are longer than an output line to be truncated, we can allow the lower input module to lose characters when it is reading a string that is longer than the *String* data type permits. Of course, the *String* data type must be able to accommodate all output lines.

Figure TEXT_INPUT shows a lower input module that arises from these considerations.

Figure TEXT_INPUT Low-level Input Module

Discussion Abstracts a textual input file so that unsigned integers and strings of nonblank characters, as well as single characters, can be input. Integers which do not end with a blank or an end of line cannot be input— not as integers

Coupling *String* (variable-length string of fixed maximum length)

State Space A state consists of a four way condition:
first_of_line/farther_down_line/end_of_line/end_of_file
a character *NEXT_CHAR*, a *String LAST_STRING,* and an *Integer LAST_INTEGER.*
Note that *NEXT_CHAR* is defined iff first_of_line or farther_down_line is set.

Probes
end_of_line
  export: *Boolean*
  description: export true iff end_of_line is set
has_data
  export: *Boolean*
  description: export true iff end_of_file is not set
first_of_line
  export: *Boolean*
  description: export true iff first_of_line is set

Figure TEXT_INPUT *(continued)*

next_char
    preconditions: first_of_line or farther_down_line has been set
    export: *Character*
    description: export *NEXT_CHAR*
last_integer
    preconditions: *adv_integer* must have been invoked
    export: *Integer*
    description: export *LAST_INTEGER*
last_string
    preconditions: *adv_string* or *adv_nonblank_string* must have been invoked
    export: *String*
    description: export *LAST_STRING*

Operations
initialize
    description: **either**
                        set end_of_file or end_of_line
                or
                        set first_of_line
                        NEXT_CHAR ← ?
                end
adv_string
    precondition: end_of_file is not set
    description: **if** end_of_line is not set **then**
                        LAST_STRING ← string beginning with *NEXT_CHAR*
                        set end_of_line
                else
                        LAST_STRING ← empty string
                fi
    Note that input characters may be lost in satisfying the end-of-line condition.
adv_nonblank_string
    preconditions: end_of_file is not set
    description: **if** first_of_line or farther_ down_line is set
                        and next_char ≠ " "
                    then
                        LAST_STRING ← string beginning with *NEXT_CHAR*
                                        and containing no blanks
                    either
                        set farther_down_line
                        NEXT_CHAR ← " "
                    or
                        set end_of_line
                    end
                else
                        LAST_STRING ← empty string
                fi
    Note that input characters may be lost in satisfying these
conditions.
adv_integer
    preconditions: end_of_file is not set
    description:
        if (first_of_line is set)
            and *NEXT_CHAR* is a digit

Figure TEXT_INPUT *(continued)*

then
    LAST_STRING ← largest integer beginning with NEXT_
                            CHAR that
                                is within implementation-dependent range
    either
        set farther_down_line
        NEXT_CHAR ← nondigit
    or
        set end_of_line
    end
  fi
  Note that input characters may be lost in satisfying these
conditions.
adv_char
  preconditions: end_of_file may not be set
  description:
    either
        {end_of_line was set}
        set end_of_file or end_of_line
    or
        {end_of_line was set}
        set first_of_line
        NEXT_CHAR ← ?
    or
        {first_of_line or farther_down_line was set}
        set farther_down_line
        NEXT_CHAR ← ?
    or
        {first_of_line or farther_down_line was set}
        set end_of_line;
    end
skip_blanks
  precondition: end_of_file is not set
  description: **if** first_of_line or farther_down_line is set
                        and NEXT_CHAR = "
                    then
                either
                    set end_of_line
                or
                    set farther_down_line
                    NEXT_CHAR ← a nonblank character
                end
                    fi

This module chart describes input characteristics that may or may not be
present in the actual input file. For example, each input line, including the last,
must end with an end_of_line marker. The end_of_file condition can only be
reached in *adv_char* and only when *adv_char* begins with the end_of_line condition. An implementation of this module must act as if an end_of_line marker
precedes the end_of_file marker, even if that is not the case in the input text. A
module implementor has the responsibility of ensuring that the module definition
is satisfied, even though the module's imports and inputs are unusual.

We have already seen in Figure PAGE_OUTPUT of Section 4.4 a low-level output module that starts a new page when the current one is full. Point 3 under Pagination specifies such behavior. Some of the behavior specified by other points (the ejection of pages at the beginning, at the end, and whenever an input command so requests) is also supported by the PAGE_OUTPUT module, so it makes a good starting place to think about the lower-level output module.

As mentioned earlier, an output buffer will be incorporated into the design to allow the page decision required by the nasty complication in point 4 to be delayed. One way to accomplish timing for the delay is to mark the beginnings and endings of display text in the buffer. When the buffer is full, an automatic page-printing action can print everything in the buffer down to the beginning, if any, of that display text whose ending is not in the buffer. If this display text does not already begin at the top of the buffer, then the buffer can be reformatted so that it does. There will be more room for data at the bottom of the buffer. If this display text already begins at the top of the buffer, there is no way to avoid dividing the display between two pages, and the entire buffer should be printed.

Actually, only one mark is required to accomplish the plan of the last paragraph. It would mark the beginning of the text, if any, that should be saved when automatic page ejection takes place. Text that should be saved is, of course, display text that begins below the first line and whose ending has not yet been entered into the buffer.

We must decide whether the buffer belongs in the upper or the lower output module. The upper module will deal with words and lines and commands to eject pages. What will the lower module deal with?

The purpose of the output modules can be said to be to add white space to the words and lines of the text—vertical white space to lines and horizontal white space to words. To place both these functions in one module is to create a module that is too complex.

A separation of these functions requires that one module pack words into lines and another pack lines into pages. Because words are available at the top and must be packed into lines before lines can be packed into pages, the upper module should pack words.

This means that the upper module will deal with horizontal space, and so the lower module should deal with vertical space.

The lower-level output module will accept only fixed-length lines. Its job will be to place those lines on output pages., Figure PAGE_BUFFER shows how that job is accomplished. The marking of text to be saved is accomplished through *save* and *unsave* operations: *save* is to be invoked whenever display mode is begun, and *unsave* whenever pack mode is begun.

Figures TEXT_INPUT and PAGE_BUFFER provide a false bottom of twelve operations and six probes for dealing with input and output, all of which were tailored to the problem at hand but not to the language of words, lines, sentences, and paragraphs found in the specification. The upper false

Figure PAGE_BUFFER   Converts Output to Pages

Discussion   Paginates output. Output is delayed in a buffer until a page ejection operation is invoked or an attempt to write beyond a page's capacity is made. Text in lower part of the buffer can be marked "save." The page ejection operation causes the contents of the buffer to be placed on an output page. An automatic page ejection causes the text that is not to be saved to be placed on an output page. The buffer is then flushed of the text that was output, and the save mark is removed from the buffer.

Coupling   *String* (variable-length string of fixed maximum length).

External Data Object   A textual output file. Because output always consists of an entire page, exact output actions are not specified. Instead, this metastep

[ ] ← a sequence of lines

is written to mean that the lines are copied in sequence to the output file with appropriate spacing at the top and the left. The spacing is known from two parameters *TOP_MARGIN* and *LEFT_MARGIN* of this module's state space.

State Space   A state consists of *Integer* parameters: *LEFT_MARGIN*, *TEXT_WIDTH*, *TOP_MARGIN*, and TEXT_LENGTH; a two-way condition: save/no_save; *Integers ROW* and *SAVE_ROW;* and a sequence

$$S = L_1, L_2, \ldots, L_{ROW}$$

of strings of length *TEXT_WIDTH* characters called lines.
Note that $0 \leq ROW \leq TEXT\_LENGTH$.

Probes

Operations
initialize
   imports: *LEFT_MARGIN, TEXT_WIDTH, TOP_MARGIN, TEXT_LENGTH*
   description: **if** imported parameters won't fit on output page or
                         TEXT_LENGTH is too large for this module's
                         implementation
                   then
                      error abort
                fi
                $S \leftarrow$ the empty sequence
                set no_save

eject_page
   description: [ ] ← S
                [ ] ← page-eject command
                set no_save

line
   imports: *String, LINE*
   description: **if** save is set **then**
                      [ ] ← $L_1, L_2, \ldots, L_{SAVE\_ROW}$
                      remove first *SAVE_ROW* elements from S and relabel
                      set no_save
                      [ ] ← page-eject command

Figure PAGE_BUFFER   (*continued*)
> **elsif** *ROW* = *TEXT_LENGTH* **then**
> > *eject_page*
> **fi**
> add *LINE* to *S* on right

filler_line
> description: **if** 0 < *ROW* < *TEXT_LENGTH* **then**
> > add empty line to *S* on the right
> **fi**

save
> description: **if** no_save is set **then**
> > *SAVE_ROW* ← *ROW*
> > set save
> **fi**

unsave
> description: set no_save

bottom should be planned to allow the top-level metacode to deal with these natural concepts.

The top-level metacode must deal with words, lines, and commands. The actual strings which contain the words and lines can be available from the string input module. Manipulating the string input module so as to obtain the correct strings means seeking lines or words while watching out for commands. These commands must be recognized:

$$\text{set\_pack, set\_display, do\_eject, finish\_line, and do\_nothing} \qquad (5.1)$$

The last arises when an erroneous command line is discovered. When a new word is sought, it is necessary to determine whether the new word begins a paragraph or a follow-up sentence. The complications involved with obtaining this kind of information do not belong at the top level, but the information does.

A word input module which hides the details of identifying kinds of words and recognizing when commands are present between words will be useful. Recognition of commands, however, is properly a function of a command input module. Let's look at command input first.

The command input module views input as a sequence of commands. A probe *command_line* reports whether the text input module is positioned at the beginning of a command. A *get_command* operation—working through the text input module—interprets the rest of the present input line as a command. The state of command module contains the last command that was interpreted. When the *get_command* operation has been invoked on an input line that cannot be interpreted as a command, it will set the do-nothing command. Figure COMMAND_INPUT shows the command input module.

The word input module views the input file as a sequence of words, but it will not pass up a command line when searching for the next word.

The word module's state can contain a four way condition:

no_word/ordinary_word/sentence_word/paragraph_word

Figure COMMAND_INPUT   Command Input Module

Discussion   Views input file as a sequence of commands.

Coupling   *Command* (includes representations of set_pack, set_display, finish_page, finish_line, and do_nothing).

Modules Used   Text input module.

State Space   A state consists of a *Command COMMAND* and a two-way condition: command_line/other_line
Note: command_line is set iff *text_input.first_of_line* is true and *text_input.next_char* = ">".

Probes
command
  export: *Command*
  description: export *COMMAND*
command_line
  export: *Boolean*
  description: true iff command_line is set

Operations
initialize
  description: *COMMAND* := do_nothing
get_command
  precondition: *command_line*
  description: *text_input.adv_char*
             if *text_input.next_char* represents a command **then**
                 COMMAND ← that command
             else
                 COMMAND ← do_nothing
             fi
             text_input.adv_string;
             text_input.adv_char;

which explains the status of the last word to have been found. A probe can make this available to the top level. The word itself can remain available through *text_input.last_string*.

For the word module to ascertain the word-status condition, it must remember whether the previous word was a possible end of sentence. This knowledge word can be saved in the word module's state as a *Boolean MAYBE_END_OF_SENTENCE*.

Figure WORD_INPUT defines a module that uses the text input module and the command input modules. It explains probes and operations in terms of its own state and the probes and operations of these modules. For example, the operation *get_word* ends in one of three mutually exclusive situations:

1 The *command_input.command_line* is false and ordinary_word, sentence_word, or paragraph_word is set.
2 The *command_input.command_line* is true and no_word is set.
3 The *text_input.end_of_file* is true and no_word is set.

Figure WORD_INPUT   Word Input Module

Discussion   Views input file as a sequence of words. Words that begin
paragraphs or follow-up sentences can distinguished from words
which do not. This module uses the text input module and requires that
program units external to itself not alter the state of the text input
module when *kind* ≠ no_word.

Coupling   *WordKind* (includes representations of no_word, ordinary_word,
paragraph_word, sentence_word).

Modules Used   Text input module and the command input module.

State Space   A state consists of a *WordKind KIND*.

Probes
kind
    export: *WordKind*
    description: export *KIND*

Operations
initialize
    description: *KIND* ← no_word
get_word
    preconditions: not (*command_input.command_line* or
                            text_input.end_of_file)
    description: **either**
                        arrange for *command_input.command_line* to be false
                        arrange for *text_input.last_string* to contain
                            the next input word
                        KIND ← ordinary_word, sentence_word, or paragraph_word
                    or
                        arrange for *command_input.command_line* to be true
                        KIND ← no_word
                    or
                        arrange for *text_input.end_of_file* to be true
                        KIND ← no_word
                    end

The intention is that (1) should arise when it is possible to input a word
without meeting a control line, (2) should arise when a control line is found in
the search for a word, and (3) should arise when the end of the file is discovered
in the search for a word. The intention is not stated because a precise statement
requires that the input file be described in greater detail than is desirable. As
with many modules in this book, this one assumes that the problem statement
is part of the shared knowledge of the communicator/designer and the
communicatee/implementor.

According to previous decisions, the upper-level output module (or modules)
is concerned with vertical spacing, i.e., the packing of words into lines and
the output—through PAGE_BUFFER—of the packed lines.

There are three ways in which a word can be packed. They depend on the
kind of word: Does it begin a paragraph or a follow-up sentence? If so, the
packing is different from that for ordinary words. Figure LINE_FORMATTER
shows an output module that arises from these few considerations.

Figure LINE_FORMATTER   Output Side of the Higher False Bottom

Discussion   Enables the formatting of output lines. Operations for the output of words exist that allow words to be packed into lines. Different operations are available for the beginnings of follow-up sentences and of paragraphs. It is assumed that the maximum string length is five less than the parameter *TEXT_WIDTH*. Used with PAGE_BUFFER, this module enables output of text that is formatted into lines and pages.

Coupling   *String* (a variable-length character string with a fixed maximum).

Modules Used:Page buffer module.

State Space   A state consists of an *Integer* parameter *TEXT_WIDTH*, an *Integer P*, and a *sequence LINE* of *P Characters*.
   Note that $0 \le P \le TEXT\_WIDTH + 5$.

Probes

Operations
initialize
   imports: *Integer, TEXT_WIDTH*
   description: *LINE* ← empty sequence
word
   imports: *String W*
   description: **if** P + (length of *W*) + 1 > *TEXT_WIDTH* **then**
              page_buffer.line using *LINE*
              LINE ← empty
           elsif $P > 0$ **then**
              add a blank to right of *LINE*
           fi
           add *W* to right of *LINE*
sentence_word
   imports: *String W*
   description: **if** P + (length of *W*) + 2 > *TEXT_WIDTH* **then**
              page_buffer.line using *LINE*
              LINE ← empty
           elsif $P > 0$ **then**
              add two blanks to right of *LINE*
           fi
           add *W* to right of *LINE*
paragraph_word
   imports: *String W*
   description: **if** $P > 0$ **then**
              page_buffer.line using *LINE*
              LINE ← empty
           fi
           page_buffer.filler_line
           add five blanks to right of *LINE*
           add *W* to right of *LINE*
finish_line
   description: **if** $P > 0$ **then**
              page_buffer.line using *LINE*
              LINE ← empty
           fi

After all the work that has gone into designing the two false bottoms, the writing of top-level metacode is almost anticlimactic. Figure TEXT_FOR-MATTER shows the top level; it relies on probes and operations of the five modules in the two bottoms.

Figure TEXT_FORMATTER   Performing the Task of Figure SPECIFICATION

```
assume pack mode
initialize input modules
using the text input module and advancing to the second line
    obtain LEFT_MARGIN, TEXT_WIDTH, TOP_MARGIN, TEXT_LENGTH
if  TEXT_WIDTH + 5 > maximum String length or
        it wasn't possible to obtain four unsigned integers
        then
    error abort
fi
initialize output modules using LEFT_MARGIN, TEXT_WIDTH, TOP_MARGIN,
    and TEXT_LENGTH
repeat while text_input.has_data
  {note both input and output are at line beginnings}
  if command_input.command_line then
  command_input.get_command
  take appropriate action, if any, based on command_input.command
  —action may involve changing assumption of pack mode
  elsif pack mode is assumed then
    word_input.get_word
    if word_input.kind ≠ no_word then
      repeat
        take appropriate action based on word_input.kind
        word_input.get_word
      again until word_input.kind ≠ no_word
      line_formatter.finish_line
    fi
  else {it's a display line}
    text_input.adv_string
    page_buffer.line(text_input.string)
    text_input.adv_char
  fi
again
page_buffer.eject_page
```

The design for a text formatter is now complete. Although a lot of detail has been included, a lot of detail has been abstracted away from the design. To illustrate how much work is left for the implementor, consider Figure WORD_INPUT which contains detailed metacode for the *get_word* operation. This detail normally would not be included with the design because an implementor could work it out alone.

Because the TEXT_INPUT module is the main module to be interfaced by the word input module, it probes and operations are referenced in Figure GET_WORD without prefix.

Figure GET_WORD   Possible Metacode for *word_input.get_word*

```
MAYBE_END_OF_SENTENCE ← KIND ≠ no_word and
    last_string ends with ".", "?", "!", ")", or a quotation mark
INDENT ← first_of_line and next_char = " "
repeat
    skip_blanks
exit when not end_of_line
    adv_char
    INDENT ← next_char = " "
again
if end_of_file or command_input.command_line then
    KIND ← no_word
else
    adv_nonblank_string
    if INDENT then
        KIND ← paragraph_word
    elsif MAYBE_END_OF_SENTENCE and
            last_string begins with an uppercase letter,
            a quotation mark, or a "("
        then
        KIND ← sentence_word
    else
        KIND ← ordinary_word
    fi
fi
```

This design has been revised more than once to eliminate the errors and increase clarity. As mentioned in the beginning of this chapter, that process of revision is as much a part of problem solving as any of the considerations used in developing the false bottoms. In the false-bottom approach, the need to revise almost always occurs when the top-level metacode is written. False bottoms must be tailored to the metacode they serve. Even carefully planned ones will often require a few alterations when the shape of that metacode is finally made explicit.

However, had this design been done top-down, then almost certainly it would have been necessary to make revisions while the three input and two output modules were being defined. Although the flexibility offered by object modules might have allowed any stupidities in the top level to be accommodated, a cleaner design arises when the designer is willing to rewrite.

A statement "I designed this bottom-up," or " I designed this top-down" is thus nothing more than a statement of the order in which the first draft was written. The end result usually arises from an interplay between the top and the bottom that comes about during the subsequent drafts. Viewed in this way, there isn't much difference between the two design techniques. Both result in metacode which depends on object modules, some of whose steps may again depend on metacode, etc.

EXERCISES

Exercises 5.3.3, 5.3.5, and 5.3.7 ask for changes in the design which require careful consideration of where information belongs and how it should be shared between modules.

5.3.1 Implement and test the text formatter of this section.

5.3.2 This design has described input without the use of an external input object. (See Section 4.4 for more information about the use of input files as external data objects.) Define external input object, and rewrite the string input module, using it in place of the five-way condition. Which version do you like better? Why?

5.3.3 Alter the specification so that the output text may be double- or single-spaced and the set of commands may allow for the spacing to be switched from one to the other. Alter the design to match your new specification.

5.3.4 Alter your text formatter implementation to match your design of exercise 5.3.3.

5.3.5 Alter the specification so that an optional automatic output page number can be requested. Alter the design to match your new specification.

5.3.6 Alter your text formatter implementation to match your design of exercise 5.3.5.

5.3.7 This exercise assumes that output page numbering is in effect. There are some places in this design where truncation of input can happen. Alter the specification so that a truncations file is kept while the formatting takes place. This file should contain, for each instance of a truncation, the output page number on which the truncated material appears and the characters that have been truncated. Alter the design to match your new specification.

5.3.8 Alter your text formatter implementation to match your design of exercise 5.3.7.

CHAPTER 6

DESIGN GOALS

The creation of quality software requires more than the writing of a design, implementation of matching code, and execution of a few test cases. Quality software should be appropriate, friendly, simple, flexible, robust, constructible, verifiable, and parsimonious.

"Appropriate" is a brief way of saying that the software should perform a useful function as an integrated part of a larger system that may contain other machines, people, and even bureaucratic procedures. Normally a software project begins with the writing of a set of requirements and a specification of what the software is to do, and the problem of creating appropriate software is considered to be one of getting the requirements and specification right. Sometimes a prototype is written to test the original ideas.

"Friendly" is a brief way of saying that the software should be easy for people to use and not conducive to human error. The design of user-friendly computer systems has been lacking in the past, but is now receiving more attention. It is not easy—a study of what works well, and what does not, combines a knowledge of computer systems with psychology and an ability to draw correct conclusions from the experiences of users.

"Simple" is a goal in its own right. As in the case with all human creations, software works better when it is simple. Unfortunately, simplicity is most important when it is most difficult. It is not easy to break a complex task into a cooperating set of simple tasks and to keep the nature of the cooperation simple as well. For software designs, the concept of object module does help. Simplicity is discussed in Section 6.1.

"Flexible" is a brief way of saying that the software should not be unduly hard to modify. Software that is useful is very often pressed into further service with additional capacity. Often it outlives the machine for which it was designed. The design of flexible software is discussed in Section 6.2.

"Robust is a brief way of saying the executing software should respond gracefully to unexpected input. Software should protect its users, not the other way around. Designing software that will discover and recover from unexpected situations is discussed in Section 6.3.

"Constructible is a quality of a design rather than of the finished software. A constructible design is one that can be built and tested in stages. One way to be sure your design is constructible is to make a separate design for each of those stages. When object modules are used, it is possible to create an earlier stage by creating simple implementations of some of the modules which run too slowly, use too much memory, don't handle error cases correctly, assume simplified input, lack some of the more complicated operations, etc. By specifying that a system of these simplified modules be implemented first, a designer ensures that the implementation team will have early experience with making the modules fit together and that a skeleton system is available to help test more complex versions of individual modules.

"Verifiable" is a brief way of saying not only that the software must be correct but also that there must be some way of knowing it is correct. The method by which this knowledge will be obtained must be planned during or before the design stage. A carefully written problem statement will state verifiable objectives. Without any standard by which to compare the end result, the only verification method is to take a vacation when the system is installed and see whether the users become mad enough to track you down. When there are verifiable objectives, the designer can pursue three verification methods: Make the design clearly understandable and have a peer review it for correctness, plan test data which is likely to find deviations from the objectives, and, finally, create a document that explains why the design is correct.

"Parsimonious" is a brief way of saying the software should not waste resources. Usually this means that neither time nor money should be wasted. Often there is a tradeoff between the two, and the creation of parsimonious software involves an appropriate balancing of resource use for the expected work load. There are two approaches to the creation of parsimonious software, strategic and tactical. The design techniques of this book should help a designer to plan strategic considerations. As mentioned in the introduction to Chapter 4, tactical maneuvers should not be attempted until a working program exists.

The importance of these goals increases as the size of the software project increases. If a program that takes 2 days to design and implement is found to be incorrect and unfriendly, one can redo the work from scratch. The process of doing the design and implementation twice may well produce a better result than could be achieved had a careful attempt been made to achieve all the goals at once.

However, if a project requiring the work of ten people for 2 years is found to be incorrect and unfriendly, then there will be a lot of needless suffering. (Often it seems to be the innocent user who does the suffering.) A discipline called *software engineering* has grown up so that these and other goals can be achieved on all projects and on schedule.

Very expensive lessons had to be learned before the need for software engineering become apparent. One was learned by IBM almost two decades ago. IBM dominated the computer market. Its human resources included talented, experienced people. An ambitious new line of machines was being created. The time seemed ripe for ambitious software projects. OS/360 was begun. It was rightfully expected that this operating system would receive widespread use. It was a surprise that OS/360 became an example of how not to run a software project.

The progress of the project has been described by one of its managers [BRO]: "The effort cannot be called wholly successful, however. Any OS/360 user is quickly aware of how much better it should be. . . . Furthermore, the product was late, it took more memory than planned, the costs were several times the estimate, and it did not perform very well until several releases after the first."

Further, the OS/360 cost $200,000,000 to build, and each new release had an estimated 1000 bugs [BOE]. An expensive lesson indeed! One that made evident the need for software engineering. IBM pulled an acceptable product from that morass, one that has been widely relied on. A lesser company could not have.

Many books about software engineering have been written, and many colleges teach a course on the subject. But there is too much to fit into one book, and several books now cover various subtopics. This book is of that genre, discussing the use of abstraction in the design process, and this chapter touches on achieving the goals of simplicity, flexibility, and robustness in object module designs. It does no more than touch on these topics because this book is about using abstraction to design software, not about what constitutes quality software.

Remark: Although the subject matter of this book properly belongs to the field of software engineering, the principles of that field do not allow an assumption that the problem statement is part of the common understanding of the designer and the implementor. However, such an assumption has been made consistently in the examples of this book.

Software engineering must deal with colossal programs (programs measured in the tens of thousands of lines). Such programs require a formalized definition of what the designer and the implementor share. This definition cannot say, "Both know all about the problem."

Although the techniques of this book are useful for all but the smallest programs, this not a text in software engineering, and there has been no discussion of the special problems of designing colossal programs. The emphasis is on ordinary programs (programs measured in the thousands, hundreds, or sometimes even tens of lines). Implementors of ordinary programs usually have access to problem statements.

6.1 SIMPLICITY

Some high school students, it has been said, are writing computer programs that are more complex than Einstein's theory of relativity. Supposedly, this means that programming computers is complicated and requires genius. Actually, it only means that some high school students have been excited by computers without receiving a good education in how to program them.

When we find ourselves admiring complicated programs rather than simple ones, it is useful to remember two elementary points (1) Any programmer can add complication to any given computer program. (2) Any programmer can complicate any given program beyond her own or anybody else's ability to fathom it.

These points help to put the difference between complexity and simplicity into perspective and to explain why many compute programs are overly complex for the jobs they perform. I have often seen such programs in teaching programming to computer science students. Even yet, I sometimes design them myself. Achieving simplicity is not a simple task!

When a mathematician admires another's elegance, she is not admiring the other's trickiness or even her clothes. She is admiring the other's ability to create simple solutions. When a software designer admires another's elegance, it should be the same way.

Abstraction is used in designing computer programs to simplify the designs—not to make them unreadable by high school students, although that may be a side effect because abstraction does not convey meaning unless the writer and the reader share adequate concepts.

Complexity appears in our designs in the form of complex action abstractions, complex data abstractions, or complex interactions between abstractions. Before considering these appearances in detail, let's consider what "complex" means.

One simple-minded definition says "complex" means that there are ten or more things to consider at one time.

An interesting paper written by a psychologist in the 1950s is entitled "The Magical Number Seven, Plus or Minus Two: Some Limits on Our Capacity for Processing Information." Because of its interest to program designers in the 1980s, it was reproduced in a book of readings about software engineering [MIL].

The paper presents example after example of situations where people's ability to make an accurate judgment is limited by M possible judgments and people's ability to remember with accuracy a sequence of things is limited to sequences of M things. In both cases M is the magical number. The paper cites evidence that this number is 7 plus or minus 2. The magical number also appears in our history in provocative ways: we distinguish seven days to a week, seven deadly sins, and seven notes to a (diatonic) musical scale.

The likelihood that our abiity to do a good job of remembering and making judgments is limited to situations with fewer than ten alternatives suggest that to deal with more complicated situations (such as the twelve notes of the chromatic scale) we ought break the situation down into pieces having at most seven multifaceted parts (like the seven notes of the common diatonic scale which can be sharp, natural, or flat). This conclusion will be referred to as the *magical-number rule*.

Although there is, as yet, no scientific basis for believing that the magical-number rule can be applied beneficially to program design, I have an interpretation of it that has worked well for me. I count data items, metatests, and metasteps in a metacode segment. I do not lump these counts together, but rather consider them separately. When any one reaches seven, I begin to ask myself whether some simpler way could be found. I do not allow any count to exceed nine unless I can find a substantial justification for such an excess.

These counts make up a kind of measurement of the underlying complexity of a design, but they must not be confused with the complexity itself. A judicious application of the magical-number rule can reduce complexity—a blind application only reduces measured complexity. (And it may not even do that if another measurement of complexity is used.)

As mentioned, this application of the magical-number rule limits a program unit to fewer than ten data items, fewer than ten metatests, and fewer than ten metasteps. Contructs for repetition and selection do not count as metasteps—their metatests are counted instead. The rule also limits an object module to fewer than ten data items, fewer than ten probes, and fewer than ten operations. (Drivers count as operations.)

"Data item" refers to any unit of information that is manipulated. A data record counts as one data item if it is manipulated as a unit. Otherwise, each part of the record that is manipulated separately counts as one data item, and the entire record is not counted even if it is also manipulated as a unit. A vector, on the other hand, counts as one data item—regardless of the way it is manipulated (because the elements of a vector are essentially interchangeable). An N-dimensional array counts as one for each dimension that is actually used.

These rules place no limit on the number of modules. However, since a metastep that invokes a module operation is verily a metastep, the number of modules that can be used in any one context is limited.

When metacode becomes too complex, it can be simplified by introducing another level of abstraction. This is done, as shown in Sections 2.2 and 2.3, by replacing metacode with new, more abstract metasteps.

When a module definition becomes too complex, the module should be fissioned into smaller modules. Usually, a way to define these smaller modules can become apparent by looking carefully at the complex module's state and

Figure HIERARCHY   Pattern of Invocations

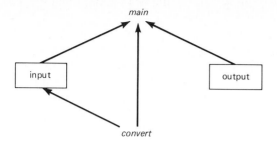

dividing it into relatively independent sets of information. Each of these becomes the nucleus for a smaller module.

The probes and operations of the complex module can be divided among the smaller modules. Often module fissioning forces the addition of new probes and operations. When action in smaller module A requires information about the state of smaller module B, a probe is added to B which will provide that information. If an operation in A must make a change in B's state, then an operation is added to B which can be invoked from A to make the necessary change.

Although there are no examples of module fissioning per se in this book, there are lots of examples of the creation of modules. The points made in Section 4.3 are particularly helpful in deciding how the smaller modules should be defined.

Complex interactions between abstractions can be seen in the pattern of invocations of module probes and operations. This pattern is visible in a drawing that shows the module names, with arrows drawn from modules whose probes and operations are invoked to the other modules which must invoke one or more of those probes and operations. Since some program units are *freestanding*, i.e., are not part of modules, these are shown in the drawing as well.

For example, if a program unit *main* invokes an input module and an output module and the input module invokes another program unit *convert*, then the pattern of invocations would be that shown in Figure HIERARCHY. Note that module names are placed in boxes while freestanding program units are not. The probes, operations, and drivers of the input and output modules are program units which are a part of some module, and so they do not appear on the chart.

It is also possible to have boxes with one side missing. These open boxes represent external data objects whose actions are listed in the module charts. Arrows will never point toward an open box because an external data object never invokes an action of the new design.[1]

---

[1] Such an invocation might make sense if the design dealt with interrupts, but that topic is beyond the scope of this book.

Roughly speaking, the messier this drawing, the messier the design. When your designs start to produce messy charts, you should be thinking about ways to simplify them.

A *hierarchy chart* is a drawing of this type that has been augmented with information about the particular probes, operations, and drivers which are invoked and information about data couplings. It is called a hierarchy chart because the drawing almost always can be organized so that invoking entities appear above those that are invoked. (Some reasons why this should be so

Figure BOWL_HIERARCHY   A Hierarchy Chart for the Bowling Scorekeeper of Section 5.2

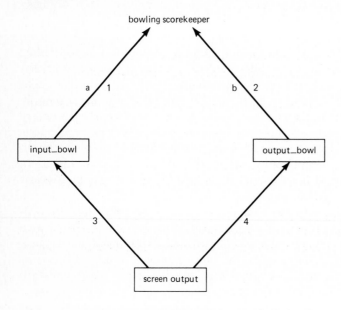

		Invocations			Couplings
Reference	Probe	Operation	Driver	Reference	Data type
a	*Pin_counts*	*get_counts* *get extra*	*initialize*	1	*PinCounts* *Player* *Frame*
b	*initialize*	*update* *update_extra*		2	*PinCounts* *Player* *Frame*
				3	*String*
				4	*String* *PinCounts* *Player* *Statue*

are given in Section 6.2.) Figure BOWL_HIERARCHY is an example of a hierarchy chart.

The invocations of particular probes, operations, and drivers are shown in an *invocations* table below the drawing. Each arrow that represents a module invocation appears with a letter. This letter references a place in the invocations table. The table reference lists all the module's probes, operations, or drivers which are invoked by the program unit at the top of the arrow.

Data couplings are shown in a *couplings* table below the drawing. If an arrow rises from an object module, then the data coupling consists of all data types that are imported, exported, or updated by those probes, operations, or drives listed in the invocations table. If an arrow rises from a program unit, then the data coupling consists of all data types that are imported, exported, or updated by the program unit. The couplings table shows exactly what this coupling is for each arrow. Each arrow appears with a positive integer that references a place in the couplings table.

As was the case in the couplings section of a module chart, the data types *Real, Integer, Character,* and *Boolean* are ignored in the couplings table of a hierarchy chart. Although this does prevent some information from being visible, this problem can be avoided by naming all data types—even those which are to be implemented as one of the four basic data types.

Data-type modules do not appear in a hierarchy chart, but the types they support may appear in the couplings table.

Sometimes a module or a freestanding program unit *A captures* another module or freestanding program unit *B*; that is, *B* is invoked in *A* and nowhere else. When this happens, *A* and not *B* will appear in the hierarchy chart and an auxiliary hierarchy chart will be drawn to show how *B* is invoked by *A*. The concept of capture is a design concept. It is different from the concept of support unit (see Section 4.1) which is an implementation concept. Support units do not appear in hierarchy charts.

The RECORD_BOWL module of Section 5.2 is used by the OUTPUT_BOWL module to save information about past bowling frames. No other module or freestanding program unit invokes actions of the output table module, so this module is not found in Figure BOWL_HIERARCHY. Instead, it appears in an auxiliary hierarchy chart given in Figure EXPAND_OUTPUT.

When an auxiliary hierarchy chart is drawn for a module and its captures, the probes, operations, and drivers of that module appear across the top of the drawing as if they were freestanding program units. Otherwise, an auxiliary hierarchy chart is made just like a main hierarchy chart.

A hierarchy chart and its auxiliaries give a picture of the interactions between modules and freestanding program units. They are useful for two reasons. First, the complexity of the drawing(s) and the size of the tables give us a view of the underlying complexity of the interactions between abstractions of the design. Second, a hierarchy chart provides a map into the design, a map which helps the designer, the implementor, and those who come later to find their way in the design.

Figure EXPAND_OUTPUT   An Auxiliary Hierarchy Chart for the OUTPUT_BOWL Module

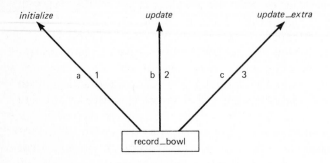

	Invocations			Couplings	
Reference	Probe	Operation	Reference	Data type	
a		*initialize*	1		
	Pin_counts	*record*	2	*Player*	
b	*bonus*			*PinCounts*	
	total			*Frame*	
	pin_counts	*record*	3	*Player*	
c	*bonus*			*Pin_counts*	
	total			*Frame*	

When it is necessary to fission a module, the hierarchy chart may be of further help because it shows the patterns of usage for the module's probes, operations, and drivers. For example, if two probes of the module to be fissioned are used in different parts of the hierarchy, then perhaps they belong in separate, smaller modules.

This section has discussed the value of simple designs and has shown how a map of a design, called a hierarchy chart, can be drawn. Simple designs are identified as those having simple hierarchy charts and which satisfy the magical-number rule. These measurements of simplicity/complexity in designs are somewhat unusual. More common measurements are the Halstead effort metric [HAL] and the McCabe metric [MCC]. Those metrics have not been shown here because they were originally defined for programs that did not use subroutines and so can penalize the object module style of design.

Whatever measurement of complexity is used, an overly complex design should never be justified by pointing to measurements which say it isn't complex. This kind of justification is a confusion of the measurement with the complexity that it attempts to measure. Rules that this or that measurement be kept within bounds are like rules of grammar: Strict enforcement or wanton abandonment will hurt the final product. Indeed, creating clean, simple designs is a lot like creating clean, simple prose: There are no shortcuts to learning how it's done. The learning method that works is to try and try again.

Remark: Another way to draw a hierarchy chart is to let the arrows represent the *uses* relationship [PARN]. A program unit or module *A* is said to use another program unit or module *B* in case the correct execution of *A* requires the correct execution of *B*. The uses relationship is more useful in designing systems programs than the invokes relationship described in this section. To exemplify the difference, note that an operating system may invoke a compiler without using one. An applications program may use a scheduler without invoking it.

EXERCISES

6.1.1 What is the magical number? What is its significance?

6.1.2 What is the magical-number rule? How is it applied?

6.1.3 The diagram in a hierarchy chart consists of nodes connected by arrows. What are the three kinds of nodes? Can one of these kinds of nodes be used to represent object-type modules?

6.1.4 Write a hierarchy chart for the design represented in Figures TEXT_FORMAT-TER, TEXT_INPUT, PAGE_OUTPUT, WORD_INPUT, COMMAND_IN-PUT, and LINE_FORMATTER of Section 5.3. (Some readers will have skipped over Section 5.3 on first reading, but they can do this exercise just as well as if they had read the section. The work may even make a subsequent reading of that section a little easier.)

6.1.5 Write a hierarchy chart for your design of exercise 4.5.12. Check your design against the criteria of this section. Alter it to meet those criteria. If necessary, redraw the hierarchy chart. Do not implement.

6.1.6 Write a hierarchy chart for your design of exercise 5.1.6. Check your design against the criteria of this section. Change it to meet those criteria. If necessary, redraw the hierarchy chart. Do not implement.

6.2 FLEXIBILITY

There seem to be two kinds of software: worthless software and software that undergoes some changes during its useful life.

Yet designing software for change is not a part of our computer science education. To paraphrase D. L. Parnas [PARN], there are two major reasons for this: the computer science professor and the mathematics professor.

I have been both, and I am a confessed sinner. The examples of this very book follow the computer science professor's style of talking about *the* problem and how to write *a* program that solves *it*. When a mathematics professor, I taught that theorem A is generally better than theorems B and C if it gives the same results as B and C and applies to a wider range of situations.

With teachers like me, it is no wonder that designers have seldom thought about probable future changes to their programs and, when they have, they have inserted all kinds of bells and whistles in the hope that the program would be able to play all anticipated future tunes.

A generally applicable program is, according to Parnas, analogous to a TV set that can be used in North America or in Europe. Such a TV would be too complicated. Present technology avoids the complication by having components that can be changed for the two different electric currents and broadcast characteristics.

With this book, I am doing things that may aid future program designers in creating designs flexible enough to withstand the demands for improving, porting, and integrating valuable software. First, I am emphasizing the object module concept, a concept which aids in producing flexible software. Second, I am writing this section about achieving flexibility in software designs.

Consider a situation analogous to the TV set example: A generally applicable income tax preparation program would deal with the taxes of any state. Such a program is too complicated. Object module technology avoids[2] the complication by having a component that can be changed for different state income tax systems. This component is an object module with operations that act on pertinent information and probes that report the results of those actions. The set of probes and operations used for this module would be standardized, but their functions would not. A probe that is very important for one state tax system might always export zero for another. To move the program from one state to another would only require that the state tax module be replaced.

The use of object modules for input and output often increases flexibility. Figures INPUT_INTEGER, INPUT_F, and INPUT_P of Section 4.4 demonstrate this point. A program which has been based on an INPUT_INTEGER kind of module need not be altered when the underlying kind of input is changed from FORTRAN style, as in INPUT_F, to Pascal style, as in INPUT_P. Only the module that performs the input must be changed.

This section contains ten pointers for designing flexible object modules.

The first pointer is to *plan ahead*. Try to identify those design decisions which are volatile. Then isolate each in an object module or type module. Ideally, the isolation will be so complete that only one module will need to be altered if the design decision is changed. Examples of design decisions which are likely to be changed are as follows:

1 The coding language or hardware configuration
2 The source of input
3 The place where output is to be put
4 The format of the input or output
5 The amount of error checking of the input
6 A choice of data structure (easy to implement, memory saving, machine-time saving)
7 Internal versus external storage
8 Batch versus interactive processing
9 Action to be taken when error condition is discovered

---

[2] To my knowlege such a tax preparation program has not been written, but there seems no reason why it could not be.

This pointer was used in Section 5.2 where it was necessary to choose between using an object module for input and using freestanding program units. The latter was possible because no information needed to be shared between the necessary program units, but a decision for the former was made because the use of an input module allows changes of the types listed in decisions 2, 4, and 8 to be made more easily.

The second pointer is to *create a design with several versions.* Plan a motor scooter version that does less than the user requires but enough to prevent her from being too unhappy if your schedule slips and the motor scooter is all you can provide on time. Plan a basic two-door version which is the least you can talk your user into. Plan a four-door luxury version that does everything your user has mentioned which isn't outrageous.[3] Plan a couple of custom-built versions that will extend the present project in directions which are likely to be necessary. These directions may contradict each other. Now integrate your plans so that fancier versions can be built by adding capacity to the next simpler version. This may require a redefinition of the various versions. That's OK, but be sure to explain to your user what you are doing and why.

Your fanciest versions will differ from your simplest in that they will have more modules, probes, operations, and drivers or more sophisticated implementations of some existing modules. When you build the four-door version, you will be reusing a lot of code from the two-door version. For this reason and because of the experience you have gained in making the two-door version, the time it takes you to get it right will be less than if you tried to build it directly.

Next year when you add capacity to the system, the planning for the custom-built versions should be very useful, although it is unlikely that the added capacity will be exactly what you had anticipated.

The third pointer is to *accept dummy probes and drivers.* Often you can identify probes or drivers which are not necessary for the present version but which are required for other versions. If those other versions are likely to be used, then include the dummies now. The *initialize* driver of Figure INPUT_BOWL in Section 5.2, which is a no-op, is an example of a dummy. It is of no use unless the input requirements of the program are changed. Its presence allows major input changes without affecting the top-level code.

The *full* probe of the STACK example in Section 4.2 is an example of a potential dummy because it is possible to implement a stack so that a test for fullness is impossible. With such an implementation *full* must always return false. If the stack contains a *full* probe and the *push* operation contains a precondition that *full* must be true, then a switch from one implementation to the other can be made without changing any program unit that uses the stack module.

---

[3] The explanation of this pointer confuses the writing of a design with the writing of a requirements specification. To avoid this confusion, think of the four-door version as the requirements specification. The other versions are then created with both requirements and design considerations in mind.

One driver that is occasionally useful and, therefore, should perhaps be included in all object modules is an *epilogue* driver which must be invoked after any other operation is invoked. This driver would be a dummy for most of the examples of this book, but its presence would facilitate problem changes that force modules to clean up after themselves. The change in Section 5.1 from an algorithm that works with a vector to one that works with a data file exemplifies the usefulness of an *epilogue* driver.

The fourth pointer is this: *do not be afraid of specialized probes*. A probe which answers a weird question about a module's state does not hurt the flexibility of an object module, as long as it does not force the state to be specialized. The *is_pure* probe of the TANK module in Section 4.1 is quite specialized: it exports true iff some brand comprises 90 percent of the tank. The decision that 90 percent is important is an example of a volatile design decision. It is also easily changed. Only the probes dealing with the 90 percent brand need to be changed. In general, a specialized probe can easily be replaced with another.

The fifth pointer is to *build defaults into the* initialize *operation and override them with extra single-purpose operations*. Suppose, for example, a module handles screen output and is set for a default screen size. This default should be set during initialization. Many programs use the default. Those which require a different screen size can invoke a specialized operation whose only purpose is to alter the screen size. Thus only programs which override the default need to pay for the effort to do so. The specialized override operation simply isn't used by others. If almost all programs are overriding the default, then maybe it is an inappropriate default. Perhaps there should be no default, and the initialize operation should always import the relevant values as parameters.

The sixth pointer is that *recursion should be avoided in the invocation of module probes or operations*. Or, there should be no loops in the drawing of the hierarchy chart which involve object modules. It should not be possible to trace your finger in the direction of the arrows and end up where you began—unless the tracing completely avoids object modules in favor of freestanding program units. This pointer is the reason that the hierarchy chart is aptly named. Without loops, it is always possible to arrange the object modules so that any module that invokes another appears above it.

Recursion is an important programming tool for some kinds of problems. It is disallowed for object modules in order to achieve greater independence between modules. If module A invokes module B but B does not invoke A, then it is conceivable that the purpose of A could be drastically changed without requiring a change to B. Furthermore, there is a chance that B may be reused in another software system that does not need A.

Recursion is disallowed for object modules, but it is not disallowed for object module design. Freestanding program units can be recursive, so can support units. Object modules can be invoked by recursive program units. The only restriction is that there should be no loop in the hierarchy chart involving object modules.

The seventh pointer is to *think of your design as a series of layers*. Each layer contains modules that make the problem easier to solve; i.e., each is a virtual machine that adds to the original language or machine some operations and probes which are helpful in solving the original problem. Lower layers correspond to lower levels in the hierarchy chart. (The rule that there be no loops among the object modules in the hierarchy chart ensures that there will be a hierarchy of layers.)

A module in an upper layer may be useful only for the present version of the problem. But the lower a module is in the hierarchy, the more useful to other, related problems it ought to be.

The layer approach can be contrasted with the series-of-transformations approach. When the design is created as a series of transformations from input to output, then it loses flexibility. The reason is that often it is impossible to remove a transformation from the middle of the series because the format of its import is different from that of its export.

The eighth pointer is to *be wary of interconnections that skip from a higher layer to a lower layer*. Look at your hierarchy chart. Is there a probe, operation, or driver at the bottom that is invoked at the top? How many layers does it jump over? Why is such a large jump necessary? If you can get rid of the jump, then the bottom and top are more independent of each other, and it will be more likely that one can be replaced without affecting the other. The same point applies to probes and drivers.

This pointer also applies to specialized data types. If a *Widget* is used all the way up and down the hierarchy chart, then it seems that the level of abstraction isn't increasing with the level in the chart. Why not? Perhaps the top and the bottom are too interdependent.

This pointer, of course, does not apply to designs whose charts have only a few levels.

The ninth pointer is that *if you are in doubt about whether one or two modules are required, then design two*. The more specialized your modules are, the easier they are to replace. If this proliferation of modules makes too much complication at the top level, then create an additional amalgamating module that combines the functions of two or more specialized modules. If the specialized modules are captured by the amalgamating module, then the main hierarchy chart need not indicate their existence.

The tenth pointer is to *resolve questions of whether module A should invoke module B or vice versa* with these criteria:

1 Is module A or module B be more likely to be useful without the other? That module ought go on the bottom.

2 Is module A or module B made much simpler if it can invoke the other? That module ought go on the top.

If criteria 1 and 2 produce contradictory results, then some module A is simpler if it invokes another module B and it is likely to be useful without the function which B performs. In this case, have module A invoke module B. A simple version of B can always be created to integrate with A in that application which does not require the function which B performs. Criterion 1 is the less important. It is also less important than the eighth pointer, which limits interconnections between higher and lower layers.

To say criterion 1 is less important is not to say it is unimportant. Often a different division of functions into modules will allow all flexibility goals to be satisfied. Do not ignore criterion 1 without considering other possible divisions of function into modules.

The value of flexible designs isn't quantifiable because the degree of flexibility gained by following these ten pointers isn't known. However, the amount of flexing of existing designs that is done is considerable. A recent estimate states that 50 percent [PARI] of the software dollar goes to the correction and alteration of existing programs. This gives some idea of how much time is spent maintaining old programs. It doesn't reveal how much time is lost because tools weren't created that would make it unnecessary to develop new programs entirely from the beginning. Even if we cannot quantify the benefit gained from following these ten pointers, we can see that the potential for a large benefit is there.

EXERCISES

6.2.1 An explanation is given in this section for the decision in Section 5.2 to create the input module in Figure INPUT_BOWL rather than use freestanding program units for input. Expand this explanation.

6.2.2 List the ten pointers of this section in order of decreasing interest to you. Explain why the top and bottom of your list are the most and least interesting, respectively.

6.2.3 Eight of the ten pointers involve object modules. Which of these involve
  a Probes
  b Operations
  c Invocation of one module by another
  d State space

6.2.4 Does your design of exercise 6.1.5 satisfy the ten pointers for achieving a flexible design? If not, rewrite it so that it does. Include an updated hierarchy chart in your revision, and make sure that the simplicity criteria of Section 6.1 are still met. Do not implement.

6.2.5 Does your design of exercise 6.1.6 satisfy the ten pointers for achieving a flexible design? If not, rewrite it so that it does. Include an updated hierarchy chart in your revision, and make sure that the simplicity criteria of Section 6.1 are still met. Do not implement.

6.3 ROBUSTNESS

Compare these two stories:

In the first story, Irate User stormed into Hapless Programmer's office. A pile of output hit the desk with a loud crack, and there was silence but for the rustling of papers as Irate User sought the damaging evidence. When it was found, she said, "Look at this!" There were asterisks where numbers belonged. "That should be no problem," said Hapless Programmer. "Some number is out of range." "If it is no problem for you, then why wasn't it done right in the first place?" asked Irate User. "Its a big problem for me. These reports were due yesterday!"

Hapless Programmer soon found the offending variable. Finding why it had gotten out of range, however, was another matter entirely. It was necessary to search through the nooks and crannies of a year-old program. It seemed like the problem lay with one or another input value that had suddenly become a little larger. "All inputs are essentially the same as before," said Irate user when Hapless Programmer asked her on the next day. Still . . . the third day, Hapless Programmer went into Irate User's department and talked with the people responsible for collecting the data. Sure enough, an input value was now larger than Hapless Programmer had understood it would ever be. The correction was made on that same day.

In the second story, Disturbed User rushed into Prudent Programmer's office with a stack of output, saying, "I needed this report yesterday, and now look what has happened!" The words "Input Range Warning" appeared on the top page of output, but Disturbed User was uninterested. There was silence while she sought her problem within the large stack of output. When it was found, she said, "Look at this!" There were asterisks where numbers belonged. "How long have you been getting that input range warning?" asked Prudent Programmer. "About 3 months," said Disturbed User. "Nothing seemed to be wrong, so we forgot it." "Well, something is wrong now," said Prudent Programmer, "and even if the large input value is unrelated to the asterisks, the warning should be fixed. What is a reasonable maximum for that input value?" "Don't know," said Disturbed User, "we never thought it would get as high as it has." They discussed the input value and decided on a better way to check its range.

Prudent Programmer spent the rest of the morning tracking and fixing the link between the large output value and the large input value. She set up new input checks to help monitor the use of the program and gave the results to Disturbed User that very afternoon.

Hapless Programmer lost 3 days from her current schedule because of the unexpectedly large input item. Prudent Programmer lost less than 1 day. Irate User was never completely convinced that Hapless Programmer had not been at fault. Disturbed User knew the input warning should have been reported to the programmer long before. The moral is clear: Design your programs so that input items are checked for reasonableness and appropriate warnings are printed whenever an unreasonable input item is discovered.

Don't be a spineless designer. Insist on doing it right, and design only robust software. Robust software is software that performs gracefully in the face of the unexpected, and it will save you and your company time in the long run.

The determination of how to make a computer system perform gracefully in the face of unexpected failures in input, software, and hardware is an extremely complicated subject. But the practices of doing sanity checks on all input and of checking all preconditions of modules are not so complicated, and they comprise a large first step in achieving the goal of robust software.

For each input value, the designer should determine an acceptable range. Each input action should check its input for compliance with the range restrictions.

When it is assumed that input values satisfy certain relationships among themselves, then those relationships should be checked as well. For example, if it is assumed that a sequence of integers is in nondecreasing order, the input module should check whether they really are in nondecreasing order.

Three types of things may be done when input is found to flunk these tests: Attempt a correction, log an error message, or abort.

Input data correction can be done interactively as in the example of the bowling scorekeeper of Section 5.2. That scorekeeper was designed to reject unreasonable data and to prompt the user for new input.

Automatic replacement of bad input with estimated values can be attempted when there is some redundancy in the input data. In such cases, unreasonable data can be ignored or can be replaced with estimates derived from the other input data. A program which must continually check some temperature reading is an example. A temperature reading that is too far from its predecessor is probably a mistake and should be ignored until corroborating evidence comes in.

When input is corrected as in the last paragraph, there may be no need for an error log. In almost all other situations, an error log should be kept. Where should this log be kept or printed? Should there be different logs for different kinds of errors? Who gets to see the error reports? These are decisions that may change from time to time, so the use of an object module to receive and dispose of error messages is advocated. This module can be altered as decisions about error logs are remade.

Planning robust software is not just a matter of planning for unacceptable input. Preconditions on each probe, operation, driver, and significant freestanding program unit should be written, and plans should be made for corrective action when the preconditions are violated. These sanity checks at the module and freestanding program unit level are important for two reasons. First, many programs are complicated, and the relationship among the parts is not always as clear-cut as the designer assumes. Many existing programs misperform when an unexpected concatenation of circumstances arises. Some of these make mistakes that are never detected! Second, object modules are meant to be reused. Conditions in the new program may not be the same as in the old, and preconditions can be violated inadvertently. Modules that check their own preconditions are easier to reuse because they protest when misused.

The action taken when a sanity check fails should sometimes be to abort and print an error message. Since a graceful abortion is rather a contradiction in terms, designers of robust software often ignore this option. But when a sanity check is done to verify a condition that is believed to be impossible, such an abortion can be more graceful then continuing as if nothing had gone wrong.

Robust software is not achieved through object modules that permit unacceptable changes to their states or export eccentric values. These things must be avoided even when unanticipated circumstances arise. Thus an operation should not alter the state of its module until its precondition has been checked. Operations whose preconditions have been violated may alter their states only if a plan for an acceptable alteration has been incorporated into the design. Likewise, probes whose state has been violated should export default or estimated values. The value **undef** can be used as a default that signals something is wrong.

Many of the module charts in this book contain a note at the bottom of the State Space section. This note gives conditions that should always be satisfied by the state after any operation has executed. The *integrity* of the module depends on the continued satisfaction of these conditions regardless of the way the module is used or misused. A designer of robust software will spend some time defining module integrity in sufficient detail to ensure that all important properties of the state are noted and preserved. The axiomatic approach given in Section 7.2 shows a good way to accomplish this detail.

This section has suggested that all inputs and imports should be checked for reasonableness. Unreasonable data should be corrected or should cause some kind of error report to be generated, or both. A module's integrity should also be preserved, even when preconditions of operations are violated. It is more acceptable to abort execution than to violate module integrity. But if aborted execution would cause a disaster or the violation might arise directly from input that is out of range, the robust design must provide for the module's integrity in another way.

Of course, a module chart must document how these things are accomplished. Documentation helps other designers who use the module to know how it will perform, but it does not ensure that they will understand and remember well enough to use the module. To achieve this, the error-handling actions must be *consistent:* they must be applied on a modulewide basis. If each possible precondition violation is handled in a different way, the resulting module is like a city like a completely different set of traffic rules posted for each intersection. You can drive in such a traffic system, but you will either make mistakes or move very slowly. A module's Discussion section should explain just one kind of error-handling action for probes and, possibly, a second for operations. These actions should apply to all probes and operations in the module.

The principles of a simple design must not be sacrificed in the name of robust software!

EXERCISES

6.3.1 What two kinds of sanity checks does this section advocate?

6.3.2 When a sanity check reveals a problem, what kinds of actions are possible? What circumstances justify each action?

6.3.3 What is module integrity, and how is it protected?

6.3.4 Rewrite your design of exercise 6.2.4 to add the standards of robustness given in this section. Make sure the simplicity criteria of Section 6.1 and the flexibility criteria of Section 6.2 are still met. Implement and test your design. Your testing not only should demonstrate proper behavior for good data, but also proper error handling for all possible error situations.

6.3.5 Rewrite your design of exercise 6.2.5 to add the standards of robustness given in this section. Make sure the simplicity criteria of Section 6.1 and the flexibility criteria of Section 6.2 are still met. Implement and test it. The testing, of course, should create all the possible error situations as well as test for proper behavior when the data is good.

REFERENCES

[BOE]: Boehm, B. "Software and Its Impact: A Quantitative Assessment," reprinted in Freeman and A. I. Wasserman (eds), *Tutorial on Software Design Techniques,* 3d ed., IEEE Computer Society, Los Angeles, 1980, pp. 5–17.

[BRO]: Brooks, Jr., F. P. "The Mythical Man-Month," reprinted in Freeman and Wasserman (eds), *Tutorial on Software Design Techniques,* 3d ed., IEEE Computer Society, Los Angeles, 1980, pp. 17–24.

[HAL]: Halstead, M. H. *Elements of Software Science,* Elsevier North-Holland, Amsterdam, 1977.

[MCC]: McCabe, T. J. "A Complexity Measure," *IEEE Transactions on Software Engineering,* March 1976, pp. 308–316.

[MIL]: Miller, G. A. "The Magical Number Seven, Plus or Minus Two: Some Limits on Our Capacity for Processing Information," reprinted in E. N. Yourdan (ed.), *Writings of the Revolution—Selected Readings on Software Engineering,* Yourdan Press, New York, 1983, pp. 443–460.

[PARI]: Parikh, G., and Zvegintzov, N. *Tutorial on Software Maintenance,* IEEE Computer Society, Los Angeles, 1983, p. 1.

[PARN]: Parnas, D. L. "Designing Software for Ease of Extension and Contraction," reprinted in Freeman and Wasserman (eds.), *Tutorial on Software Design Techniques,* IEEE Computer Society, Los Angeles, 1983, pp. 226–236.

CHAPTER 7

MATHEMATICS MAKES BETTER ABSTRACTIONS

There are two reasons for looking at designs from an even more abstract point of view than in previous chapters. Both have to do with the ability of abstraction to separate the wheat from the chaff.

Wheat, of course, is where we get our daily bread, and chaff is the stuff we find between us and the harvested wheat.

For a software designer, the daily bread comes from designs, and the chaff is the inclusion in designs of unnecessary detail and mistakes. Abstraction helps to winnow out details. That is reason one for desiring an even higher level of abstraction; some of our previous action and data abstractions have involved more detail than is necessary. It is easier to check abstract descriptions for errors than it is to check detailed descriptions, because the checking can take place in an environment that is more relevant. That is the second reason for desiring an even higher level of abstraction; we need all the help we can get in preventing errors.

To achieve a higher level of abstraction, we turn, of course, to mathematics. Section 7.1 describes some mathematical concepts that are useful in stating precisely what an action does. These concepts can often aid the designer in finding a suitable level of abstraction for expressing an action.

Section 7.2 applies the language of Section 7.1 to data abstractions. Axioms are written which state precisely what can be expected from the probes and operations of an object or type module. Axioms such as these are often easier to write than are the kinds of descriptions used in Chapters 4 and 5. This is not to say that it is easier to write mathematical axioms that are precise than it is to write English. Rather, it is easier to write abstract axioms than it is to write abstract English.

Armed with the concepts of Sections 7.1 and 7.2, a designer will have less trouble in communicating many of her designs.

Remark: The axiomatic approach described here is essentially that of theoretical mathematics. A good set of axioms for a data abstraction describes something which can be built (i.e., is consistent), contains a minimum of redundancy (i.e., is independent), and provides enough detail to exclude the building of things which the axiom creator doesn't intend (i.e., is complete).[1] The terms in parentheses have technical mathematical meanings; they represent concepts which mathematical logicians take seriously. Writing axioms of mathematical systems that satisfy these properties is not easy. Often it isn't possible. Even when it is possible, not just anybody can do it. Mathematicians don't learn to write good sets of axioms until graduate school, if then. Why should we think that the axiomatic approach is a good technique for the average program designer?

The reason lies in the different ways these professionals will use axioms. This difference is apparent in the ways the two kinds of professionals would write axioms for a fraction data type. A program designer would be mainly concerned with describing the conditions in which the various operations are defined and would assume underlying arithmetic properties. A mathematician would be mainly concerned with the more abstract properties of rational numbers—properties that explain the essence of a system of rational numbers.

Not all aspects of a design should be axiomatized. This can lead to unnecessary complication of simple things. All mathematics must be axiomatizable.

The need for independent axioms in program design is not very great. A little redundancy won't hurt, and it may even ensure that the implementor gets the point.

The program designer is not creating axioms to explain a theory. She is writing down properties of a program she intends to build. Her axioms are closer to concrete concepts than the mathematician's.

For these reasons many more people ought be able to write axioms about program designs than are able to write axioms about traditional mathematical systems.

This is not to say that there are no difficult axiomatic problems associated with computer science. There are, in fact, many such problems. One example is the description of the underlying properties of those rational numbers which can be represented in a computer as real numbers. Such problems, however, are not normally a part of program design.

---

[1] These are unusual characterizations of a consistent, independent, and complete set of axioms, but they can be interpreted in a way that is equivalent to the usual definitions.

7.1 DESCRIBING ACTION ABSTRACTIONS

One reason we often do not use mathematics in describing programming actions and action abstractions is the difficulty inherent in describing this standard programming concept:

$$X \leftarrow X + 1$$

The difficulty arises because one of the basic properties of a mathematical expression is that repetitions of the same symbol are representations of the same value. The assignment operation does violence to this property. It is made for a world in which variables change values within the same context.

A piece of metacode can be understood by the changes it describes for a set of variables. A particular set of values for the variables is a state, and the set of all possible values is a state space. The effect of "executing" a piece of metacode is to change the state.

Restated in terms of a state, the assignment statement given above becomes "X's part of that state which exists just after the assignment is 1 larger than X's part of that state which exists just before the assignment."

In this section the only states of interest are the one just before a metastep begins, which is denoted by "^{B}", and the one just after a metastep ends, which is denoted by "^{A}". With this convention the assignment statement can be written

$$X^A = X^B + 1$$

And a more abstract assignment of a vector V of integers could be written

$$V^A = V^B \text{ sorted into nondecreasing order}$$

(After reading this section, you should be able to restate this sorting metastep in mathematical notation.)

Another reason mathematics is seldom used is that it must be learned first. This section contains a brief presentation of the relevant aspects of mathematics. It assumes a knowledge of functions, relations, and sets as is taught at the beginning of many mathematically oriented texts and a knowledge of the use of truth tables as is shown in the tutorial on boolean expressions at the end of Section 1.1. The notation is used in many areas of mathematics; it is taught formally in mathematical logic.

Some of the basic expressions used in mathematical logic are the same as the boolean expressions of programming languages but with a more compact notation. We shall write "~" for "not," "|" for "or," and "&" for "and." So if we wanted to say that a metastep causes X to remain the same or to become the negative of what it was, we would write

$$X^A = X^B \mid X^A = -X^B$$

Notice that this assertion does not state that X becomes the absolute value of itself. Variable X could stay the same for both positive and negative values, and still the assertion would be satisfied. To assert that X becomes the absolute value of itself, we need a clause about X^A being nonnegative as, for example, in

$$(X^A = X^B \mid X^A = -X^B) \ \& \ X^A \geq 0 \tag{7.1}$$

The concept in mathematical logic which is analogous to **if** . . . **then** . . . is called *implication*. Implication is denoted by "$\Rightarrow$". An example is

$$X^B < 0 \Rightarrow X^A = -X^B \tag{7.2}$$

which, of course, means that X becomes the negative of itself—if it starts out negative. We would read the expression this way: "X-before less than 0 implies that X-after equals minus X-before." Any analogy that might exist between mathematics and poetry sure doesn't extend to reading aloud! A more complex expression is even more difficult to read aloud because we must say things like "begin paren" and "end paren" to indicate where the parentheses are.

Consider this detailed metacode:

```
if X < 0 then
    X ← −X
fi
```
$$\tag{7.3}$$

which seems to have a meaning similar to expression (7.2). The metacode explains how X is given a new value. It uses programming concepts. Expression (7.2), however, simply asserts a relationship between the before and after values of X. It uses a concept which is not as familiar to us as programming concepts are and which has yet to be defined. Let's rectify that oversight by defining $P \Rightarrow Q$ in terms of concepts known from *Boolean* expressions:

$$P \Rightarrow Q \quad \text{iff} \quad {\sim}P \mid Q$$

The expression P is called the *antecedent,* and the expression Q is the *consequent.* The definition says that we can find out the truth of the assertion on the left by evaluating the expression on the right; they are logically equivalent. The meaning of the definition lies in the pattern of truth values for P and Q which it accepts, i.e., which combinations it say are true.

Figure IMPLICATION   Truth Table for $\Rightarrow$

P	Q	$P \Rightarrow Q$	${\sim}P \mid Q$
true	true	true	true
true	false	false	false
false	true	true	true
false	false	true	true

Figure IMPLICATION shows a truth table for implication. The columns for $P \Rightarrow Q$ and $\sim P \mid Q$ are the same. Since the combination of P being true and Q being false is the only row that shows a false in these columns, an assertion that $P \Rightarrow Q$ holds is an assertion that the combination of the antecedent being true and the consequent being false is impossible. Clearly, such an assertion cannot be made about just any antecedent and consequent.

It is time to remember that both the antecdent and the consequent themselves represent logical expressions. Think of them as *Boolean* expressions using variables $X_1, \ldots, X_N$. Then the assertion $P \Rightarrow Q$ is an assertion that there are no possible values of $X_1, \ldots, X_N$ which will cause both P to be true and Q to be false.

Consider, for example, this implication:

$$X > 1 \Rightarrow X + 1 > 1$$

where X is any real number. The antecedent is $X > 1$, and the consequent is $X + 1 > 1$. To say that this implication is true is to say that for no X is $X > 1$ *and* $X + 1 \leq 1$.

The truth table definition of implication tells us what we can conclude when an implication is known to be true. In that case, the second row of the table is impossible for any values of $X_1, \ldots, X_N$.

Now if P is true, for example, if $X > 1$, then our attention is limited to the top two rows. Given also that the implication is true, the second row is prohibited, and so we can see that Q, for example, $X + 1 > 1$, must be true. If, however, P is false ($X \leq 1$), then our attention is limited to the bottom two rows. Because neither of these is prohibited by the truth of the overall implication, we can conclude nothing about Q ($X + 1 > 1$).

Thus when we analyze the truth table definition of implication, we see that it is consistent with our intuitive understanding.

Now consider this assertion:

$$(X < 0 \,\&\, X > 0) \Rightarrow (X \times X = -1)$$

Since the antecedent for this implication is always false, the second row of the truth table is prohibited. This means the implication must be true—we know this before we look at the consequent. For any real number X the consequent for this particular implication is also false, but that is irrelevant. The implication itself is still correct. This property of logical implication may seem strange at first, but it is OK because we will never be foolish enough to conclude that a consequent is true because an antecedent is false. (It is tempting sometimes to make the equally foolish conclusion that the consequent is false because the antecedent is false, but we have seen that the truth table definition of implication prohibits this foolishness.)

Now let's think about whether assertion (7.2) describes the effect of metacode (7.3). If $X^B < 0$, then (7.3) will cause X^A to be $-X^B$ and (7.2) states that X^A

$= -X^B$ must be true. If $X^B \geq 0$, then (7.3) will cause X^A to be X^B, but (7.2) states nothing about the truth of $X^A = -X^B$. Since the antecedent is false, the consequent may be either true or false. This means that (7.3) does satisfy (7.2) but (7.2) is too permissive to do a good job of describing the effect of (7.3). For example, the following metacode also satisfies (7.2):

$$X \leftarrow -X$$

To describe the metacode in (7.3) we should also state what the result is when $X^B \geq 0$. This isn't difficult:

$$(X^B < 0 \Rightarrow X^A = -X^B) \; \& \; (X^B \geq 0 \Rightarrow X^A = X^B)$$

This expression, of course, describes the obtaining of an absolute value, which is the same thing that (7.1) describes. Because (7.1) places more emphasis on the properties of X^A and less on the relationship between X^A and X^B, it is preferable to this version.

The symbols $\sim$, $\&$, $|$, and $\Rightarrow$ are called *logical connectives*. Another logical connective is useful. It corresponds to "iff" and is written $\Leftrightarrow$. A definition is

$$P \Leftrightarrow Q \text{ iff } (P \Rightarrow Q) \; \& \; (Q \Rightarrow P)$$

Figure LOGICAL_PRECEDENCE gives the precedence hierarchy of the logical connectives. This is used in the same way as the precedence hierarchy of the operators in a programming language is used to allow unambiguous expressions that are not overly parenthesized.

Figure LOGICAL_PRECEDENCE **Logical Connectives Listed in Order of Precedence**

$\sim$
$\&$
$|$
$\Rightarrow$
$\Leftrightarrow$

Even with five logical connectives, we have no way to say that a vector V of N integers is sorted into nondecreasing order because there is no way to say that $V(I) \leq V(I + 1)$ for every I with $1 \leq I < N$. Such a reference to all values of a particular set requires what is called the *universal quantifier*. The universal quantifier is written "$\forall$," and when we see it, we read "for every." Using *Integer* to denote the set of all integers, we can write

$$\forall I \in Integer \; (1 \leq I < N \Rightarrow V(I) \leq V(I + 1)) \qquad (7.4)$$

to mean "for every I that is an element of *Integer*, $1 \leq I < N$ implies that $V(I) \leq V(I + 1)$." A somewhat more natural way of saying the same thing is:

For every *Integer I* with $1 \leq I < N$, it is the case that $V(I) \leq V(I + 1)$

but this naturalness is not available in our mathematical notation. Even though (7.4) is not stated in the most natural way, it makes a statement about precisely the correct indices *I*.

We shall use *Integer, Real, Boolean,* and *Char* to represent the sets of integers, reals, booleans, and (printable) characters, respectively. In a context where a data type *Item* is known, we use *Item* to represent the set of all items—indeed, many authorities would insist that this is exactly what a data type is.

Before the universal quantifier can be used with any precision, a definition must be known. As with other features of mathematical logic, the universal quantifier is defined by stating a way to know whether an assertion that contains it is true. For a data type X and assertion P that contains no quantifiers, the assertion

$$\forall I \in X(P)$$

is defined to be true iff each time all the I's which appear in P are substituted with the same element of X, the resulting quantifier-free assertion evaluates to true. The variable I in P is said to be *bound* by $\forall I$.

For example, the assertion

$$\forall L \in Boolean(\ L \mid \sim L \ ) \tag{7.5}$$

is true because both of the following substitutions are true:

$$\text{true} \mid \sim\text{true}$$

and

$$\text{false} \mid \sim\text{false}$$

When P is any assertion and X any set,

$$\forall I \in X(P)$$

is defined to be true iff each time all those I's that are not bound by quantifiers inside P are substituted with the same element of X, the resulting expression evaluates to true. (This evaluation will, of course, require the consideration of other substitutions for the variables bound by quantifiers within P.) Occurrences of I in P that are not bound by a quantifier that is itself in P are said to be bound by $\forall I$.

Variables of an assertion which are not bound by quantifiers in the assertion are said to be *free* in the assertion. Variables superscripted with B or A will always be free in the entire expression because it makes no sense to quantify them.

There are two abbreviated ways to write quantified expressions. First, it is possible to quantify multiple variables at once. For example,

$\forall I,J \in X(P)$

means

$\forall I \in X(\forall J \in X(P))$

and

$\forall I,J,K \in X(P)$

means

$\forall I \in X(\forall J \in X(\forall K \in X(P)))$

etc. Second, "$\in$ *Integer*" can be omitted. For example,

$\forall I(P)$

means

$\forall I \in Integer(P)$

As an example of the use of $\forall$, let's write an assertion that a metastep will export the largest integer I whose square is less than or equal to an imported X. This assertion must say that I is an integer, that I's square is less than or equal to X, and that I is largest with respect to this property. "Largest with respect to this property" means that no larger integer exists whose square is less than or equal to X. This assertion does the trick:

$$I^A \in Integer \ \& \ I^A \times I^A \leq X^B \ \& \ \forall J(J \times J \leq X^B \Rightarrow J \leq I^A) \tag{7.6}$$

Here the final part of the assertion has been turned around. Rather than directly stating that there is no larger integer whose square is less than or equal to X, it states that any integer whose square is less than or equal to X is not larger.

Another quantifier, the *existential* quantifier, makes it unnecessary to turn concepts around in this fashion. The existential quantifier is written "$\exists$," and when we see it, we read "there exists." An assertion

$\exists I \in X(P)$

is true iff there is an element of X which can be substituted for all free I's in P to make P true.

The universal quantifier would require that substitution of all free I's in P with each element of X produce a true assertion. This definition differs in that only one X need make the assertion true. In both cases substitution is limited to the variables that become free when the quantifier is removed. The concepts of bound and free variables apply to the existential quantifier in the same way as to the universal quantifier. The same abbreviations apply to both quantifiers.

Besides these similarities there is a more direct relationship between the universal quantifier and the existential quantifier. To say that there is an element of X which can be substituted for all the I's in P to make P true is the same thing as saying that it is false that every element of X will, when substituted for all the I's in P, make P false. More succinctly,

$$\exists I \in X(P) \Leftrightarrow {\sim}\forall I \in X({\sim}P)$$

It is this relationship which allows us to avoid turning things around when writing assertions. Assertion (7.6), for example, can be phrased in a more straightforward manner:

$$I^A \in \textit{Integer} \ \& \ I^A \times I^A \le X^B \ \& \ {\sim}\exists J(\ I^A < J \ \& \ J \times J \le X^B)$$

By saying "there is no J which is larger than I and whose square is less than or equal to X," this assertion seems closer to the original concept than does (7.6). Of course, the two assertions are logically equivalent.

Even with five logical connectives and two quantifiers, it is quite difficult to assert something like the following: "vector V^A is a rearrangement of V^B." A way to match up the elements of V^A and V^B is required for this assertion. The relevant mathematical concept is, of course, a one-to-one, onto function, or *bijection*. Notation to handle the more general concept of function is useful for many kinds of assertions. Two more notational conventions are required. First, we write *Function* to mean the class of all functions. Second, for a function f, we write

$$f : X \to Y$$

to mean that f has domain X and codomain Y. If f is one-to-one, that fact is denoted with an $\to$ to the left of the $\to$; and if f is onto, that fact is denoted with an $\to$ to the right of the $\to$. Thus

$$f : X \to\!\!\to Y$$

means that f is an onto function from X to Y and

$$f : X \to\!\to\!\to Y$$

means that f is a bijection from X to Y.

A metastep which rearranges a vector V of N elements can be described with this assertion:

$$\exists f \in Function(\ f:\{1, \ldots, N\} \to \to \to \{1, \ldots, N\}\ \&$$
$$\forall I(1 \leq I \leq N \Rightarrow V^A(I) = V^B(f(I))))$$

Earlier it was said that each occurrence of a variable in the same expression represents the same value as each other occurrence of that same variable. Strictly speaking, that isn't true. Rather, each occurrence of a variable in the same *context* represents the same value. The context of a free variable is established by the text surrounding the assertion. It consists of one or more complete assertions. The context of a bound variable is established by the rules of binding explained above. All variables bound by the same quantifier lie within the same context. A bound variable context is often only part of an expression. It never extends beyond one complete assertion.

A variable can be bound twice in the same assertion. For example,

$$\forall I(\ 0 < I < 10 \Rightarrow I \times I < 100)\ \&\ \exists I(\ I > 100\ \&\ I - 2 < 100) \tag{7.7}$$

contains two bindings of I. The expression is equivalent to

$$\forall I(\ 0 < I < 10 \Rightarrow I \times I < 100)\ \&\ \exists J(\ J > 100\ \&\ J - 2 < 100)$$

The variable I has been changed to J in one of its contexts. Bound variables can be switched in this manner without changing the meaning of an assertion. Free variables cannot.

Another way a variable can be bound twice is to nest the bindings. For example,

$$\forall I(\ I > 10\ |\ \exists I(\ I < I\ )\ |\ I < 100) \tag{7.8}$$

contains two contexts of I, and one lies inside the other. To substitute I with 11 in the outermost context, for example, would give

$$11 > 10\ |\ \exists I(\ I < I\ )\ |\ 11 < 100$$

(This is the kind of substitution that must be considered when the truth of the statement is evaluated.) Variable-to-variable substitutions for I in each context give an equivalent expression:

$$\forall K(\ K > 10\ |\ \exists J(\ J < J\ )\ |\ K < 100\ )$$

The rules of binding by quantifiers define a pattern of which occurrences of a variable are the same and which are different. The pattern is very similar to that generated by the declaration rules in Pascal, Algol, or PL/I. The binding of variables is analogous to the declaration of variables in subprograms.[2]

Three final examples can help to clarify the material of this section.

Assertion (7.7) is a proper logical assertion, but is it true? Assertion (7.7) is true iff all substitutions of I in the first context and some substitution of I in the second context make it true. Consider the first context. For any fixed integer I, the expression

$$0 < I < 10 \Rightarrow I \times I < 100$$

is true because the rules of algebra force all integers that satisfy the antecedent to also satisfy the consequent. Thus the first quantified expression is true. If the integer 101 is substituted for I in the second context, the expression becomes true; thus the second quantified expression is true. Since (7.7) is the combination of two true expressions with &, expression (7.7) is true.

Assertion (7.8) is also a proper logical assertion, but is it true? Assertion (7.8) is true iff any substitution of I in the outer context leaves one of $I > 10$, $I < 100$, or $\exists I(I < I)$ true. Since any integer is either greater than 10 or less than 100, substitution by any integer leaves one of these three expressions true—even though an evaluation of $\exists I(I < I)$ gives false.

Finally, let's describe a metastep which exports true (through a variable P) iff a variable M is a prime.

A positive integer is prime iff it is not the product of two numbers other than itself and 1; or, a number M is prime iff

$$\sim \exists I,J(\, 1 < I < M \,\&\, 1 < J < M \,\&\, I \times J = M) \tag{7.9}$$

Actually, the expression $1 < J < M$ is redundant since any I and J that satisfied the other two would also satisfy $1 < J < M$.

The desired assertion forces P to be true iff the simplified version of (7.9) evaluates to true. This assertion is

$$P^A \Leftrightarrow \sim \exists I,J(\, 1 < I < M^B \,\&\, I \times J = M^B)$$

This section has developed a language for making assertions about metasteps. Readers who have not dealt with similar languages will find it a little heavy, and it is. But notice that it is usually much easier to use this language to describe a metastep than it is to write detailed metacode of the corresponding metastep. That is one thing we want from any design language.

Another desirable aspect of a design language is the avoidance of descriptions of how something is done. The design should only describe the results. That too is a feature of the language of assertions. When the language is applicable, it is ideal. And it is applicable often enough to be worth learning.

---

[2] Many computer scientists use "binding" in a slightly different sense that means "establishing a value for."

EXERCISES

7.1.1 Demonstrate the truth or falsity of each of the following assertions:

    a $X \times X \times X < 0 \Rightarrow X < 0$

    b $X < 0$ and $X > 0 \Rightarrow X = 0$

    c $X \times Y = M \mid U \times V = Y \Rightarrow X \times U \times V = M$

7.1.2 Use a truth table to see whether $P \Rightarrow Q$ is equivalent to

    a $Q \Rightarrow P$

    b $\sim Q \Rightarrow \sim P$

7.1.3 Write a truth table definition of $P \Leftrightarrow Q$.

7.1.4 Determine the truth or falsity of the following assertions:

    a $\forall X \in Real(\ \exists Y \in Real(\ X^2 = Y\ )\ )$

    b $\exists Y \in Real(\ \forall X \in Real(\ X^2 = Y\ )\ )$

    c $\exists I(\ I > 10 \mid \exists I(\ I > I\ ) \mid I < 100\ )$

    d $\exists I(\ I > 10 \mid \exists I(\ I < 10\ ) \mid I \times I < 10\ )$

    e $\exists I(\ I > 10 \mid \exists I(\ I < 10\ ) \mid I < 10\ )$

    f $\exists f \in Function(\ f\mathord{:}\{1, \ldots, N\} \mapsto \to \to \{2, \ldots, N+2\}\ )$

    g $N \in Integer\ \&\ N > 1 \Rightarrow \exists f \in Function($
        $f\mathord{:}\{1, \ldots, N\} \to \to Boolean\ \&\ \forall I(\ 1 \leq I \leq N \Rightarrow (f(I) \Leftrightarrow \exists J(\ 2 \times J = I)))$

7.1.5 Letting $A(X,Y)$ stand for "you can fool X at time Y," *People* be the set of all people, and *Time* be the set of all times, translate the following into the language of mathematical assertions. (Assume that time is measured in days and "some of the time" means at least 1 day.)

    a You can fool some of the people all the time.

    b You can fool all the people some of the time.

    c You can't fool all the people all the time.

7.1.6 Write an assertion that describes the action of this metacode:

```
if X > 0 then
    IX ← 1
elsif X < 0 then
    IX ← −1
fi
```

7.1.7 Write an assertion that describes the action of this metacode:

```
if X < 2 × Y and Y > 10 then
    X ← X × X
elsif Y > 10 then
    Y ← 10
else
    X ← −X
fi
```

7.1.8 Write an assertion that describes the action of this metacode:

```
I ← 1
repeat while X(I) ≠ K and I < X_SIZE
    I ← I + 1
again
FOUND ← X(I) = K
```

7.1.9 Write an assertion to describe a metastep that sorts a vector of real numbers into nondecreasing order.

7.2   DESCRIBING DATA ABSTRACTIONS

Section 4.1 presented data abstractions as sets of cooperating actions. Section 7.1 presented a language of abstractions for describing actions. In this section the two concepts are combined to obtain a truely abstract description of data.

The first data abstraction in this book is the tank module found in Figure TANK of Section 4.1. A translation of TANK to mathematical symbols involves defining the state space in completely mathematical terms and writing a list of mathematical assertions that the probes and operations must satisfy.

The original definition of TANK's state was as follows: "A *Real* parameter, *SIZE*, and a set of brands together with the amount of gas attributable to each. The available brands are those in the *Brands* data type and an extra unknown brand which is different from any in *Brands*."

The set of brands, call it *SB* is easily described mathematically:

$$SB = Brand \cup \{unknown\}$$

where unknown symbolizes an entity which is not an element of *Brand*. The phrase "together with" corresponds to the mathematical concept of function. Let

$$amt : SB \rightarrow Real$$

and interpret $amt(B)$ to be the amount of gas attributable to brand B.

A direct translation of Figure TANK to mathematical notation is now easy. The probe *pure_brand,* for example, exports a brand B (if there is any) which satisfies

$$amt(B) \geq 0.9 \times SIZE$$

The variables in the expression (and those used in any expression that describes a probe) do not require the before/after notation of the previous section. Probes do not reassign values to variables.

Operations do redefine variables and functions in the state. Variables and functions belonging to the state, therefore, should be superscripted with B or A when they appear in the description of an operation. However, since state parameters are given a value once by *initialize* and not by any other operation, there is no need to use the superscript notation with them.

The *refill* operation can, then, be described with amt^B, amt^A, $SIZE$, and SB. Letting the imports be *Brand B* and *Real R*, a description of *refill* is

$$(Z \neq B \Rightarrow amt^A(Z) = amt^B(Z) \times (SIZE - R)/SIZE)$$
$$\& (Z = B \Rightarrow amt^A(Z) = R + amt^B(Z) \times (SIZE - R)/SIZE)$$

Figure TANK_PRE_AX shows the finished translation of Figure TANK into the notation of the previous section.

Figure TANK_PRE_AX   Module of Figure TANK, Rewritten with Mathematics

Defines   *TANK*

Coupling   *Brand*

State Space   An *Integer* parameter *SIZE*, a set
$$SB = Brand \cup \{unknown\}$$
and a function
$$amt : SB \rightarrow Real$$
where these properties hold:
$$\sim unknown \in Brand \qquad \Sigma_{B \in SB} amt(B) = SIZE \qquad \text{and} \qquad \forall B \in SB(\, amt(B) \geq 0 \,)$$

Probes

pure
 exports: *Boolean, B*
 description:
$$B \Leftrightarrow \exists Z \in Brand(amt(Z) \geq 0.9 \times SIZE \,)$$

pure_brand
 precondition: *pure*
 exports: *Brand, B*
 description: $amt \, (B) \geq 0.9 \times SIZE$

Operations

initialize
 imports: *SIZE*
 precondition: *SIZE* > 0
 description:
$$amt^A(unknown) = SIZE$$
$$\forall X \in Brand(amt^A(X) = 0)$$

refill
 imports: *Real, R; Brand, B*
 precondition: $0 < R \leq SIZE$
 description:
$$\forall R \in Real(\, \forall Z \in SB(￼$$
$$(Z \neq B \Rightarrow amt^A(Z) = amt^B(Z) \times (SIZE\text{-}R)/SIZE)$$
$$\& \, (Z = B \Rightarrow amt^A(Z) = R + amt^B(Z) \times (SIZE\text{-}R)/SIZE)))$$

The mathematical assertions in Figure TANK_PRE_AX are essentially axioms. Any implementation that satisfies them is an implemented TANK. The state is obviously an abstraction of the information which an implementation must keep for its probes and operations. It does not overspecify the module in that the mathematical entities in the state are clearly unsuitable for implementation. Few programmers, for example, will be tempted to implement *amt* as a function.

However, the full power of mathematical notation has not been applied in Figure TANK_PRE_AX. A lot of information is missing from the mathematics. Preconditions are missing, and many symbols are bound by the text in which the mathematics appears rather than by the mathematics itself. For these reasons, it is impossible to know much about what is going on by only reading the mathematics.

Further, the form of the mathematics of Figure TANK_PRE_AX does not allow for direct assertions about interactions between probes and operations.

Modules do have interactions between their various actions. If these interactions cannot be described directly with the axioms, then the entire burden of their description falls upon references to the state space. In many cases, this burden will cause an overspecification because the state will contain greater detail than is desirable.

In a fully mathematical specification of an object module, an operation is a mathematical function which maps the module's state onto a new state. If the operation has an import, it is a multivariate function.

For example, the *refill* operation of the tank module would be exhibited this way:

$$refill : Tank\_State\_Space \times Real \times Brand \rightarrow Tank\_State\_Space$$

The use of $\times$ indicates that the domain of this function consists of triplets whose first element is a *Tank_State_Space*, whose second is a *Real*, and whose third is a *Brand*. Thus the *refill* function is to be applied to three variables of three data types (*Tank_State_Space*, *Real*, and *Brand*) and it will produce another *Tank_State_Space*. As the name implies, *Tank_State_Space* is just the state space of the tank module. Operations, not probes, are represented by functions with the state space in their codomains.

The *refill* operation, however, does not always produce a valid *TANK_STATE_SPACE* because its effect is undefined if its precondition is not satisfied. The symbol **undef** is used to indicate an undefined state. The undefined state is not an element of the state space. Using this symbol, we see that the codomain of *refill* and become $TANK\_STATE\_SPACE \cup \{\textbf{undef}\}$.

The *initialize* operation can be exhibited this way:

$$initialize : Real \rightarrow Tank\_State\_Space \cup \{\textbf{undef}\}$$

which shows that the *initialize* function represents an operation because *TANK_STATE_SPACE* is in the codomain. The *initialize* operation is the only operation which does not have the state space as a factor of its domain.

The effect of the *refill* operation is to alter the *amt* function. This alteration is described in Figure TANK_PRE_AX with references to amt^B and amt^A. However, the A and B superscripts are inappropriate if we are to be able to write axioms invoking multiple probes and operations. A satisfactory alternative is to describe *refill* with references to $amt(T,Z)$, which represents the amount of brand Z when the tank is in state T, and $amt(refill(T,B,R),Z)$, which represents the amount of brand Z after R units of brand B have been used to refill a tank that was in state T.

By using this method, every part of the state space which can change will be represented as a function whose domain contains *Tank_State_Space* as a factor.

In the tank module, the set *SB* remains unchanged and the number *SIZE* remains unchanged but for initialization. Because *SIZE* can change, we ought to represent it as a function:

SIZE : Tank_State_Space → Real

An expression saying that *SIZE* is set during initialization would be

SIZE(initialize(R)) = R

where *R*, clearly, is *initialize*'s import. An expression saying that *SIZE* is not changed by *refill* would be

SIZE(refill(T,B,R)) = SIZE(T)

To use axioms to describe where parameters, such as *SIZE*, are changed would be unnecessarily tedious. This tedium is not necessary if we assume a priori knowledge on the part of the reader of the module chart: Parameters are imported by the *initialize* operation and remain unchanged during every other operation. A parameter, such as *SIZE*, can then appear as a free variable in all the axioms rather than as a function.

The principle is that all entities of the state space are fixed; they remain unchanged during the module's existence. Parameters are given their values at the instant *initialize* is invoked. If *initialize* is invoked a second time, the original module dies and another takes its place. State changes are shown not by letting the state space symbols change their values but by viewing them as functions of the state.

To return to the development of an abstract module chart for the tank module, the probes are easily exhibited thus:

pure : Tank_State_Space → Boolean

and

pure_brand : Tank_State_Space → Brand ∪ {**undef**}

Because probes do not have the state space in their codomains, they cannot change the state. Probes do have the state space in their domains. This is required because all probes must access the state. For these two probes, the domain is the state space because there are no imports. Probe *pure* does not have **undef** added to its codomain because it is defined for all states.

Figure TANK_AX describes the tank module with this notation. The exhausting name *Tank_State_Space* has been shortened to *Tank*. The axioms have been listed together in their own section away from the probes and operations.

The axioms in Figure TANK_AX are mostly rephrasings of those in Figure PRE_TANK_AX. One difference is the way preconditions have been included in TANK_AX. The axioms state that a precondition violation makes the functional value of a probe or an operation equal to **undef** and that a satisfied precondition makes the functional value equal to a defined member of the codomain.

Figure TANK_AX   Module of Figure TANK Rewritten in Axiomatic Style

Defines Type   *Tank*

Coupling   *Brand*

State Space   A *Real* parameter *SIZE*, a set
$\qquad$ *SB* = *Brand* ∪ {unknown}
and a function
$\qquad$ *amt* : *Tank* × *SB* → *Real*
where ~unknown∈*Brand*

Probes
pure : *Tank* → *Boolean*
pure_brand : *Tank* → *Brand* ∪ {**undef**}

Operations
initialize : *Real* → *Tank* ∪ {**undef**}

refill : *Tank* × *Brand* × *Real* → *Tank* ∪ {**undef**}

Axioms
$SIZE{>}0 \Rightarrow$ *initialize(SIZE)*∈*Tank* &
$\qquad\qquad$ *amt(initialize(SIZE),unknown)* = *SIZE* &
$\qquad\qquad$ ∀*B*∈*Brand*(*amt(initialize(SIZE),B)* = 0)
$SIZE{\le}0 \Rightarrow$ *initialize(SIZE)* = **undef**
∀*T*∈*Tank*(∀*R*∈*Real*(∀*B*∈*Brand*(0<*R*≤*SIZE* ⇔ *refill(T,B,R)*∈*Tank*)))
∀*T*∈*Tank*(∀*R*∈*Real*(∀*B*∈*Brand*(∀*Z*∈*SB*(
$\quad$ (*Z* = *B* ⇒ *amt(refill(T,B,R),Z)* = *R* + *amt(T,Z)* × (*SIZE-R*)/*SIZE*) &
$\quad$ (*Z*≠*B* ⇒ *amt(refill(T,B,R),Z)* = *amt(T,Z)* × (*SIZE-R*)/*SIZE*)))))
∀*T*∈*Tank*(*pure(T)* ⇔ *pure_brand(T)*∈*Brand*)
∀*T*∈*Tank*(*pure(T)* ⇔ *amt(T,pure_brand(T))*≥0.9 × *SIZE*)
∀*T*∈*Tank*(*pure(T)* ⇔ ∃*B*∈*Brand*(*B*≥0.9 × *SIZE*))

The use of *Tank* variables causes TANK_AX to appear more like a type module than an object module, because a tank-type module would show type *Tank* in its data coupling. In fact, if "State Space" were replaced with "Supported Data Types," then TANK_AX would essentially fit the form given in Section 4.5 for an object-type module.

The reason for this similarity is that we have reached a level of abstraction in which the difference between the two kinds of modules disappears. It becomes an implementation detail. As with all implementation details, the choice of whether to make a *Tank* type explicit in the code or to make it implicit with the use of a tank object module can vary from one implementation to another.

The rules for probes and operations of object and type modules were manifestations of the same restrictions. They can be restated in terms of the notation of this section. In the following list, the original object module rules are followed by their mathematical equivalents in the notation of axiomatic description. These equivalents are written under the assumption that no part of the state space is altered by a probe or an operation except the *initialize* operation whose imports are the state space parameters.

All probes and operations of an object module must have something to do with the state—all probes and operations must include the state space as a factor of their domains or codomains.

A probe of an object module must not alter the state and must export exactly one data type—the codomain of a probe must be exactly one data type, and this data type may not be the state space. (The codomain, however, may be augmented with **undef.**)

An operation of an object module must alter the state and may export or update nothing—the codomain of an operation must be the state space. The state space is not a factor of an operation's domain iff that operation is *initialize*. (Again, the codomain may be augmented with **undef.**)

Axiomatic specifications can be given to external interface modules, but more effort is required than for containment modules. (See Section 4.4 for the difference between these kinds of object modules.) The pagination module of Figure PAGE_OUTPUT in Section 4.4 is a fairly representative example of an external interface module. The purpose of that module is to divide character output into pages both automatically and under control of the invoking program unit. The state space consists of two integers: *ROW*, which keeps track of the position of the last line to be output, and *MAX_ROW*, which is the maximum number of lines that may appear on a page. There is an external object which is an output device that accepts commands to output single characters, start new output lines, and eject pages. Although the number of pages per line is limited, this module places no limitation on the number of characters per line.

For axioms to describe the effect of this module, i.e., to show the places in the output where the page breaks occur, a way to describe the output is needed. Since the only aspects of the external medium with which PAGE_OUTPUT deals are characters, new lines, and new pages, a satisfactory view of output is a sequence of characters interspersed with end-line and end-page markers. Axioms that make statements about output are possible if this view of output is incorporated into the state space. The state space, therefore, should contain not only entities that correspond to *MAX_ROW* and *ROW* but also a function, call it *printed,* which identifies the particular sequence that belongs to a given state.

To put the function *printed* in the state space is to move the external object into the state space. This eliminates the concept of external object from the module. The effect, of course, is to raise the level of abstraction to a point where it is impossible to distinguish between output and manipulations of sequences. Of course, such distinctions are made. They are part of the common understanding between the designer and the implementor.

An extra function *elt* is useful for identifying the particular symbols that have been output; *elt(S,I)* is the *I*th element of the sequence *S*.

Let's call the data type defined by the axiomatic page output module simply *Output*.

Consider the *new_page* operation. In Chapter 4 its description was as follows:

```
ROW ← 0
[] ← new-page command
```

Letting $P \in Output$ and K be the number of entities output so far, the effect of the second line on the output sequence can be described with

```
∀I∈Integer(
  (elt(printed(new_page(P)),I) ≠ elt(printed(P),I)⇔
   I = K + 1 & elt(printed(new_page(P)),I) = new_page ))
```

The integer K is easy to find because it is the place where the sequence *printed(P)* starts having undefined elements.

Figure PAGE_AX shows an axiomatic module chart arising from these considerations.

As yet, no example has shown how interactions of probes and operations can be expressed without reference to a state. Such interactions are expressed through the concept of composition of functions.

A quick review is in order. Examples of functions are

$$f(X,Y) = X^{1/2} + Y^2$$

and

$$g(Z) = Z^2$$

and a possible composition of *f* and *g* is

$$h(Z,Y) = f(g(Z),Y) = |Z| + Y^2$$

This kind of composition of functions is shown in multivariate calculus books. A more formal version involving univariate functions is shown in the first few chapters of many other mathematics and discrete-structures texts. A formal multivariate version can be found in books about category theory. The calculus text version will suffice for our purposes with the difference that our functions normally will not be dealing with real numbers.

An example involving operations of the tank module is as follows:

refill(initialize(20), SuperBurn,10)

Figure PAGE_AX Axiomatic Description of Page Output Module

Defines type   *Output*

State Space   An *Integer* parameter *MAX_ROW,* and functions *row* and *printed* such that
   row : Output → Integer   and   *printed : Output → Seq*
where *Seq* is the set of all finite sequences whose elements are characters, new_line symbols, or new_page symbols.
   Also, a function *elt* with
   elt : Seq × *Integer → Char* ∪ {new_line,new_page,**undef**}
is assumed that returns the element of the sequence at the indicated position or returns **undef** if there is none.

Probes
roomfor : Output × *Integer → Boolean*

Operations
initialize : Integer → Output ∪ {**undef**}
new_page : Output → Output
new_line : Output → Output
out_char : Output × *Char → Output*

Axioms
MAX_ROW>0 ⇒ *initialize(MAX_ROW)*∈*Output* &
                    row(initialize(MAX_ROW)) = 0 &
                    printed(initialize(MAX_ROW)) = empty
MAX_ROW≤0 ⇒ *initialize(MAX_ROW)* = **undef**
∀*P*∈*Output*(∃*K*∈*Integer*(∀*I*∈*Integer*(
   (0<*I*≤*K* ⇔ *elt(printed(P),I)*≠**undef**) &
   ∀*C*∈*Char*(
   (*I*≤0 ⇒ *elt(printed(out_char(P,C)),I)* = **undef**) &
   (0<*I*≤*K* ⇒ *elt(printed(out_char(P,C)),I)* = *elt(printed(P),I)*) &
   (*I* = *K* + 1 ⇒ *elt(printed(out_char(P,C)),I)* = *C*) &
   (*I*>*K* + 1 ⇒ *elt(printed(out_char(P,C)),I)* = **undef**)))))
∀*P*∈*Output*(∃*K*∈*Integer*(∀*I*∈*Integer*(
   (0<*I*≤*K* ⇔ *elt(printed(P),I)*≠**undef**) &
   (*I*≤0 ⇒ *elt(printed(new_page(P)),I)* = **undef**) &
   (0<*I*≤*K* ⇒ *elt(printed(new_page(P)),I)* = *elt(printed(P),I)*) &
   (*I* = *K* + 1 ⇒ *elt(printed(new_page(P)),I)* = new_page) &
   (*I*>*K* + 1 ⇒ *elt(printed(new_page(P)),I)* = **undef**))))
∀*P*∈*Output*(∃*K*∈*Integer*(∀*I*∈*Integer*(
   (0<*I*≤*K* ⇔ *elt(printed(P),I)*≠**undef**) &
   (*I*≤0 ⇒ *elt(printed(new_line(P)),I)* = **undef**) &
   (0<*I*≤*K* ⇒ *elt(printed(new_line)(P)),I)* = *elt(printed(P),I)*) &
   (*I* = *K* + 1 ⇒ *elt(printed(new_line(P)),I)* = new_line) &
   (*I* = *K* + 2 & *row(P)*<*MAX_ROW* ⇒
     elt(printed(new_line(P),I) = **undef**) &
(*I* = *K* + 2 & *row(P)* = *MAX_ROW*) ⇒
     elt(printed(new_line(P)),I) = new_page) &
   (*I*>*K* + 2 ⇒ *elt(printed(new_line(P)),I)* = **undef**))))
∀*P*∈*Output*(∀*C*∈*Char*(*row(out_char(P,C,))* = *row(P)*))
∀*P*∈*Output*(*row(new_page(P))* = 0)
∀*P*∈*Output*(
   row(P)<*MAX_ROW* ⇒ *row(new_line(P))* = *row(P)* + 1)
∀*P*∈*Output*(
   row(P) = *MAX_ROW* ⇒ *row(new_line(P))* = 0)
∀*P*∈*Output*(∀*I*∈*Integer*(
   roomfor(P,I,) ⇔ *row(P)* + *I*≤*MAX_ROW*))

This is a composition of functions that is exactly analogous to the example with f and g above. In that example, the first argument of f required a *Real* value, and g provided it. In this example, the first argument of *refill* requires a *Tank*, and *initialize* provides it. The expression states that the tank has been initialized with 20 units of an unknown brand and then refilled with 10 units of SuperBurn.

Any module state is obtainable with the execution of a sequence of operations, and this sequence of executions can be represented with a mathematical expression of the kind shown in the previous paragraph.

As mentioned, it is desirable to write a module description which avoids overspecification in the state space. The most elegant axiomatic specifications of modules involve interactions of probes and operations and are *state-light*, i.e., say almost nothing about a state space. These specifications are not emphasized in this section because they are considerably more difficult to achieve. The difficulty usually manifests itself in specifications that allow implementations which do not perform as intended.

However, when state-light specifications can be written, the resulting module chart is simpler and less likely to provide an overspecification.

Figure QUEUE of Section 4.2 shows an object module that defines a queue of *Items*. This module has operations for initializing and entering *Items* into a queue and for removing *Items* for a queue. These operations are described in terms of a state that is a sequence of *Items*. To show that this sequence depends on the paticular *Queue* whose state it is, we could represent it as a function:

$i : Queue \times Integer \rightarrow Item \cup \{\textbf{undef}\}$

Another function

$k : Queue \rightarrow Integer$

would then be useful in keeping track of where the sequence ends. Thus, if $Q \in Queue$, then

$$i(Q,1), i(Q,2), \ldots, \quad i(Q,k(Q))$$

is the sequence of *Items* in the state of Q and $i(Q,J) = \textbf{undef}$ for all *Integers* J less than 1 or greater than $k(Q)$.

A mathematical description of the *remove* operation would then be written in the same style as seen in the tank example:

$$i(remove(Q),1), \cdots, i(remove(Q),k(remove(Q)))$$
$$=$$
$$i(Q,2), \cdots, i(Q,k(Q))$$

Unfortunately, this seems to imply moving data, and to the extent that an implementor perceives, even subconsciously, that data is to be moved around, this is an overspecification.

The virtue of the state-light approach is that it can free the description of first-in, first-out from the tangential concept of redefining the sequence in the state.

Figure QUEUE_AX shows a state-light description of a queue. First consider its probes and operations, and ignore, for the moment, its axioms. The expression

front(remove(enter(enter(initialize,I),J)))

makes syntactic sense with those probes and operations. It says to *initialize* a queue, *enter Item I* into it; *enter Item J* into it, *remove* it, and then find the *front*. Of course, the *front* should be *J*. The expression

front(enter(remove(enter(initialize,I)),J))

should yield the same result, and so should this one:

front(remove(enter(enter(enter(initialize,I),J),K)))   (7.10)

Figure QUEUE_AX   State-Light Axiomatic Description of a QUEUE

Defines Type   *Queue*

Coupling   *Item*

State Space   empty

Probes
front: *Queue* → *Item* ∪ {**undef**}
full : *Queue* → *Boolean*
empty : *Queue* → *Boolean*

Operations
initialize : ∅ → *Queue* ∪ {**undef**}
enter : *Queue* × *Item* → *Queue* ∪ {**undef**}
remove : *Queue* → *Queue* ∪ {**undef**}

Axioms
∀Q∈*Queue*(∀I∈*Item*(~*empty*(Q) & ~*full*(Q) ⇒
  remove(*enter*(Q,I) = *enter*(*remove*(Q,I))))
∀Q∈*Queue*(∀I∈*Item*(*empty*(Q) ⇒ *empty*(*remove*(*enter*(Q,I))))))
∀Q∈*Queue*(∀I∈*Item*(~*empty*(Q) & ~*full*(Q) ⇒ *front*(*enter*(Q,I)) = *front*(Q)))
∀Q∈*Queue*(∀I∈*Item*(*empty*(Q) ⇒ *front*(*enter*(Q,I)) = I))
∀Q∈*Queue*(∀I∈*Item*(*full*(Q) ⇔ *enter*(Q,I) = **undef**))
∀Q∈*Queue*(Q = *initialize* ⇔ *empty*(Q) ⇔ *remove*(Q) = **undef** ⇔ *front*(Q) = **undef**))
∀Q∈*Queue*(~(*empty*(Q) & *full*(Q)))

These observations provide a feel for what first-in first-out means in the context of mathematical expressions of queue probes and operations. This feeling seems to be expressed thus: "The value of any expression in which *front* is the last action is found by counting the *remove*'s and then skipping, from left to right, the same number of *Items*. The next *Item* to be seen in the left-to-right order is the value."

The problem with this formulation is that it is difficult to express with the mathematics we have taken so much trouble to develop. Further, there is an easier way.

The achievement of a state-light description seems to require either luck or the knowledge of a relevant trick or both. In this case, there happen to be two equations that go a long way toward resolving the essential meaning of an expression involving the operations of *remove* and *enter*:

$$\sim empty(Q) \ \& \ \sim full(Q) \Rightarrow remove(enter(Q,I)) \ = \ enter(remove(Q),I)$$

and

$$empty(Q) \Rightarrow empty(remove(enter(Q,I)))$$

The idea is that the rightmost *remove* can be moved rightward in the expression by the first axiom until it reaches an *enter* which operates on the empty queue. Then the second axiom says that the *remove* and the *enter* cancel each other.

When this moving and cancellation is finished for each *remove* operation, the expression will be reduced to an equivalent one containing no *remove* operations, some number (possibly 0) of *enter* operations, and an *initialize*. If there are no *enter* operations, the queue should have no front. Otherwise, one of these equations will show that the front is

$$\sim empty(Q) \ \& \ \sim full(Q) \Rightarrow front(enter(Q,I)) \ = \ front(Q)$$

and

$$empty(Q) \Rightarrow front(enter(Q,I)) \ = \ I$$

These two equations are used by applying the first one, over and over, until there is only one *enter* left—this will be when *enter* operates on *initialize*. The second equation then states what the front of the queue is.

Figure EVALUATE shows how these four equations are applied to the queue represented in (7.10).

Figure EVALUATE   Use of Axioms to Evaluate the Front of a Queue

```
front(remove(enter(enter(enter(initialize,I),J),K)))   =
front(enter(remove(enter(enter(initialize,I),J)),K))   =
front(enter(enter(remove(enter(initialize,I)),J),K))   =
front(enter(enter(initialize,J),K))                    =
front(enter(initialize,J))                             =
J
```

Axioms made from these equations would go a long way toward describing a queue because they essentially explain what the front of any queue is.

Application of these four axioms, of course, requires a knowledge of which queues are full and which queues are empty. Empty queues are those equal to that created by *initialize*. There is no way to characterize which queues are full.

Luckily, we don't need to know which queues are full. What we need to know is the front of any queue. If we have a queue, we have something that has been created with a sequence of operations that don't break the rules. One of the rules must be

$$full(Q) \Rightarrow enter(Q,I) = \textbf{undef}$$

Thus, if we are considering a particular queue and an invocation of *enter* that was used in creating that queue, then that invocation of *enter* was not applied to a full queue.

Consider now the axioms in Figure QUEUE_AX. The first five have been discussed. The sixth tells us about the empty queue, and the seventh ensures that all queues will hold at least one item.

These axioms completely describe the concept of queue because they make it possible to figure out what the front of any queue is. This is done by writing down a mathematical expression describing the sequence of operations that created the queue and then applying the reductions demonstrated above.

It seems that axiomatic descriptions—not necessarily state-light axiomatic descriptions—can be written for essentially any object or type module that can be viewed with the containment paradigm.

Modules that interface with external objects must be rewritten without the interface to be fully described with the techniques of this section. Figure PAGE_AX is an example of this.

Axiomatic descriptions can also support a high level of abstraction. Figure QUEUE_AX is an example.

Axiomatic descriptions need not support a high level of abstraction. The tank module of Figure TANK_ABS of Section 4.1 is more abstract than the axiomatically described tank module in Figure TANK_AX.

On balance, however, it is often easier to achieve a high degree of precision and of abstraction with axiomatic descriptions than without them.

You can read more about state-light descriptions of object-type modules in [GUT].

EXERCISES

7.2.1 Consider the properties listed at the end of the State Space section of Figure TANK_PRE_AX. Some are redundant; i.e., they will be satisfied whenever the module is used according to the descriptions in the operations. Identify the redundant properties, and explain how you know they are redundant.

7.2.2 What aspects of the tank module's behavior can be concluded from the mathematical assertions in Figure TANK_AX that cannot be concluded from the mathematical assertions in Figure TANK_PRE_AX?

7.2.3 Review the rules for object modules. All these rules must be known by designers of modules, but some need not be known by the implementor of a module that has been given an axiomatic description. The reason is that the stated axioms enforce those rules. For each rule, state which kind it is.

7.2.4 Add a *lines_left* probe to the module in Figure PAGE_AX. This probe should report the number of unprinted lines on the current output page. Exhibit the probe in a function, and write an extra axiom to describe what it does.

7.2.5 Restate each of the following as a single mathematical expression involving composition of functions from the relevant module chart:

a Export the brand that comprises more than 90 percent of a tank that is initialized to 20 gallons and then filled with 19.5 gallons of SuperBurn.

b Initialize for output, print a line with "HI" on it, and finally start a new page.

c Export the front of a queue that has had "H" then "I" added to the initial empty queue and then has had the front removed.

7.2.6 Find the front of the following queues with the method shown in Figure EVALUATE:

a *remove(remove(enter(enter(initialize,J)))*

b *remove(enter(enter(remove(enter(initialize,I)),J),K))*

7.2.7 Revise the output page module in Figure PAGE_AX so that output lines are limited in length. When an attempt is made to put one character too many on an output line, there should be an automatic beginning of a new line.

7.2.8 Revise the module chart in Figure STACK of Section 4.2 to the style of Figure QUEUE_AX.

7.2.9 Revise the module chart in Figure TEXT_OPERATIONS of Section 5.1 to the style of Figure TANK_AX.

7.2.10 Revise the module chart in Figure COPY_OPERATIONS of Section 5.1 to the style of Figure PAGE_AX.

REFERENCES

[GUT]: Guttag, John. "Abstract Data Types and the Development of Data Structures," reprinted in P. Freeman and A. I. Wasserman feds.), *Tutorial on Software Design Techniques*, 4th ed., IEEE Computer Society, Los Angeles 1983.

FORTRAN
IMPLEMENTATIONS

Appendix F shows how FORTRAN code can implement the designs of this text. It is divided into these sections:

MATCHING SELECTIONS AND REPETITIONS IN CODE

Metacode selections are similar to FORTRAN selections. Here is a FORTRAN example:

```
IF METATEST1() THEN
    CALL S1
    CALL S2
ELSEIF METATEST2() THEN
    CALL S3
    CALL S4
ELSE
    CALL S5
    CALL S6
ENDIF
```

Do *not* change the pattern of indentation. A different pattern of indentation makes it quite difficult to match the metacode with the code. This metacode pattern shown in this book has been copied from [KER]. It lets the eye quickly see exactly how many alternatives there are, and there is less creep to the right side of the page or screen with this pattern than with many others. Use it.

Figure REPETITION_EQUIVALENCES shows the four metacode structures and FORTRAN equivalents. Just the **repeat for** structure has an analogue in ANSI standard FORTRAN. Three of the structures must be constructed from other things. The constructions shown here are not the only possibilities. In fact, the particular dialect of FORTRAN which you use may have nonstandard structures for repetition. If so, you can avoid some of the abominations in Figure REPETITION_EQUIVALENCES. However, if you choose different ways to represent these repetitions, then you ought to use the same construction every time so the correspondence between your code and your metacode will be clear.

Figure REPETITION EQUIVALENCES   **Metacode Repetition Constructs and Equivalent FORTRAN Constructs**

Metacode		*FORTRAN*
repeat while *M*	*	repeat while *M*
.	#	IF(*M'*)THEN
.		.
.		.
again		.
	*	again
		GOTO #
		END
repeat for *I* ← *J*, . . . , *K*		DO # I = J,K
.		.
.		.
.		.
again	#	CONTINUE
repeat	*	repeat
.	#1	CONTINUE
.		.
.		.
.		.
exit when *M*	*	exit when *M*
.		IF(*M'*) GOTO #2
.		.
.		.
again	*	again
		GOTO #1
	#2	CONTINUE
repeat	*	repeat
	#	CONTINUE
.		.
.		.
.		.
again until *M*	*	again until *M*
		IF(.NOT.(*M'*)) GOTO #

Where *M* indicates a metatest, *M'* indicates the corresponding FORTRAN logical expression, and # indicates a statement number.

SUBROUTINES FOR INPUT

The FORTRAN examples in this appendix are written in a modular style that matches the design methodology of the book. The methodology requires a different approach to input than FORTRAN programmers are used to.

Consider, for example, the program in Figure ADD_EM which reads an unknown number of integers and prints their sum. Two subroutines ININIT, "input number initialize," and INADV, "input number advance," handle the actual input. These subroutines are called file *operations*. They will be placed where the comment "declare file operations" is. They do their work by manipulating the file and altering variables called file *probes*. File probes are declared and placed in COMMON inside the main program where the comment "declare probe variables" is. An identical declaration is placed in each of the two file operations—again where the comment "declare probe variables" is.

The variables INCUR, "current input number," and INHAS, "input has a number," are the file probes of this example. Because they are placed in COMMON/INPRB/, a common area of memory that the file operations and the main program share, the variables are available to both the file operations and the main program. (See "Introduction to FORTRAN COMMON" at the end of this section, if necessary.)

File probes are meant to provide the main program with input data. In this case, INCUR sequences through the integers that appear on the file. It becomes the first integer when ININIT is called and becomes the next integer each time INADV is called.

When INCUR is the last integer and INADV is invoked, INCUR becomes undefined. After initialization with ININIT, INHAS is true iff INCUR is defined.

Figure ADD_EM   A Main Program that Depends on an Input Module

```
      PROGRAM ADDEM
*     declare probe variables   —integer input file
      INTEGER SUM
      CALL ININIT
      SUM = 0
*     REPEAT WHILE THERE IS ANOTHER INTEGER
  100 IF ( INHAS )THEN
          SUM = SUM + INCUR
          CALL INADV
*     AGAIN
        GOTO 100
        ENDIF
      PRINT *, 'THE SUM IS: ', SUM
      END
*     declare operations     —integer input file
```

Probes may not be assigned or otherwise given values outside the file operations. Thus a probe is used in the main program in essentially the same way as an argumentless function. In fact, it is permitted for probes to be functions instead of variables. These functions may import data with arguments.

Manipulation of an input file by any means other than file operations is not permitted.

Figure ADD_CONTEXT shows the variable declarations and subprogram definitions which are to be inserted in the code in Figure ADD_EM.

The program in Figure ADD_EM is not quite equivalent to its Pascal counterpart in Appendix P because input lines can contain more than one integer for the Pascal version but may not for the FORTRAN version. To achieve complete equivalence, it would be necessary for the input operations to read a whole line at a time into a string variable and then obtain any integers from that string variable. Since the string variable would have to be a state variable, as explained in the next example, an equivalent implementation would detract from this example. The point is, however, that the use of file probes and operations is an effective way of separating the way in which input happens from the top-level FORTRAN code that uses input.

The two subroutines ININIT and INADV happen to be essentially identical. This is because the example is a simple one and there is no need to OPEN the system standard input file. In most cases, there will be some difference between the implementations of the two subroutines.

Of course, an input file is not always so simple as to be a sequence of integers. For example, a list off names and telephone numbers, one of each per line, might need to be read. This could be done by having three probes— INNAME, "input name," INPHON, "input telephone number," and INHAS, "input has values"—and by advancing over a line at a time.

An input module can also be used to convert the existing input to a more congenial form. For example, consider a program which reads a file of real numbers but has no use for the numbers per se; instead the successive

Figure ADD_CONTEXT   Implementing an Input Module

```
*    probe variables                                      —integer input file
        INTEGER INCUR
*                      : THE CURRENT INTEGER ON THE INPUT FILE
        LOGICAL INHAS
*                      : THE STATUS (HAS OR NOT) OF INCUR
        COMMON /INPRB/ INCUR, INHAS
*    operations                                           —integer input file
        SUBROUTINE ININIT
*        declare probe variables                          —integer input file
        PARAMETER( INFILE = 5 )
*                      UNIT NUMBER OF INPUT FILE
        READ(INFILE,*,END = 100) INCUR
        INHAS = .TRUE.
        RETURN
100   INHAS = .FALSE.
        RETURN
        END

        SUBROUTINE INADV
*        declare probe variables                          —integer input file
        PARAMETER( INFILE = 5 )
        READ(INFILE,*,END = 100) INCUR
        INHAS = .TRUE.
        RETURN
100   INHAS = .FALSE.
        RETURN
        END
```

differences between two consecutive input numbers are required. (An example of this situation appears in Section 3.2) a main processing loop that deals with differences is shown in Figure USE_DIFF. Note that this is essentially the same form as that of ADD_EM.

Figure USE_DIFF   Using Differences between Input Values

```
        PROGRAM USEDIF
*        declare probe variables    —input of differences
        CALL DFINIT
*        REPEAT WHILE ANOTHER DIFFERENCE IS AVAILABLE
100   IF( DFHAS )THEN
*            do the necessary processing with DFCUR
            CALL DFADV
*        AGAIN
          GOTO 100
          ENDIF
        END
*        declare operations         —input of differences
```

The file operations to support this loop are now more complicated because of the need to have two consecutive input values available at all times, so that their difference can be calculated. The two input values ought be local to the module in the sense that the main program has no use for them, and they ought be global to the module in the sense that both DFINIT and DFADV must deal with them. This is accomplished in Figure DIFF_CONTEXT by placing them in COMMON /DFSTATE/, an area of memory that is common to the file operations but not to the main program. (Readers who are not acquainted with the FORTRAN 77 standard should review the use of the SAVE statement in the material about COMMON at the end of this section.)

Unfortunately, these rules are not enforced by FORTRAN:

1 Files may be manipulated only by file operations,
2 Probes may not have their values changed outside of file operations.
3 State variables may not be accessed outside of file operations.

Figure DIFF_CONTEXT

```
*    probe variables        —input of differences
         REAL DFCUR
*           : THE CURRENT DIFFERENCE BETWEEN CONSECUTIVE
            : INPUT VALUES
         LOGICAL DFHAS
*           : THE STATUS (HAS OR NOT) OF DFCUR
         COMMON /DFPRB/ DFCUR,DFHAS
*    state variables        —state variables
         REAL OLD
*           : THE OLDEST AVAILABLE INPUT ITEM
         REAL NEW
*           : THE MOST RECENTLY INPUT ITEM
         COMMON /DFSTAT/ OLD,NEW
         SAVE /DFSTAT/
*    operations        —input of differences
       SUBPROGRAM DFINIT
*      declare probe variables   —input of differences
*      declare state variables    —input of differences
       PARAMETER( INFILE = 5 )
*        UNIT NUMBER OF STANDARD INPUT FILES
       READ(INFILE,*,END = 100) OLD,NEW
       DFHAS = .TRUE.
       DFCUR = NEW − OLD
       RETURN
 100 DFHAS = .FALSE.
       RETURN
       END

       SUBROUTINE DFADV
*      declare variable probes   —input of differences
*      declare state variables    —input of differences
       PARAMETER( INFILE = 5)
       OLD = NEW
       READ(INFILE,*,END = 100) NEW
       DFCUR = NEW − OLD
       RETURN
 100 DFHAS = .FALSE.
       RETURN
       END
```

The programmer must take care that they are followed.

The technique of this section probably seems a little heavy-handed. It is, but not as much as would appear at first reading. Several points made throughout the book explain why this is so. As you read, you will see that some classes of problems become easier from the point of view exemplified by the input file modules of this section. For now, note that this technique allows matching input loops to be written in FORTRAN and Pascal, and so it allows the kind of flexibility often required when programs are ported from one machine to another. It is, therefore, a technique that is worth learning.

INTRODUCTION TO THE FORTRAN COMMON STATEMENT

This short introduction describes how labeled COMMON can be used to implement probe and state variables in FORTRAN.

The COMMON statement is far more flexible than described here. Like the GOTO statement, it is too flexible and has been much maligned. The reason is that it allows secret communication between subprograms, a condition which can cause no end of devilry. (Devilry is not uncommon with people who depend on secrets.) This devilry arises because of the difficulty of figuring out which subprogram has responsibility for what. The problem of secret communication is such a serious one that many professors have been participating in a conspiracy to eradicate the concept of COMMON from the minds of computer science students. This means, of course, that many readers of his book are reading about the COMMON statement for the first time, right now.

And therein lies a danger. The COMMON statement is not a tool to pick up and use in a wanton manner. An undisciplined use can negate many of the benefits of the modular style advocated in this book. Since all subprograms linked by a COMMON statement share variables, the question "what value does this variable X have?" cannot be answered without first answering "which subprogram used it last?" This could make subprograms tougher to debug than would be the case if all information were shared via parameter lists. But it won't—not if the use of COMMON statements is strictly limited to the style and purpose shown here. (Section 4.3 gives some of the rationale for the kind of intersubprogram communication required by the modular style if this book.)

All probe variables of a module must be declared in all program units that use the module and in all operations of that module. The same declarative statements should be reproduced in each of these places. These declarations are the usual FORTRAN declarations followed by

COMMON /<list name> / <list of probes>

where <list name> is a FORTRAN identifier chosen as a name for the list of probes and <list of probes> is a list of all the module's probe variables, separated by commas. Wherever these declarations are reproduced, the same probe variables will be available. The programmer is responsible for making sure that the values of probes are altered only within the operations of the module and not in the program units which use the module.

Figures ADD_EM and ADD_CONTEXT show an example of probe variables labeled INPRB. Their declarative statements appear in ADD_CONTEXT and are to be reproduced once in the main program in ADD_EM and once in each of the operations in ADD_CONTEXT.

State variables are declared in almost the same way. They have their own labeled COMMON statement:

COMMON / <list name> / <list of state variables>

and their declarative statements are never reproduced in invoking program units. For this reason, a FORTRAN run-time system may not save the values of the state variables from one execution of an operation to another. To make sure the values are saved, a SAVE statement

SAVE / <list name> /

is added immediately after the COMMON statements. The identifier <list name> must be the same in both statements and different from that used for the list of probe variables.

The declarative statements for state variables (including the SAVE statement) are reproduced in each operation. (If any probes are implemented as subprograms, the declarative statements must be reproduced there as well.)

Figures USE and USE_DIFF (pages 205 and 227) show an example of state variables labeled DFSTAT. Their declarative statements appear in USE_DIFF. These should be reproduced in two places, one for each operation.

Of course, in a program that uses more than one module, each will have its own name. No COMMON statement will be reproduced in the operations of a module to which it doesn't belong.

Note that a FORTRAN compiler will not check whether each use of a COMMON statement with the same name has the same variables, declared the same way and listed in the same order. The programmer must see to this. Strange things may happen if she does not.

F3

SOME EXAMPLES MATCHING METACODE IN CHAPTER 2

The correspondence between detailed metacode and FORTRAN code is illustrated by showing FORTRAN code in Figure COUNT_CODE that matches FIGURE COUNT_DETAIL of Section 2.2.

Figure COUNT_CODE   FORTRAN Code Matching Figure COUNT_DETAIL

```
      DO 100 I = 1,26
         LCOUNT = 0;
 100  CONTINUE
      I = 1;
*     repeat while
 200  IF( I.LE.SLNGTH )THEN
         ILETTER = ICHAR(S(I:I)) − ICHAR('A') + 1
         LCOUNT(ILETTER) = LCOUNT(ILETTER) + 1
         I = I + 1
*     again
      GOTO 200
      END
```

The major variables used in Figure COUNT_CODE could be declared thus:

```
CHARACTER S*(SLNGTH)
INTEGER LCOUNT(26)
```

This implementation isn't quite as good as could be written in FORTRAN, but we cannot improve on it while matching the metacode in Figure COUNT_

DETAIL. If we were implementing Figure COUNT_ABS, we could do a better job of using FORTRAN. Figure FORTRAN_COUNT shows how.

Figure FORTRAN_COUNT   FORTRAN Code Matching Figure COUNT_ABS

```
      DO 100 I = 1,26
        LCOUNT = 0;
 100  CONTINUE
      DO 200 I = 1, SLNGTH
        ILETTER = ICHAR(S(I:I)) − ICHAR('A') + 1
        LCOUNT(ILETTER) = LCOUNT(ILETTER) + 1
 200  CONTINUE
```

The file-merging algorithm of Section 2.3 provides the second example of this section. In this version two character files, containing customer records for branches A and B, are merged and copied into one file of customer records. The output file is not character-oriented. It consists of a sequence of customer records—each is stored in the same format that would be used internally in the computer.

This example shows how a data-type dictionary influences the declaration of variables in FORTRAN. Variable declarations in the FORTRAN code are organized around the concept of data entity—not around basic FORTRAN data types. In one context, variables representing counts of apples and of apple pickers might both be of type INTEGER, but they have little else in common. The practice of declaring them together leads to confusion. FORTRAN allows multiple uses of INTEGER, REAL, CHARACTER, LOGICAL, etc. This permissiveness is the key to declarations which make sense. What is needed is to make the FORTRAN variable declarations for each data entry resemble entries in the data-type dictionary. See the Probe Variables section of Figure CUSTOMER_INPUT to see how this is done.

With Figure DATA_DICTIONARY, a customer record in an input file is assumed to consist of the following eleven lines:

Name—35 characters
Social security number—11 characters
Phone number—8 characters
Street—50 characters
Town/state—60 characters
Zip Code—5 characters
Number of accounts—*Integer*
Account type—1 character
Account number—8 characters
Balance—*Real*
Date of last transaction—8 characters

The input operations in this example must deal with two files. This causes no difficulties in FORTRAN. The INADV operation and both probes will import file unit numbers.

This example shows one of the differences between "import" and "pass as an argument." The file probes are, in fact, file variables, and they have no arguments. However, they are vectors indexed by file unit numbers. When they are referenced, the file unit numbers are imported.

Figure DATA_DICTIONARY establishes account types as savings, checking, or NOW. This is accomplished in FORTRAN by declaring symbolic constants SAVINGS, CHCKNG, and NOW as the integers 1, 2, and 3. See the Coupling section of Figure CUSTOMER_INPUT.

The input operations in this example transform the nature of input. In particular, account types are expressed as single letters on the input files and as SAVINGS, CHCKNG, and NOW within the program. Only the input operations show an awareness of the single letters.

FORTRAN code matching Figure FILE_MERGE appears in Figure MERGE_CODE, and the declarations and subprograms for implementing the input file operations appear in Figure CUSTOMER_INPUT.

Figure MERGE_CODE   FORTRAN Code Matching Figure FILE_MERGE

```
          PROGRAM FMERGE
*         declare coupling                        —customer input by branch
*         declare probe variables                 —customer input by branch
          OPEN(3,FILE = 'BRNCHC',STATUS = 'NEW')
          CALL ININIT
*         REPEAT WHILE BOTH FILES HAVE INPUT
   100    IF( INHAS(A) .AND. INHAS(B) ) THEN
                IF( INNAM(A) .LT. INNAM(B) )THEN
                    WRITE(3) INNAM(A), INSSN(A),INPH(A),
      +                 INSTR(A),INTWN(A),INZIP(A),INCNT(A),
      +                 (INTYPE(A,I),INNUM(A,I),INBLNC(A,I),INLDAT(A,I),I = 1,MAXACC)
                    CALL INADV(A)
                ELSE
                    WRITE(3) INNAM(B),INSSN(B),INPH(B),
      +                 INSTR(B),INTWN(B),INZIP(B),INCNT(B),
      +                 (INTYPE(B,I),INNUM(B,I),INBLNC(B,I),INLDAT(B,I),I = 1,MAXACC)
                    CALL INADV(B)
                ENDIF
*           AGAIN
              GOTO 100
              ENDIF
*         FINISH COPYING ANY REMAINING BRANCH A RECORDS ONTO BRANCH C
*             REPEAT WHILE BRANCH A HAS ANOTHER RECORD
   200        IF( INHAS(A) )THEN
                  WRITE(3) INNAM(A),INSSN(A),INPH(A),
      +               INSTR(A),INTWN(A),INZIP(A),INCNT(A),
      +               (INTYPE(A,I),INNUM(A,I),INBLNC(A,I),INLDAT(A,I),I = 1,MAXACC)
                  CALL INADV(A)
*             AGAIN
                GOTO 200
                ENDIF
```

```
*        FINISH COPYING ANY REMAINING BRANCH B RECORDS ONTO BRANCH C
*        REPEAT WHILE BRANCH B HAS ANOTHER RECORD
  300      IF( INHAS(B) )THEN
             WRITE(3) INNAM(B),INSSN(B),INPH(B),
      +         INSTR(B),INTWN(B),INZIP(B),INCNT(B),
      +         (INTYPE(B,I),INNUM(B,I),INBLNCLDAT(B,I),I = 1,MAXACC)
             CALL INADV(B)
*          AGAIN
             GOTO 300
             ENDIF
      END


*      declare operations                          —customer input by branch
```

Figure CUSTOMER_INPUT   FORTRAN Input Operations for MERGE_CODE

```
*  coupling: constants                             —customer input by branch
      INTEGER NAMSIZ,SSNSIZ,PHSIZ,STRSIZ,TWNSIZ,ZIPSIZ,ANSIZ,LDSIZ,
    +      MAXACC
*      CUSTOMER RECORD PARAMETERS
         PARAMETER( NAMSIZ = 35 )
*                    : SIZE OF A NAME
         PARAMETER( SSNSIZ = 9 )
*                    : SIZE OF SOCIAL SECURITY NUMBER
*      ADDRESS INFORMATION PARAMETERS
         PARAMETER( PHSIZ = 7 )
*                    : SIZE OF PHONE NUMBER
         PARAMETER( STRSIZ = 50 )
*                    : SIZE OF STREET ADDRESS
         PARAMETER( TWNSIZ = 60 )
*                    : SIZE OF TOWN NAME
         PARAMETER( ZIPSIZ = 5 )
*                    : SIZE OF ZIP CODE
*  ACCOUNT RECORD PARAMETERS
         PARAMETER( ANSIZ = 8 )
*                    : SIZE OF ACCOUNT NUMB
         PARAMETER( LDSIZ = 6 )
*                    : SIZE OF DATE LAST TRANSACTION
         PARAMETER( MAXACC = 5 )
*                    : MAXIMUM NUMBER OF ACCOUNT RECORDS
*  customer record data types
*  ACCOUNT TYPE
      INTEGER SAVINGS,CHCKNG,NOW
         PARAMETER( SAVNGS = 1 )
*                    : CODE FOR SAVINGS ACCOUNT
         PARAMETER( CHCKNG = 2 )
*                    : CODE FOR CHECKING ACCOUNT
         PARAMETER( NOW = 3 )
*                    : CODE FOR NOW ACCOUNT
*  file identifiers
```

```
*   BRANCHES
          INTEGER A,B
          PARAMETER( A = 1, B = 2)
*   probe variables                                    —customer input by branch
*       CUSTOMER RECORD—ONE FOR EACH BRANCH
              CHARACTER INNAM(A:B)*(NAMSIZ)
*                       : CUSTOMER NAME
              CHARACTER INSSN(A:B)*(SSNSIZ)
*                       : CUSTOMER SOCIAL SECURITY NUMBER
*             ADDRESS INFORMATION
                  CHARACTER INPH(A:B)*(PHSIZ)
*                       : PHONE NUMBER
                  CHARACTER INSTR(A:B)*(STRSIZ)
*                       : STREET ADDRESS
                  CHARACTER INTWN(A:B)*(TWNSIZ)
*                       : TOWN
                  CHARACTER INZIP(A:B)*(ZIPSIZ)
              INTEGER INCNT(A:B)
*                       : COUNT OF ACCOUNTS ACTUALLY PRESENT
*             ACCOUNTS—UP TO MAXACC ACCOUNTS ARE POSSIBLE
                  INTEGER INTYP(A:B,MAXACC)
*                       : ACCOUNT TYPE—SAVNGS, CHCKNG, NOW
                  CHARACTER INNUM(A:B,MAXACC)*(ANSIZ)
*                       : ACCOUNT NUMBER
                  REAL INBLNC(A:B,MAXACC)
*                       : BALANCE
                  CHARACTER INLDAT(A:B,MAXACC)*(LDSIZ)
*                       : DATE OF LAST TRANSACTION
*       EXISTENCE PROBE—ONE FOR EACH BRANCH
              LOGICAL INHAS(A:B)
          COMMON /INPRB/ INNAM,INSSN,INPH,INSTR,INTWN,INZIP,
        +                INCNT,INTYP,INNUM,INBLNC,INLDAT,INHAS
*   operations                                         —customer input by branch
          SUBROUTINE ININIT
*         declare coupling                             —customer input by branch
*         declare probes                               —customer input by branch
          OPEN(1,FILE = 'BRNCHA',STATUS = 'OLD')
          CALL INADV(A)
          OPEN(2,FILE = 'BRNCHB',STATUS = 'OLD')
          CALL INADV(B)
          END

          SUBROUTINE INADV(F)
*         declare coupling                             —customer input by branch
*         declare probes                               —customer input by branch
          INTEGER I
          CHARACTER*1 C
          READ(F,1,END = 200) INNAM(F),INSSN(F),INPH(F),
        +                     INSTR(F),INTWN(F),INZIP(F)
      1   FORMAT(5(A/),A)
          READ(F,*,END = 200) INCNT(F)
```

```
        IF(INCNT(F).GT.MAXACC) GOTO 200
        DO 100 I = 1,INCNT(F)
          READ(F,2,END=200) C,INNUM(F,I),INBLNC(F,I),INLDAT(F,I)
2         FORMAT(A/A/F12.0/A)
          IF( C .EQ. 'S' ) THEN
              INTYP(F,I)=CHECKNG
          ELSE IF( C .EQ. 'C' ) THEN
              INTYP(F,I)=SAVNG
          ELSE
              INTYP(F,I,)=NOW
          ENDIF
100     CONTINUE
        INHAS(F) = .TRUE.
        RETURN
200     INHAS(F) = .FALSE.
        RETURN
        END
```

APPENDIX **F4**

AN EXAMPLE MATCHING METACODE IN CHAPTER 4

One example of an object module implementation is shown here. An object module implementation follows the same form as the input operation implementations, because the input mechanism was patterned after the object module mechanism.

Essentially, an object module implementation consists of some subprograms, some state variables, and some probes.

Probes can be functions and, sometimes, subroutines as well as variables. All these things are capable of exporting information to an invoking program unit. FORTRAN implementations as variables have been demonstrated in Appendix F2.

State variables are variables necessary to represent the state or just variables that must be shared by the operations to do their jobs. A FORTRAN implementation of state variables has been demonstrated in Appendix F2.

State variables, if any, are placed in a named COMMON area that is not declared outside the subroutines of the object module. Probe variables, if any, are placed in a different named COMMON which is declared in the invoking program unit.

The data coupling of an object module consists of the probe variables, the data returned by probe functions, and the parameters of the subprograms that implement operations or probes.

This example implements the tank object module and the test program of Section 4.1. Because of the input operations, this example has essentially two object modules, a tank module and an input module.

The input module assumes that the first line of input contains a real number which is the tank size and that each additional line contains a brand letter in the first column which is followed by a real number amount. (Part of the assumption is that brands are represented by single letters.) Echo checking is done during the input operations.

Outside of the input operations *Brands* are represented with integers, 1 for 'A', 2 for 'B', etc. Inside the tank module, the unknown brand is implemented as a parameter that is set to 27.

Figure TANK_CODE contains the top-level FORTRAN code. Notice how closely it matches the metacode of the design in Figure TANK_TEST.[1] Figure FUEL_INPUT shows the input operations, and Figure TANK_MODULE contains the tank module.

Figure TANK_CODE   FORTRAN Code Implementing Figure TANK_TEST

```
          PROGRAM TNKTST

          declare coupling                                  —tank module
*         declare probe variables                           —refill input
*         declare state variables                           —tank module
          CALL ININIT
          CALL INIT(INSIZE)
*         REPEAT WHILE THERE IS MORE DATA
   100      IF(INHAS)THEN
              CALL REFILL(INBRND,INAMT)
              IF(PURE() )THEN
                WRITE(6,*) 'BRAND ',CHAR(PUREB()+CHAR('A')−1),
      +                   ' MAKES UP AT LEAST 90% OF TANK'
              ENDIF
              CALL INADV
*           AGAIN
            GOTO 100
            ENDIF
          END
*         declare operations                                —refill input
*         declare probe subprograms                         —tank module
*         declare operations                                —tank module
```

Figure FUEL_INPUT   FORTRAN Input Operations for TANK_CODE

```
*  probe variables                                          —refill input
          REAL INSIZE
*                              : TANK SIZE
          INTEGER INBRAND

*                              :INBRAND IS POSITION OF LETTER BRAND IN
*                               ALPHABET
```

[1] The nesting of function invocations shown in the WRITE statement of Figure TANK_CODE wasn't permitted by the dialect of FORTRAN which I used to test the program. I was forced to introduce temporary variables.

```
      REAL INAMT
*                           :AMOUNT OF INBRAND THAT IS REFILLED
      LOGICAL INHAS
*                         :EXISTENCE OF INPUT DATA
      COMMON /INPRB/ INBRND,INSIZE,INAMT,INHAS
* operations                                              —refill input
      SUBROUTINE ININIT
* declare probes                                          —refill input
      CHARACTER*1 C
      READ(5,*,END=1000) INSIZE
      WRITE(6,*) 'Tank Size: ', INSIZE
      READ(5,1,END=1000) C,INAMT
    1 FORMAT(A,F40.0)
      WRITE(6,*) 'Refill Input: ',C,INAMT
      INBRND = ICHAR(C) − ICHAR('A') + 1
      INHAS = .TRUE.
      RETURN
 1000 INHAS = .FALSE.
      RETURN
      END
      SUBROUTINE INADV
* declare probes                                          —refill input
      CHARACTER*1 C
      READ(5,1,END=1000) C,INAMT
    1 FORMAT(A,F40.0)
      WRITE(6,*) 'Refill Input: ',C,INAMT
      INBRND = ICHAR(C) − ICHAR('A') + 1
      INHAS = .TRUE.
      RETURN
 1000 INHAS = .FALSE.
      RETURN
      END
```

**Figure TANK_MODULE   FORTRAN Implementation of Figure
TANK**

```
* coupling: data types                                    —tank module
      LOGICAL PURE
*                         : EXPORTED BY PROBE PURE
      INTEGER PUREB()
*                         : EXPORTED BY PROBE PURE-BRAND

* state variables                                         —tank module
      PARAMETER (UNKNWN = 27 )
*                         : THE UNKNOWN BRAND
      REAL AMT(27),SIZE
*                         :AMT(I) IS AMOUNT OF BRAND I IN TANK
      COMMON /TSTATE/ AMT,SIZE
      SAVE /TSTATE/
```

```
*    probe subprograms                                        —tank module
          LOGICAL FUNCTION PURE ()
          INTEGER B
*         declare state variables                             —tank module

          B = 1
*         REPEAT WHILE . . .
    100     IF( (AMT(B).LT.0.9*SIZE) .AND. (B.LT.26) )THEN
              B = B + 1
*         AGAIN
            GOTO 100
            ENDIF
          PURE = AMT(B).GE.0.9*SIZE
          END

          INTEGER FUNCTION PUREB()
*         tank-module.pure-brand

          INTEGER B
*         declare state variables                             —tank module

          B = 1
*         REPEAT WHILE . . .
    100     IF( (AMT(B).LT.0.9*SIZE) .AND. (B.LT.26) )THEN
              B = B + 1
*         AGAIN
            GOTO 100
            ENDIF
          PUREB = B
          END

*    operations                                               —tank module
          SUBROUTINE INIT(S)
*         tank-module.initialize

          REAL S
*         declare state variables                             —tank module
          INTEGER C
          SIZE = S
          AMT(UNKNWN) = SIZE
          DO 100 C = 1,26
            AMT(C) = 0.0
    100   CONTINUE
          END

          SUBROUTINE REFILL(B,Q)
*         tank-module.refill

          INTEGER B
          REAL Q
*         declare state variables                             —tank module
          INTEGER C
          REAL P

          P = (SIZE-Q)/SIZE
          DO 100 C = 1,UNKNWN
            AMT(C) = AMT(C)*P
```

```
100   CONTINUE
      AMT(B) = AMT(B) + Q
      END
```

REFERENCE FOR APPENDIX F

[KER]: Kernighan, B. W., and Plauger, P. J. *The Elements of Programming Style*, 2d ed., McGraw-Hill, New York, 1978, pp. 32–38.

PASCAL
IMPLEMENTATIONS

This appendix shows how Pascal code can emplement the designs in the text. It is divided into these sections:

MATCHING REPETITIONS AND SELECTIONS IN CODE

Metacode selections are similar to Pascal selections. Here is a Pascal example:

```
if metatest1 then begin
    S1;
    S2
end else if metatest2 then begin
    S3;
    S4
end else begin
    S5;
    S6
end
```

Here is another:

```
if metatest1 then
    begin
        S1;
        S2
    end
else if metatest2 then
    begin
        S3;
        S4
    end
else
    begin
        S5;
        S6
    end
```

Choose one pattern and stick with it. The begin/end brackets can be omitted in certain cases, if you like. However, do *not* change the pattern of indentation. A different pattern of indentation makes it quite difficult to match the metacode with the code. This metacode pattern shown in this book has been copied from [KER]. It lets the eye quickly see exactly how many alternatives there are, and there is less creep to the right side of the page or screen with this pattern than with many others. Use it.

Three of the metacode structures for repetitions are similar to Pascal repetitions. Figure REPETITION_EQUIVALENCES shows the four metacode structures and Pascal equivalents. Only the **exit when** structure has no direct analogue and must be constructed from other things. The construction shown here is not the only possibility. If you prefer, you can use another. However, you ought to use the same construction every time, so that the correspondence between your code and your metacode will be clear.

Figure REPETITION_EQUIVALENCES Metacode Repetition
Constructs and Equivalent Pascal Constructs

Metacode	*Pascal*
repeat while *M*	while *M'* do begin
.	.
.	.
again	end
repeat for *I* ← *J*, . . . , *K*	for I := J to K do begin
.	.
.	.
again	end
repeat	{repeat} #1:
.	.
.	.
exit when *M*	{exit when *M*}
	if *M'* then goto #2;
.	.
.	.
.	
again	{again} goto #1; #2:
repeat	repeat
.	.
.	.
.	.
again until *M*	until *M'*

where *M* represents a metatest, *M'* represents an equivalent Pascal boolean expression, and # represents a statement label.

APPENDIX **P2**

SUBROUTINES FOR INPUT

The Pascal examples in this appendix are written in a modular style that matches the design methodology of the book. The methodology requires a different approach to input than is provided with Pascal's read and readln. The approach is, however, analogous to Pascal's get and reset.

The reset/get mechanism allows an input file to be seen as a sequence of characters, a sequence of integers, a sequence of customer records, or whatever. It is a handy way of dealing with input from files, but it works only when the underlying file is the desired sequence. A text file, for example, cannot be input as a sequence of integers. To do that, one must use the read procedure which behaves differently. (This difference is explained in Section 4.4.) Although the input style of this appendix mimics the reset/get mechanism, it can be applied to situations in which the input file is not a sequence of the particular things desired by the programmer.

Consider, for example, the program in Figure ADD_EM which inputs an unknown number of integers and prints their sum. Two procedures inInit and inAdvance handle the actual input. These procedures are called file *operations*. They will be placed where the comment "declare file operations" is. They do their work by manipulating the file and altering variables called *probes*. File probes are declared in the place where the comment "declare probe variables" is.

The variables inCurrent and inHas as the probe variables of this example. Like all file probes, they are meant to provide the main program with input data. The variable inCurrent sequences through the integers that appear on the file. It becomes the first integer when inInit is invoked and becomes the next integer each time inAdvance is invoked.

225

Figure ADD_EM   A Reset/Get Input Style Applied to Reading Integers from Text

```
program addEm(INPUT,OUTPUT);
{declare probes variables   —integer input file       }
{declare operations         —integer input file       }
var SUM : Integer;
begin
   inInit;
   SUM := 0;
   while inHas do begin
       SUM := SUM + inCurrent;
       inAdvance
   end;
   writeln("The sum is: ", SUM)
end.
```

When inCurrent is the last integer on the input file and inAdvance is invoked, inCurrent becomes undefined. After initialization with inInit, inHas is true iff inCurrent is defined.

Probes may not be assigned or otherwise given values outside the file operations. Thus a probe is used in the main program in essentially the same

Figure ADD_CONTEXT   File Probes and Operations for *Integer* Input

```
{file probes                        —integer input file                     }
      inCurrent : Integer;
          {sequences through integers in the input file                     }
      inHas        : Boolean;
          {true iff another integer exists                                  }
{file operations                    —integer input file                     }
procedure inInit;
begin
   while (not eof) and (input^ = ' ') do get;
   if not eof then begin
     inHas := true;
     read(inCurrent);
     while (not eof) and (input^ = ' ') do get;
   end else
     inHas := false
end;
procedure inAdvance;
begin
   if not eof then begin
     read(inCurrent);
     while (not eof) and (input^ = ' ') do get;
   end else
     inHas := false
end;
```

way as a parameterless function. In fact, it is permitted for probes to be functions instead of variables. These functions may import data with parameters.

Manipulation of an input file by any means other than file operations is not permitted.

Figure ADD_CONTEXT shows definitions of the file probes and operations which are to be inserted in the code in Figure ADD_EM.

The program of Figure ADD_EM is a subtly different from what would be likely if we had simply started to write it using read procedure without the input module style because files which consist of only blanks or of trailing blanks after the last integer will not cause error messages. All files which contain some number (possibly 0) of (reasonably small) integers separated by blanks will result in having the sum of those integers printed.

Of course, it is the use of

```
while (not eof) and (input^ = ' ') do get;
```

which ensures this property, not the use of file and operations. The point is, however, that the use of probes and operations is an effective way of separating the way in which input happens from the code that uses input.

The two procedures *inInit* and *inAdvance* happen to be essentially identical. This is because the example is a simple one and because it is not necessary to reset the input file. In most cases, there will be some differences between the implementations of these two file operations.

Of course, an input file is not always so simple as to be a sequence of integers. For example, a list of names and telephone numbers, one of each per line, might need to be input. This could be done by having three probes—inpName, inpPhone, and inpHas—and by advancing over a line at a time.

An input module also can be used to convert existing input to a more congenial form. For example, consider a program which reads a file of real numbers but has no use for the numbers per se; instead, the successive differences between two consecutive input numbers are required. (An example of this situation appears in Section 3.2.) A main processing loop that utilizes differences between consecutive input values is shown in Figure USE_DIFF. Note that this loop has essentially the same form as that of figure ADD_EM.

Figure USE_DIFF   Using Differences between Input Values

```
program useDifferences(INPUT,OUTPUT);
{declare probe variables   —input of differences      }
{declare operations        —input of differences      }
begin
   difInit;
   while difHas do begin
      {do the necessary processing with difCurrent}
      difAdvance
   end
end.
```

File operations to support this loop are now more complicated because of the need to have two consecutive input values available at all times so that their difference can be calculated. These two values ought be local to the module in the sense that the main program has no use for them and global to the module in the sense that both difAdvance and difInit must deal with them. This is accomplished in Figure DIFF_CONTEXT by placing them in a special record which is meant to be accessed only by *difInit* and *difAdvance*. Variables in this record are called state variables. It is not permitted for any statement outside of the file operations to contain a reference to the state variables.

Figure DIFF_CONTEXT   Input of Successive Differences

```
{probes                          —input of differences              }
     difCurrent : Real;
                  {current difference between input file values      }
     difHas    : Boolean;
                  {true iff there is another difference              }
{state variables                 —input of differences              }
     difState : record
          OLD : Real
                  {the second most recently input value             }
          NEW : Real
                  {the most recently input value                    }
     end;
{operations for input of consecutive differences                    }
procedure difInit;
begin with difState do begin
     while (not eof) and (input^ = ' ') do get;
     if not eof then begin
          read(OLD);
          while (not eof) and (input^ = ' ') do get(input)
     end;
     if not eof then begin
          difHas := true;
          read(NEW);
          while (not eof) and (input^ = ' ') do get;
          difCurrent := NEW − OLD
     end else
          difHas := false
end end;
procedure difAdvance;
begin with difState do begin
     if not eof then begin
          OLD := NEW;
          read(NEW);
          while (not eof) and (input^ = ' ') do get;
          difCurrent := NEW − OLD
     end else
          difHas := false
end end;
```

Unfortunately the following rules are not enforced by Pascal.

1 Files may be manipulated only by file operations.
2 Probes may not have their values changed outside of file operations.
3 State variables may not even be accessed outside of file operations.

The programmer must take care that they are followed.

The technique of this section probably seems a little heavy-handed. It is, but not as much as would appear at first reading. Several points made throughout the book explain why this is so. As you read, you will see that some classes of problems become easier from the point of view exemplified by the input modules of this section. For now, note that this technique allows matching input loops to be written in Pascal and FORTRAN, and so it permits the kind of flexibility that is often required when programs are ported from one machine to another. It is, therefore, a technique that is worth learning.

SOME EXAMPLES MATCHING METACODE IN CHAPTER 2

The correspondence between detailed metacode and Pascal code is illustrated by showing Pascal code in Figure COUNT_CODE that matches Figure COUNT DETAIL of Section 2.2.

Figure CQUNT_CODE   Pascal Code Matching Figure COUNT_ DETAIL

```
for I := 1 to 26 do LETTERwCOUNT := 0;
I := 1;
while I < SwLENGTH do begin
   ILETTER := ord(S[I]) − ord('A') + 1;
   LETTERwCOUNT[ILETTER] := LETTERwCOUNT[ILETTER] + 1;
   I := I + 1
end;
```

The major variables used on Figure COUNT_CODE could be declared this way:

```
S : packed array[1 . . SwLENGTH] of Char;
LETTERwCOUNT : array[1 . . 26] of Integer;
```

This implementation does not do Pascal justice, but we cannot do better and still match the metacode of Figure COUNT_DETAIL. If we were implementing Figure COUNT_ABS, then better use could be made of Pascal. The major variables would be declared thus:

```
S : packed array[1 . . SwLENGTH] of Char;
LETTERwCOUNT : array['A' . . 'Z'] of Integer;
```

and the matching Pascal code would be as in Figure PASCAL_COUNT.

Figure PASCAL_COUNT   Pascal Code Matching Figure COUNT_ABS

```
for C := 'A' to 'Z' do LETTERwCOUNT[C] := 0;
for I := 1 to SwLENGTH do
    LETTERwCOUNT[S[I]] := LETTERwCOUNT[s[i]] + 1
```

The file-merging algorithm of Section 2.3 provides the second example of this section. In this version two character files, containing customer records for branches A and B, are merged and copied into one file of customer records. Records in the output file match the internal storage for these records and so are not character-oriented.

This example shows how a data-type dictionary influences the declaration of variables in Pascal. A separate record is declared for each data type.

A customer record in an input file is assumed to consist of the following eleven lines:

Name—35 characters
Social security number—11 characters
Phone number—8 characters
Street—50 characters
Town/state—60 characters
Zip code—5 characters
Number of accounts—*Integer*
Account type—1 character
Account number—8 characters
Balance—*Real*
Date of last transaction—8 characters

The input operations in this example must deal with two files. This causes some difficulty in ANSI standard Pascal because file variables cannot be manipulated as ordinary variables. Although a file may be passed as a parameter to the inInit procedure, the *inInit* procedure cannot assign that file name to a file variable for use by the *inAdv* procedure. There are other alternatives; one is chosen here. A *Branch* data type is declared to be (A,B) and is used to identify the files in the invoking program unit. The *inAdv* operation, then, imports a *Branch* and selects a file based on this import.

If the end of an input file is encountered when another line is expected, inAdv will report that there are no further customers without aborting.

This example shows one of the differences between "import" and "pass as a parameter." The file probes are, in fact, file variables, and they have no parameters. However, they are vectors indexed by the *Branch* data type. When they are referenced, data of type *Branch* is imported.

The data-type dictionary requires account types to be savings, checking, or NOW. This is accomplished in Pascal with an enumeration type: (checking,savings,NOW).

The input operations in this example transform the nature of input. In particular, account types are expressed as single letters on the input files and as savings, checking, and NOW within the program. Only the input operations show an awareness of the single letters.

Pascal code matching Figure FILE_MERGE appears in Figure MERGE_CODE and the declarations and subprograms for implementing the input file operations appear in Figure CUSTOMER_INPUT.

Figure MERGE_CODE   Pascal Code Matching Figure FILE_MERGE

```
program pmerge(BRANCHA,BRANCHB,BRANCHC);

var BRANCHC : file of CustomerRecord;
{declare coupling          —customer input by branch      }
{declare probe variables   —customer input by branch      }
{declare operations for    —customer input by branch      }
begin {main}
  brInit;
  rewrite(BRANCHC);
  while has[A] and has[B] do
    if customer[A].Name < customer[B].Name then begin
        BRANCHC^ := customer[A];
        put(BRANCHC);
        brAdvance(A)
      end else begin
        BRANCHC^ := customer[B];
        put(BRANCHC);
        brAdvance(B)
      end;
        end;
      {Finish copying any remaining branch(A) records onto BRANCHC}
      while has[A] do begin
          BRANCHC^ := customer[A];
          put(BRANCHC);
          brAdvance(A)
      end;
      {Finish copying any remaining branch(B) records onto BRANCHC}
      while has[B] do begin
          BRANCHC^ := customer[B];
          put(BRANCHC);
          brAdvance(B)
      end
end.
```

Figure CUSTOMER_INPUT   Pascal Input Operations for MERGE_CODE

```
{coupling                    —customer input by branch              }
{    constants determining size of customer record                  }
  {  customer record parameters                                     }
    nameSize = 35;
```

```
    ssnSize = 11;      {size of social security number                    }
    maxNumAccounts = 5;         {maximum number of accounts per customer}
  {  address information parameters                                       }
    phoneSize = 8;         {digits in phone number                       }
    streetSize = 50;       {size of street address                       }
    townSize = 60;         {size of town address                         }
    zipSize = 5;
  {  account record parameters                                           }
    accNumSize = 8;       {digits in account number                      }
    dateTransSize = 8;    {size of transaction date                      }
{    customer record data types                                          }
    AddressInformation = record
      Phone        : packed array [1 . . phoneSize     ] of Char;
      StreetAddr   : packed array [1 . . streetSize    ] of Char;
      TownAddr     : packed array [1 . . townSize      ] of Char;
      Zip          : packed array [1 . . zipSize       ] of Char
    end;
    AccountType = (savings,checking,NOW);
    AccountRecord = record
      AccType      : AccountType;
      Number       : packed array [1 . . accNumSize    ] of Char;
      Balance      : Real;
      DateLast     : packed array [1 . . dateTransSize ] of Char
                        {date last transaction}
    end;
    CustomerRecord = record
      Name    : packed array [1 . . nameSize        ] of char;
      SSN     : packed array [1 . . ssnSize         ] of char;
      Address : AddressInformation;
      NumAccounts : Integer;
      Accounts : array [1 . . maxNumAccounts] of AccountRecord
    end;
{    internal file identifiers declared as data type                    }
      Branches = (A,B)
{    external file identifiers declared as variables                    }
      BRANCHA, BRANCHB : Text;
{  probe variables            —customer input by branch                 }
    has : array[Branches] of Boolean;
    customer : array[Branches] of CustomerRecord;
{    operations               —customer input by branch                 }
procedure brAdvance(X : Branches);
  procedure readcustomer
          (var F : Text; var C : CustomerRecord; var HAS : Boolean);
    label 0;
    var I, ACC : Integer;
      procedure endCheck;
        {if no more data then exit readcustomer with HAS = false}
        begin
          if eof(F) then begin
            has := false;
            goto 0
```

```
                    end;
                end;
                function getChar : Char;
                begin
                    getChar := F^;
                    get(F)
                end;
            begin with C do begin       {readcustomer}
                endCheck; for I := 1 to nameSize do Name[I] := getChar; readln(F);
                endCheck; for I := 1 to ssnSize do SSN[I] := getChar; readln(F);
                with Address do begin
                    endCheck;
                    for I := 1 phoneSize do Phone[I] := getChar; readln(F);
                    endCheck;
                    for I := 1 to streetSize do Streetaddr[I] := getChar; readln(F);
                    endCheck;
                    for I := 1 to townSize do Townaddr[I] := getChar; readln(F);
                    endCheck;
                    for I := 1 to zipSize do Zip[I] := getChar; readln(F);
                end;
                endCheck;
                readln(F,NumAccounts);
                if NumAccounts > maxNumAccounts then goto 0;
                for ACC := 1 to NumAccounts do with Accounts[ACC] do begin
                    case getChar of
                        'S' : AccType := savings;
                        'C' : AccType := checking;
                        'N' : AccType := NOW;
                    end;
                    readln(F);
                    endCheck;
                    for I := 1 to accNumSize do Number[I] := getChar;
                    readln(F);
                    endCheck;
                    readln(F,Balance);
                    for I := 1 to dateTransSize do DateLast[I] := getChar;
                    readln(F);
                end;
                has := true;
                0:
            end end;
begin {brAdvance}
    if X = A then
        readcustomer(BRANCHA,inCustomer[X],inHas[X])
    else
        readcustomer(BRANCHB,inCustomer[X],inHas[X])
end;
procedure brInit;
begin
    reset(BRANCHA);
    if not eof(BRANCHA) then
        inAdvance(A)
```

```
else
      has[A] := false;
reset(BRANCHB);
if not eof (BRANCHB) then
      brAdvance(B)
else
      has[B] := false;
end;
```

P4

AN EXAMPLE MATCHING METACODE IN CHAPTER 4

One example of an object module implementation is shown here. An object module implementation follows the same form as the input operation implementations, because the input mechanism was patterned after the object module mechanism.

Essentially, an object module implementation consists of some subprograms, some state variables, and some probes.

Probes can be functions and, sometimes, procedures as well as variables. All these things are capable of exporting information to an invoking program unit. Pascal implementations as variables are demonstrated in Appendix P2.

State variables are variables necessary to represent the module state or just variables that must be shared by the operations to do their job. A Pascal implementation of state variables is demonstrated in Appendix P2.

The state variables for one module are declared together in a record whose name has the word "State." This record is not accessed in the invoking program unit. In the subprograms of the module, it is accessed by being opened with the "with" statement. Probe variables are declared as ordinary variables in the invoking program unit.

The data coupling of an object module consists of the probe variables, the data returned by probe functions, and the parameters of the subprograms that implement operations or probes.

This example implements the tank object module and the test program of Section 4.1. Because of the input operations, this example has essentially two object modules, one for the tank and one for the input.

The input module assumes that the first line of input contains a real number which is the tank size and that each additional line contains a brand letter in the first column which is followed by a real number amount. (Part of the assumption is that brands are represented by single letters.) Echo checking is done during the input operations.

Representation of brands with characters is done throughout the code. Inside the tank module the unknown brand is represented with ']', the ASCII character that follows 'Z'.

Figure TANK_CODE contains the top-level Pascal code. Notice how closely it matches the metacode of the design in Figure TANK_TEST. Figure FUEL_INPUT shows the input operations, and Figure TANK_MODULE contains the tank module.

Figure TANK_CODE   Pascal Code Inplementing Figure TANK_TEST

```
program tnktst(INPUT,OUTPUT);
{ declare probe variables      — refill input        }
{ declare state variables        — tank module       }
{ declare probe subprograms   — tank module          }
{ declare operations           — tank input          }
{ declare operations           — tank module         }
begin
  inInit;
  init;
  while inHas do begin
    refill(inBrand,inAmount);
    if pure then
      writeln('Brand ',pureBrand,' represents 90% of the tank');
    inAdv
  end
end.
```

Figure FUEL_INPUT   Pascal Input Operations for TANK_CODE

```
{   probe variables             —refill input      }
      inBrand : Char;
      inTankSize,inAmount  :  Real;
      inHas : Boolean;
{   operations                  —refill input      }
procedure inAdv;
begin
    if eof then
      inHas := false
    else begin
      readln(inBrand,inAmount);
      writeln('Refill input: ',inBrand,inAmount)
    end
end;
```

```
procedure inInit;
begin
    readln(inTankSize);
    writel('Tank size input: ',inTankSize);
    inHas := true;
    inAdv
end;
```

Figure TANK_MODULE   Pascal Implementation of Figure TANK

```
{   state variables      — tank module      }
const unknown = '[';
  tankState : record
      amount : array['A'. . unknown] of Real
  end;
{   probe subprograms     — tank module      }
function pure : Boolean;
var B : Char;
begin with tankState do begin
  B := 'A';
  while (amount [B]<0.9*inTankSize) and (B<'Z') do B := succ(B):
  pure := amount[B] ≥0.9*inTankSize
end end;

function pureBrand : Char;
var B : Char;
begin with tankState do begin
  B := 'A';
  while (amount[B]<0.9*inTankSize) and (B<'Z') do B := succ(B);
  pureBrand := B
end end;
{   operations           —tank module}
procedure init;
var C : Char;
begin with tankState do begin
  amount[unknown] := inTankSize;
  for C := 'A' to 'Z' do amount [C] := 0:
end end;

procedure refill(B:Char;Q:Real);
var PROPORTION : Real;
  C : Char;
begin with tankState do begin
  PROPORTION := (inTankSize − Q)/inTankSize;
  for C := 'A' to unknown do amount[C] := amount [C] * PROPORTION;
  amount[B] := amount [B] + Q
end end;
```

REFERENCES FOR APPENDIX P

[KER]:Kernighan, B. W., and Plauger, P. J. *The Elements of Programming Style*, 2nd, ed., McGraw-Hill, New York, 1978, pp. 32–38.

EPILOGUE

From metacode, through object modules, to mathematics, this book follows a steep path toward a hazy summit. At some places along the path, wide vistas of applications can be seen. But to see them, you must look up from the path which the book provides.

The summit cannot be seen from this path: An attack on it must await better technology and a better knowledge of what lies up there. Moreover, there are fields of applications which cannot be viewed from the present path. In some cases, this is again because the technology is lacking, but in others, it is merely because one cannot walk all paths at once.

SUBJECT INDEX

SUBJECT INDEX

INDEX OF FIGURES

INDEX OF FIGURES

The labeling of figures in this book follows a principle learned from programming languages: A string is a better statement label than a number in the context of a program of reasonable length. So, too, a string is a better figure label than a number in the context of a section of reasonable length. Because each reference to a figure in this text is made in the context of a section, an index of figures isn't necessary to find referenced figures. However, it is very useful in finding unreferenced figures, that is, in finding figures you remember vaguely but whose context you don't remember.